The Campus History Series

Kansas Wesleyan University

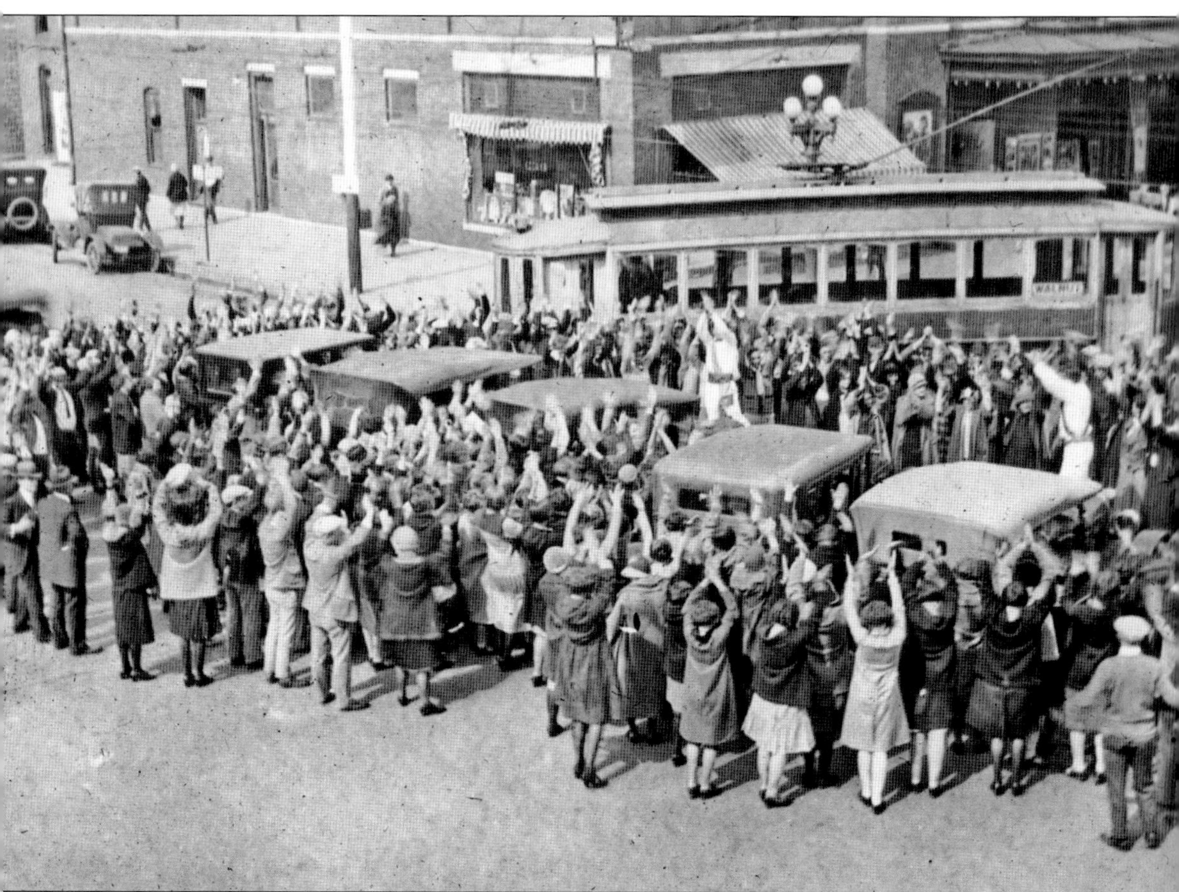

Students often gathered for pep parades in Salina at the corner of Walnut Street and Santa Fe Avenue near the Grand Theatre, across from the Kansas Wesleyan College of Commerce. In the 1926 game against Washburn, a stunt plane decorated with streamers glided over the football field and dropped the game ball. After Kansas Wesleyan beat Washburn 10-0, a pep parade led by Vernon Shahan and Kenneth Thompson traveled through downtown celebrating the victory. (Courtesy of Memorial Library Archives.)

On the Cover: Kansas Wesleyan University has often been referred to as the anchor on the south end of Salina, Kansas. The landscape and gateway signage to the university have changed over the years, but Pioneer Hall and the circular drive remain a permanent fixture and symbol of resilience. This photograph is featured in a 1950s campus brochure, *A Step Worth Taking*. (Courtesy of Memorial Library Archives.)

Cover Background: Pioneer Hall's construction was an arduous task. In 1922, excitement grew as excavation began; eight years of delays ensued. In 1924, Kansas City's Bishop Ernest Lynn Waldorf spoke during the cornerstone ceremony. His dedicatory address emphasized the importance of the university's constituency to show true spirit and support. By 1930, celebrations abounded for the building's completion. Pictured here is Pioneer Hall during the winter. (Courtesy of Memorial Library Archives.)

The Campus History Series

KANSAS WESLEYAN UNIVERSITY

JENNIFER TOELLE
FOREWORD BY BILL GRAVES

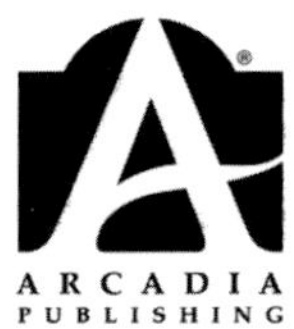

ISBN 978-1-4671-2584-0

Published by Arcadia Publishing
Charleston, South Carolina

Printed in the United States of America

Library of Congress Control Number: 2017942073

For all general information, please contact Arcadia Publishing:
Telephone 843-853-2070
Fax 843-853-0044
E-mail sales@arcadiapublishing.com
For customer service and orders:
Toll-Free 1-888-313-2665

Visit us on the Internet at www.arcadiapublishing.com

To all alumni, students, faculty, and staff, and in memoriam of the following alumni: Thomas Jewell Cravens, Powers G. Porter, Mary Campbell Palmer, and Steve Fink.

CONTENTS

FOREWORD

For anyone who has spent time as a student or part of the faculty and staff at Kansas Wesleyan University, fond memories evoke visual images of people, places, and time spent on campus. For me, those memories are quickly drawn to Carnegie Hall, where Dr. Medford Shively was teaching a business class; Dr. John Dahlquist forming a small circle of students to discuss world history; playing intramural basketball in King Gym; or the student center in the basement of Pioneer Hall, where everyone would stop by to simply see who was around. A constant presence on campus and a mentor, coach Gene Bissell would be instructing future coaches, while across the hall in Peters Science Hall, Dr. Art Neuburger would be nurturing the next generation of biologists. If I stop and close my eyes, I can see it all so very clearly and feel as if those days were not long ago.

And yet, in the 40 years since I last spent significant time on the Kansas Wesleyan campus, so much has changed. A new student center now serves as the gathering spot for today's students. King Gym and Carnegie Hall gave way to new facilities, and Pioneer Hall has undergone numerous face-lifts. Every day, hundreds of students, faculty, and staff who comprise the current Kansas Wesleyan family are creating their own memories of time spent in this wonderful place.

For 130 years, Kansas Wesleyan has anchored the south end of Salina while providing students with academic and life skills to grow both personally and professionally, eventually becoming mentors to the following generation. My great-grandfather's brother, Henry Milton Mayo, was the first graduate of Kansas Wesleyan in 1887. How proud I think he would be to know that the great-grandson of his brother became the first graduate of Kansas Wesleyan to serve as governor of Kansas. Our story is one of many examples of the university legacy that has touched countless lives and woven a tapestry of family and friends into the beautiful portrait that reflects the university of today. Shakespeare wrote, "What's past is prologue"; and it is often referenced so that we might appreciate that all that has gone on before us has helped shape today. And so very quickly, our todays will be part of what shapes future generations' tomorrows.

Kansas Wesleyan has exhibited a resilient spirit throughout its 130-year history, which should instill in us a confidence that its best days still lie ahead. I firmly believe that's true. If you look closely at these wonderful images, you'll see more than Kansas Wesleyan's significant past—you'll begin to glimpse its exciting future.

—Bill Graves '76
Former Kansas Governor

Acknowledgments

It was a pleasure to research the university's history, and this process has enriched my historical knowledge about the campus and the Salina area. The research has uncovered the heartbeat of Kansas Wesleyan's campus, generation by generation. Beginning in 1886, each decade revealed a new wave of energy and ideology of students, faculty, and staff. My appreciation goes to Dr. John Cornett, Dr. Jack Warner VanDerhoof, and Bernita Breon Mitchell for writing histories on the university. My sincere gratitude goes to those in the university community who answered inquiries and assisted in the identification of photographs.

Unless otherwise noted, all images for chapters 1 through 9 are courtesy of Kansas Wesleyan University's Memorial Library Archives. Images found in chapter 10 are courtesy of Kansas Wesleyan University and by photographer Tanner Colvin.

Special recognition goes to David Toelle, sports information director, for his unyielding support and patience during the research process and for listening without tire to each new discovery. My sincere appreciation goes to Dr. Ruth Mirtz, librarian, and Kate Wise, assistant librarian of Kansas Wesleyan University's Memorial Library for their encouragement and providing a research space. I wish to recognize Pres. Matt Thompson and the Institutional Advancement staff for assisting in getting this project off the ground. My appreciation goes to the Salina Public Library's reference staff for services they provide, access to local history materials, and for refiling the numerous rolls of microfilm.

I would like to acknowledge the following individuals and institutions: John Burchill, Jessica Coulter, Rachelle Hindman, Linda Little, Barbara Marshall, Nona Miller, Mary Jane McIntyre, Zan Popp, Steve Read, and Kay Quinn; Johnson County Museums; Sedalia Ragtime Archive; University of Denver Archives; and Topeka and Shawnee County Public Library.

Last but certainly not least, my sincere gratitude goes to the alumni, faculty, and staff—because you have provided the amazing content of this book!

INTRODUCTION

This pictorial history features the ebb and flow of Kansas Wesleyan University from its inception in 1886 through its 130th anniversary in 2016. The campus's continual progress is illustrated by each turning page. This compilation illustrates institutional history and provides a journey through time to remember students, faculty, and staff who shaped campus life generation by generation.

Access to the knowledge of university history provides an avenue to strengthen the campus community, because every community embraces human memory. College days, traditions, fundraising campaigns, and commemorations are all shared experiences. As students reminisce, professors also become fulfilled by the continual process of enriching minds and providing pathways for students. This brings profound connection to people on campus. Every footstep taken across campus connects everyone to the soil of the place. As experiences are shared, memories gently cascade and overlap, binding generations together through shared experience.

The vision for this book was reinforced after reading a passage in the 1964 *Coyote* yearbook by editor Ann Partner Nelson: "With the passage of time, the visions of college life grow dim. It is the purpose of this book and others like it to help recapture these moments and make them clear again." She also wrote "Reflections," which conveys how daily life seems insignificant until the culmination of time builds the context of milestones.

As research continued, numerous people emerged as pillars of the campus community. Individuals such as Dr. Aaron Schuyler, Rev. Milton Stolz, and Dr. Frederick Conrad Peters instilled in their students a passion for learning. Their influence provided a strong foundation for institutional permanence. This impact was mirrored by the respect others displayed towards them. An annual celebration was held to commemorate Schuyler's birthday on February 7. When Founder's Day was established on February 17, 1914, nearly a year after his death, the university discontinued the birthday celebration and declared Schuyler's birthday a holiday so preparations could be made for Founder's Day, an event typically held annually in February. While Schuyler's and Stolz's birthdays were yearly celebrations, Peters's 90th birthday was commemorated with an announcement that a new science hall would bear his name. This book features numerous individuals who were inspirational figures on campus.

The beginning chapters address the formative academic and campus development. As the chapters advance, images convey visionary goals. Andrew Perry Collins, who suggested the university's name, also promoted it nationally. Collins is quoted in his alma mater Ohio Wesleyan University's school newspaper, the *College Transcript*, in December 1888 as saying: "Aside from superintending my farm, I am trying to do something for my church and the cause of education in aiding in the establishment of K.W.U." Gratitude should be shown to individuals like Collins and his close friend Rev. John Hughes Lockwood, who spearheaded university promotion and cultivated community support.

Another strong community advocate, Christopher Eberhardt, championed Kansas Wesleyan's pursuits. Imagine his surprise as he opened a resignation from the first university president, William F. Swahlen. This came approximately one year after the university opened its doors. Swahlen's candid letter refers to his need to pursue teaching aspirations at DePauw University. Towards the end of the letter, he assures Eberhardt his replacement undoubtedly would successfully carry out Wesleyan's aims, then switches to Suetterlin script with the phrase "ende güt, alles güt," which translates "all's well that ends well." The symbolism rests in the fact that even in times of uncertainty, optimism for a joyous ending will endure. The university has experienced many times of uncertainty, which were always met with rebounding resilience. Another symbolic example of this resilience occurred as people greeted a new, young, and energetic Pres. Edward Mueller in 1894. Gathered in the university's chapel, they sang John Fawcett's "Blest Be the Tie that Binds." This song's symbolism showcases how a community can join together for strength and renewal. This type of community event continues today at annual events such as Homecoming and Founder's Day.

A 1903 photograph of the annual Lockard Sunday school picnic found in the Smoky Hill Museum's archives provided early evidence of the impact of community outreach. The image depicts a large crowd gathered at Gardner's Grove to hear Methodist ministers such as Isaiah McDowell and Charles Wesley Stevens and alumnus and one-room teacher John Corbett. Two years later, Clara Lockard, an honor student who was offered scholarships from 14 colleges in addition to a free scholarship to the University of Kansas, chose Kansas Wesleyan due to its standing within the community.

While the image of Lockard Sunday School was not chosen for the book, chapter 4 features a similar story of community engagement regarding famous alumni. Additionally, chapter 9 features the Corbett family's impact on generational legacy. No images appear of Reverend Stevens and his son Rex, yet like many alumni, Rex maintained a profound connection to his alma mater. His memorable links to his football team and coach Bill Ragle reminded captain Rex of when he led his teammates to an 11-0 victory over Friends University in 1915. While Rex is not pictured, images reflect coach Gene Bissell's influence and suggest how Rex's spirit swelled while he watched the Coyotes 50 years later in victory over Friends University in 1965.

Chapter 2 begins with an image of King Gymnasium, which highlights when trends in higher education transitioned to embrace athletics and place higher values on physical health. These trends set the stage for the integral role athletics have continued to serve on campus. Additionally, this chapter showcases inspirational and strategic leadership to carry on with fortitude through the Great Depression and two world wars. In 1915, the community welcomed a nationally known inspirational Methodist minister, John Harmon. The community had high hopes Harmon would provide an exhilarating force to propel the campus forward. He provided inspiring and comforting lectures to the central Kansas region during the grim times of World War I. Despite Harmon's brief tenure as president, his uplifting lectures lingered regionally, and he stayed connected with familial ties. After Harmon's departure, his interim successor Albert King and alumnus Charles Burch raised the flag to welcome US Army general Peyton March and his Student Army Training Corps to campus.

In the 1930s, the university had six educational goals: preparation, liberalization, specialization, integration, personality, and service. Pres. Larkin Bowers, educator and businessman, carried out these goals through a progressive approach to cultivate relationships and improve the physical campus. President Bowers suggested the construction of Pioneer Well when James William Bean, father of alumnae Edith Hageman and Dell Millikin, donated funds for a beautification project. The rationale for the well was to erect a structure for alumni to hold in high regard. The well has moved from its original location on campus but remains securely bound to university tradition. Bowers's leadership and staff were instrumental in the implementation of the Golden Jubilee Campaign to commemorate the 50th anniversary. Images of his influence are presented throughout the book, including collaborations with James Cash Penney and Earl Corder Sams. Bowers's tragic death brought forth a pause for the university, and structures like the Wishing Well and Pioneer Hall are reminders of his lasting legacy.

When Wyoming ranchman Edgar Keer Morrow pledged to lead the university, he recognized that the community was mourning a pivotal leader, yet he himself had lost his friend and classmate from undergraduate days at Ohio Wesleyan. When the board of trustees appointed

Morrow in February 1938, he spoke about riding with the campus community over a new divide where "water holes will be far apart, and storms may beat in our faces, but those invisible riders, the pioneers will be riding with us." Regrettably, presidents Morrow and Herbert Jackson Root are not pictured, but images selected represent their impact on a prosperous campus that flourished with new facilities and academic excellence. A multitude of changes are attributed to postwar plans developed under Morrow and Root, including the University Development Fund, Pfeiffer Dormitory Fund, Earl Corder Sams Fine Arts Building, and Memorial Library Fund. This foresight and planning enabled Pres. Stanley Trickett to implement these important projects. The final image in chapter 2 illustrates their continued legacy as second-generation students stand on the steps of Pioneer Hall around 1951.

The mid-1950s through the 1970s were a pivotal time of growth and academic excellence. Chapter 3 begins with Pres. Dr. D. Arthur Zook gazing upon a building model. This wonderful illustration conveys his vision to increase attendance to ensure projects advanced. Look for the image of politician Robert "Bob" Dole discussing the impending closure of Schilling Air Force Base with local college leaders. After the closure, the university drafted conceptual plans to build a new 24.5-acre main campus at the former base location, leaving the current campus as a freshman orientation campus. Although plans for a campus expansion did not materialize, the university utilized buildings on the former base for housing.

President Zook relied on the support and innovative strength of professor and academic dean Paul Renich. Renich rose to the role of university president and brought a unique, vigorous, and inspirational leadership style, firmly believing the university should be anchored by collaboration both on and off campus in the community. Renich was instrumental in the first accreditation process, fundraising campaigns, and unique initiatives such as distance learning by Electrowriter telephone courses. Renich was recognized by induction into the hall of fame at the Founder's Day Banquet in 1986.

In 1986, the university reached a milestone of 100 years, hence the title for chapter 8, "The Second Century." This is named after the successful fundraising campaign commenced in anticipation of the centennial celebration. The university experienced a renewal process and identified improvements that led to dynamic changes. Pres. Marshall Stanton wrote an article featured in the July 1986 *Wesleyan Advance* focused on how people center themselves around two contradictory poles: a need for change and also falling into the security of no change. President Stanton remarks, "The struggle between the new and old, expected and realized requires constant attention to find a satisfying balance." In comparing the recent images found in chapters 8 and 10 to earlier years, take Stanton's wise words into consideration to appreciate the distinct changes on campus and note what has remained unchanged.

Chapters 4 through 6 highlight diversified academic offerings as well as a well-rounded student experience. In the early years, President Schuyler referred to education as a way "to train the mind" and "cultivate the senses." The university's mission was to cultivate the mind by "symmetrical development of the body, mind and heart." While education remains the primary goal, campus organizations provide an enriched experience. The images featured provide a glimpse into the sphere of campus activity.

The last chapter showcases the current years and 130th anniversary. It illustrates how the campus embraces "the Power of And" and holds long-standing traditions in high regard. The final two images convey dreams realized during the dedication of the Graves Family Sports Complex. These images reinforce the book's visual historical compilation, which comprises the essence of shared experience. Shared recollections create pathways to connections and strengthen the Coyote spirit. Remember President Bowers's sage advice regarding life's journey: "the greatest joy of life comes through properly sharing the road with others and helping other travelers on the way." Turn the pages to reminisce, learn, and take pride. May this commemorative collection of images echo resilience and forever bind the Kansas Wesleyan University community.

One

The Founding Years

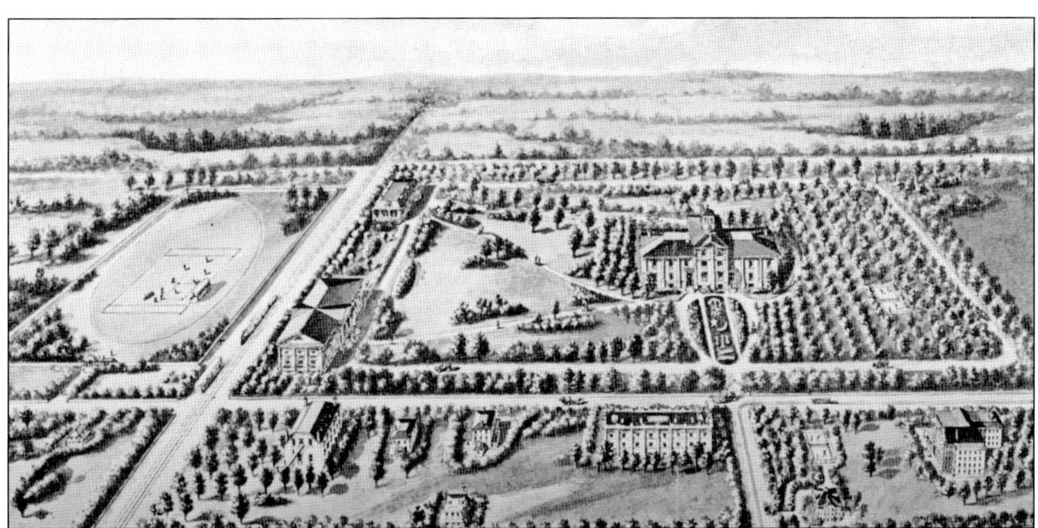

In 1885, four central Kansas communities bid for a Methodist university: Beloit, Clyde, Ellsworth, and Salina. The eagerness, enthusiasm, and strategic planning of Salinan Arthur Melville Claflin secured the bid. The board of trustees journeyed to Salina to inspect the proposed site on the southern edge of town. To see the location, they tore down a fence, crossed a potato patch, and entered a prairie field.

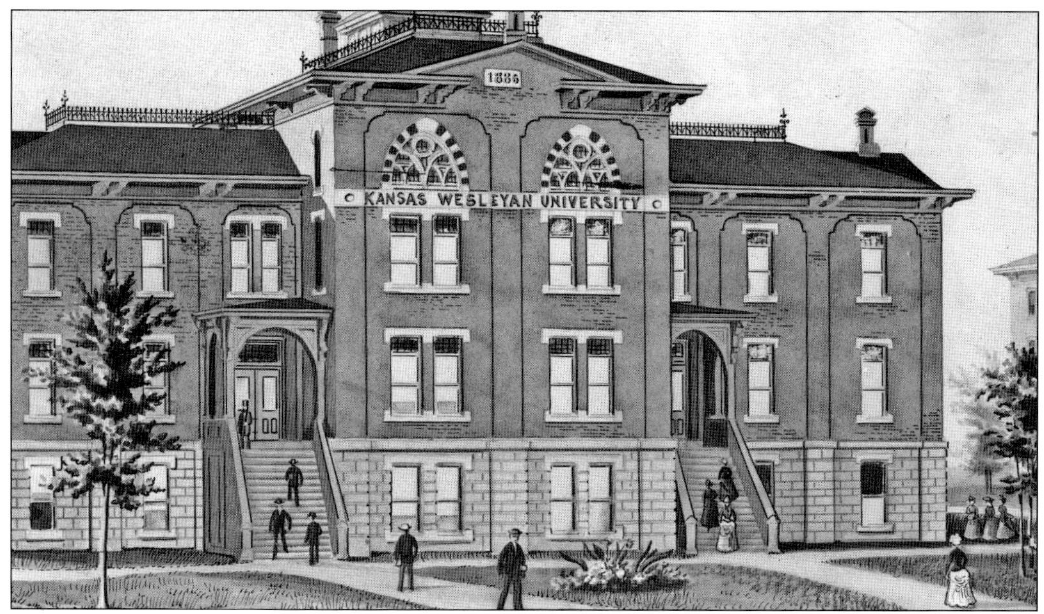

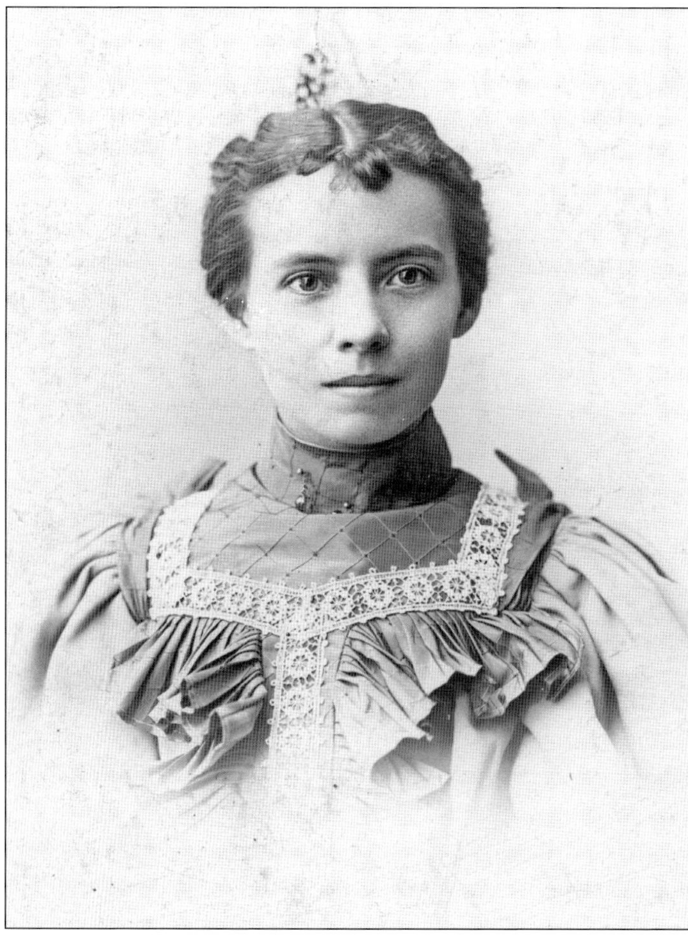

In July 1885, Andrew Perry Collins suggested the name "Kansas Wesleyan University." Collins's vision for a Methodist higher education institution in Salina became a reality when his children, Oliver and Edith, graduated from Kansas Wesleyan in 1892. To commemorate this occasion, he opened his home to the community to celebrate. Pictured is a sketch of the administration building by artist John William Caughey. Edith Collins Hagerty Bishop (left) was the first woman graduate. She married George Hagerty, university president from 1896 to 1899. Her senior essay, "Evolution of Ideas," is featured in the June 1892 *Advance*. She participated in the Ladies Athletic and Alumni Associations. She carried the Coyote Cane, an honor bestowed on the oldest living alum.

In 1886, Dr. Aaron Schuyler joined the first faculty assembled. He was often referred to as "the Grand Old Man" and the soul of the university for his deep philosophical thoughts combined with humorous anecdotes. Every February, the students would observe Schuyler Day in honor of his birthday. Schuyler served as president from 1890 to 1894.

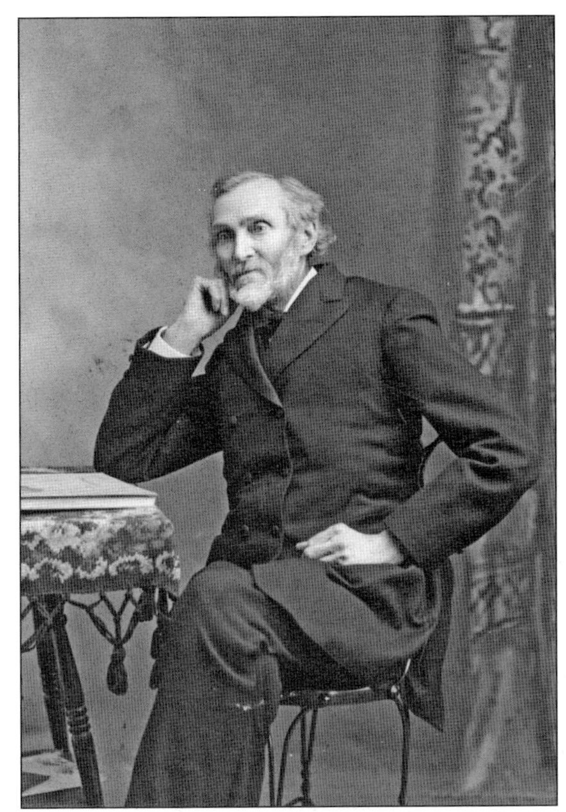

In September 1894, a reception was held in the chapel to welcome the young and energetic new president, Edward Mueller, who served as assistant pastor at Mount Vernon Place Methodist Episcopal Church in Baltimore, Maryland. He was an alumnus of Central Wesleyan College and Boston University. He was one of the youngest college presidents in the nation. Pictured here around 1892 is the faculty prior to Mueller's arrival on campus.

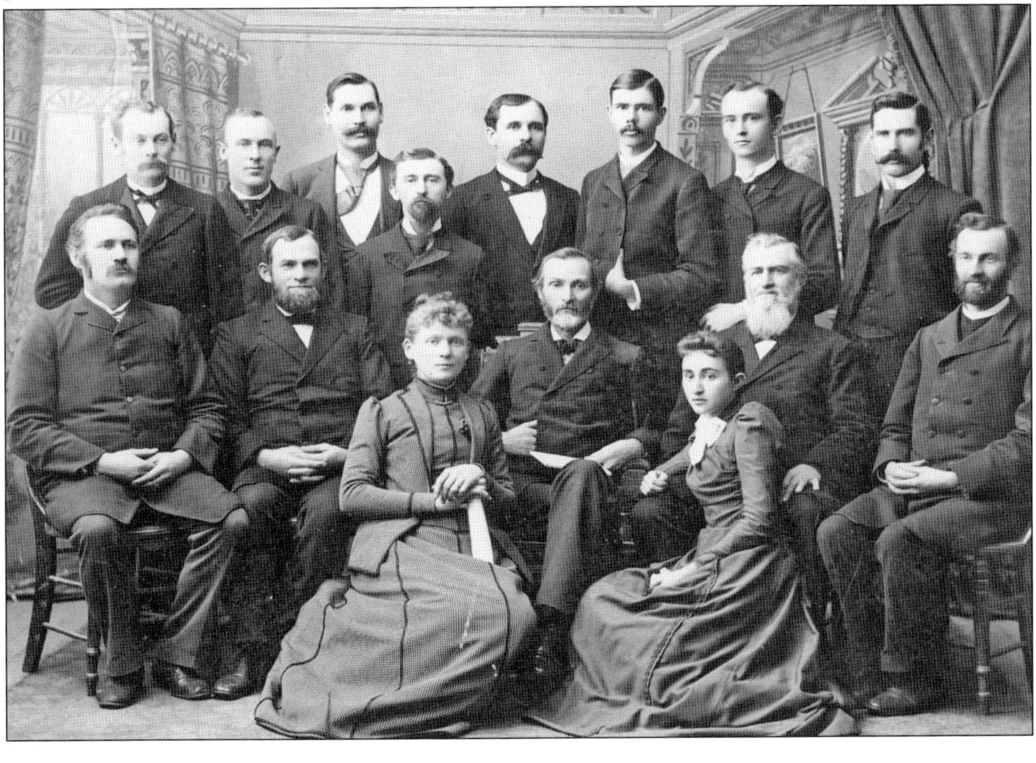

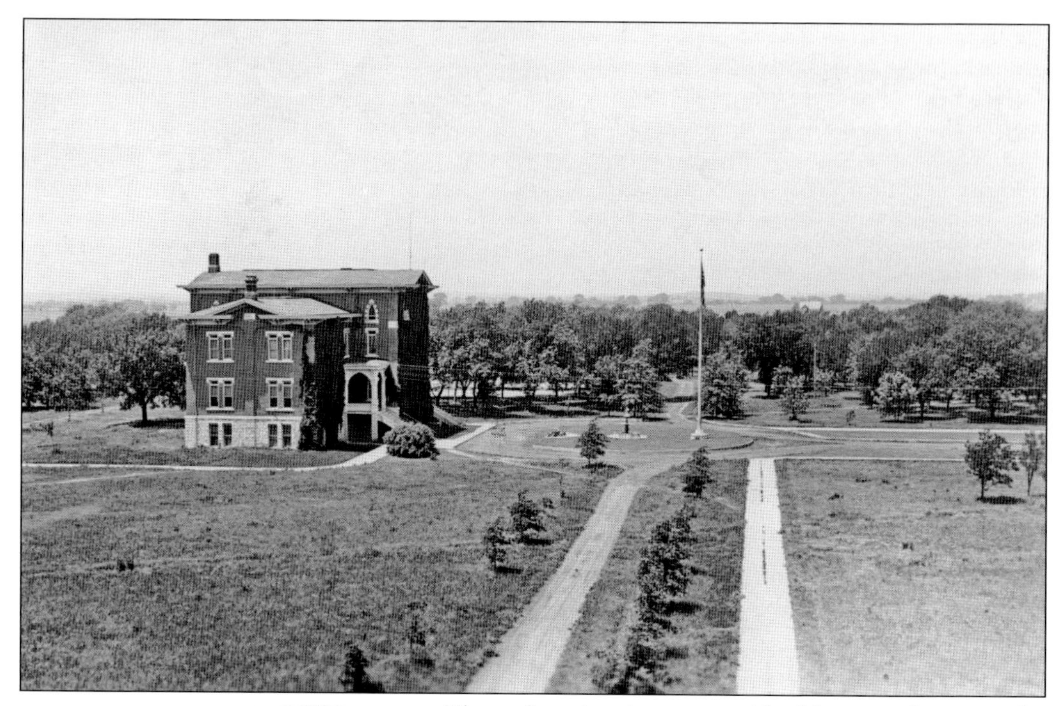

The university site was an ideal location because the South & Southwest Railroad track was positioned along the site's eastern line. This made it easy to bring construction materials and passengers to the school quickly. The Kansas Wesleyan University Aid Association collaborated with university trustees to secure the funding for the institution. The university's first building was swiftly built and opened its doors on September 15, 1886.

There were 121 students enrolled in the university's first academic year. Rev. Henry Milton Mayo, a senior enrolled in the classics course, became the first graduate in 1887. Mayo served Methodist churches primarily in Colorado. At the time of his death in 1919, he was the endowment secretary at the University of Denver. His sons and daughter-in-law Margery Reed Mayo were actively involved in leadership at the University of Denver.

In 1886, Rev. Daniel McGurk's remarkable oratorical skills secured him a position to teach elocution. He later enrolled as a student and graduated in 1893. McGurk married Rev. John Hughes Lockwood's daughter Anna in 1889. He became one of the fastest-rising Methodist ministers in the nation, and preached in Kansas City and New York. In 1901, McGurk was awarded an honorary degree, and later an annual oratorical contest was named in his honor.

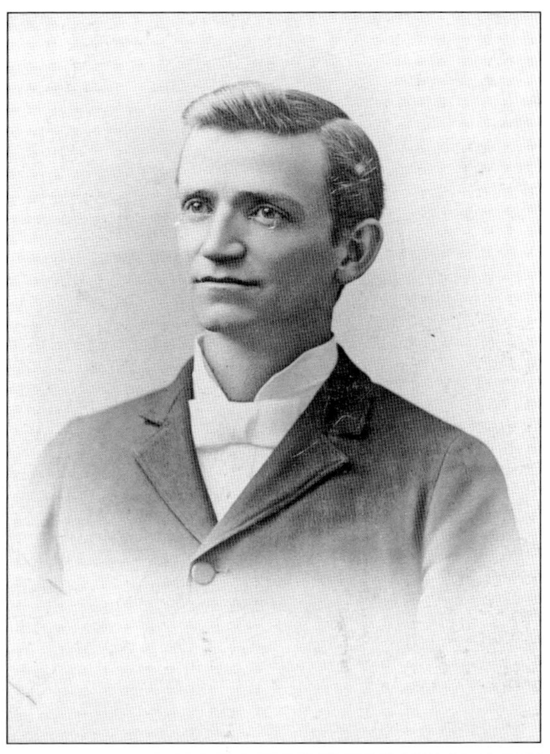

In 1893, Rev. Henry Milton Mayo, the university's first graduate, returned to Salina to deliver the invocation at the commencement ceremony. Daniel McGurk (front row, far left) delivered an oration on "Christianity and Intellectual Progress," arguing that Christianity has the ability to spark intellectual pursuits. Pictured here is the class of 1893.

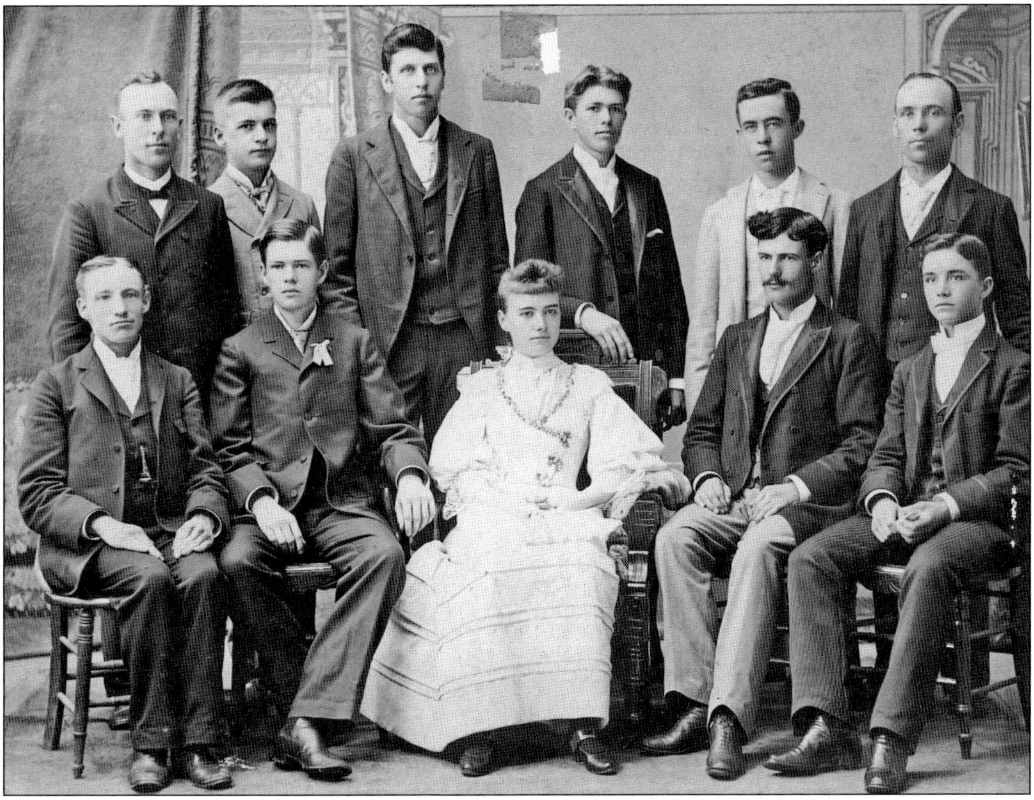

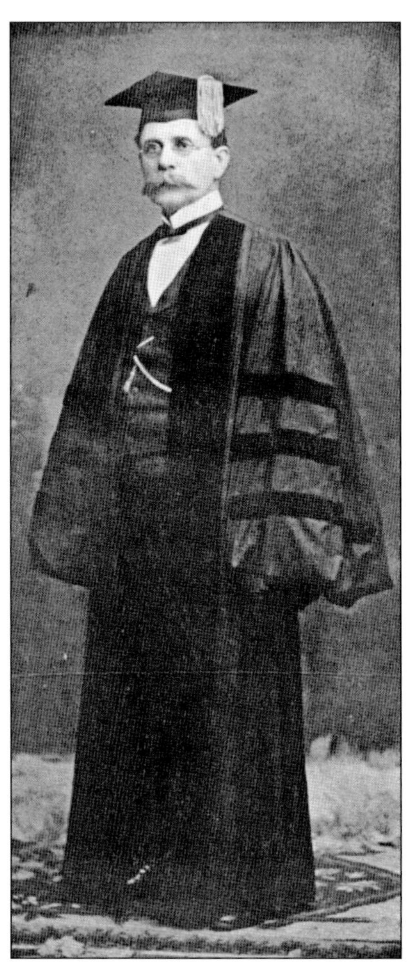

In 1890, Thomas Watson Roach (left; below, far right) resigned his school superintendent position in Cloud County, Kansas, to lead the National Commercial College of Business in Denison, Texas. In 1892, Kansas Wesleyan contracted with Roach to develop a commercial department, which became known as Kansas Wesleyan Business College, located at corner of Santa Fe Avenue and Walnut Street. The school maintained a superior level of distinction and was often advertised as one of the best business colleges in the Middle West. Roach led the entire university as president from 1903 to 1908. When Roach retired in 1913, Levi Livermore Tucker and his wife, Mary, continued the business college's pursuits until 1917. The contract was renewed periodically until 1920, when Kansas Wesleyan purchased it under the name Kansas Wesleyan College of Commerce. (Below, courtesy of the Smoky Hill Museum.)

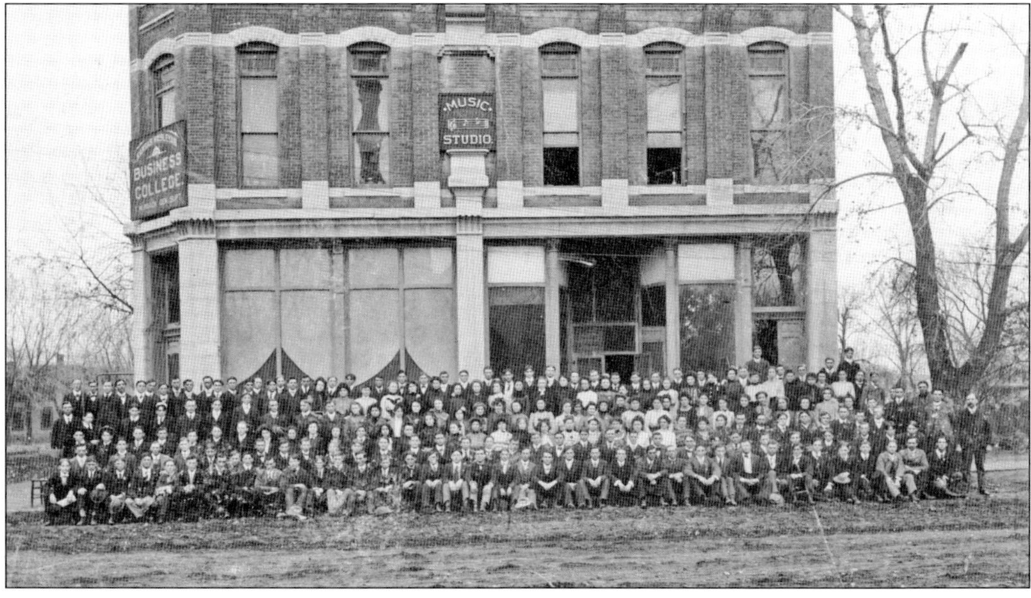

Dr. Michael Milton Stolz (right) had a distinct zeal and passion for the university. His enthusiasm and loyalty to the university was shown daily in his work. Stolz was a pioneer of Methodism in Kansas and among the first advocating church-sponsored education. As the first administration building was nearing completion, he took a dangerous fall that required crutches for several years. In 1905, Stolz retired from the Methodist ministry and higher education, but he continued to serve the university for another decade as librarian and museum curator. The museum under Stolz's care was first located on the top floor of the Carnegie Science Hall. Later, it moved back to its previous location in the administration building. The majority of the museum's collection was comprised of natural history specimens. Below is Stolz in the university museum.

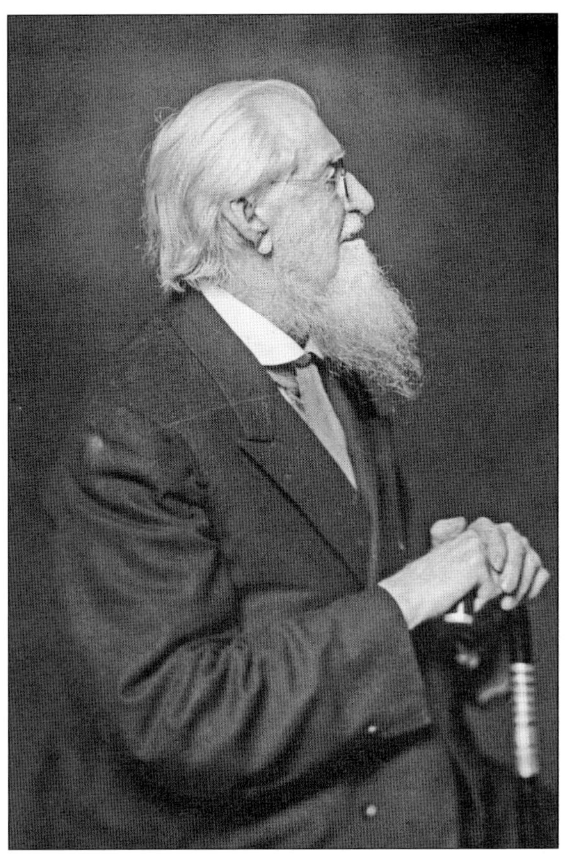

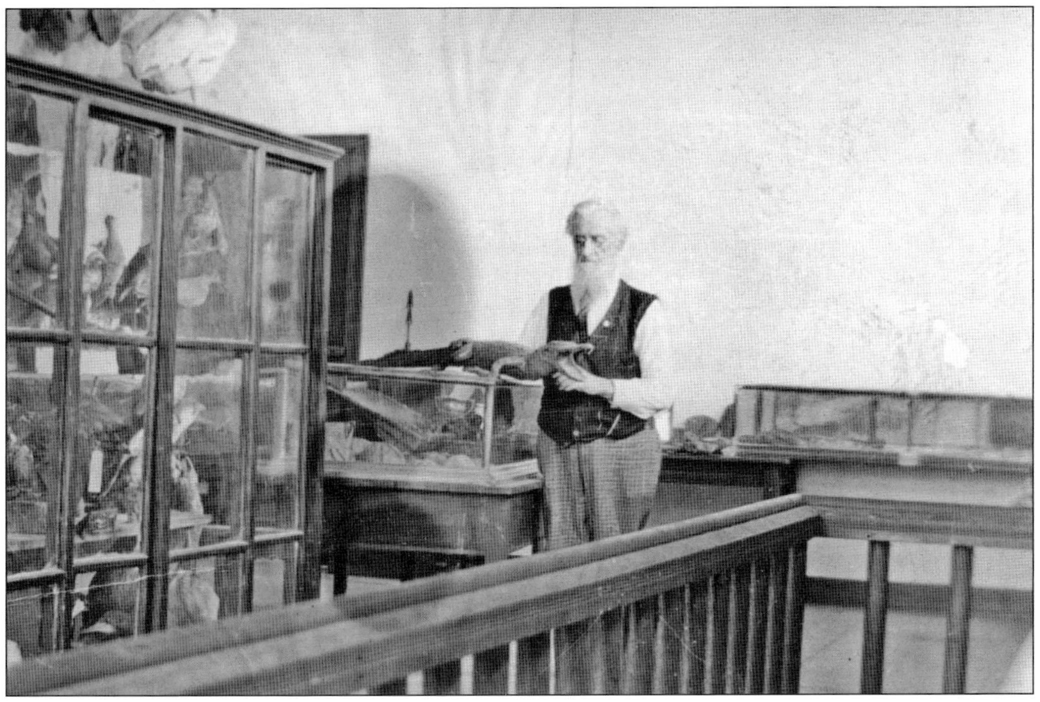

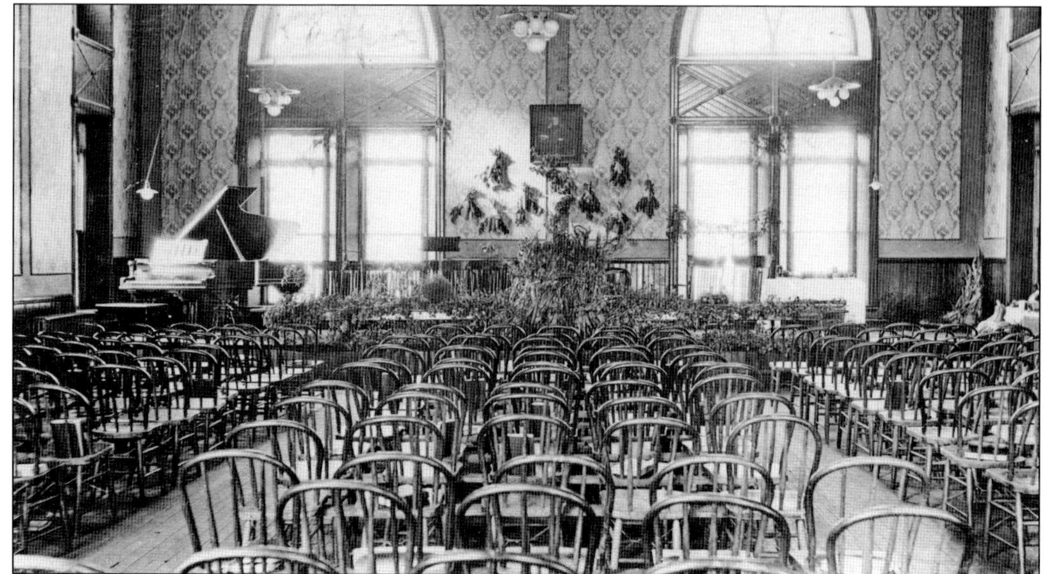

In February 1887, the reading room of the administration building became overcrowded when it was used as the university's chapel. Over the years, the chapel became a gathering place for various events, such as musical entertainment, literary society programs, theater performances, conferences, and much more. The University United Methodist Church held services here until 1917.

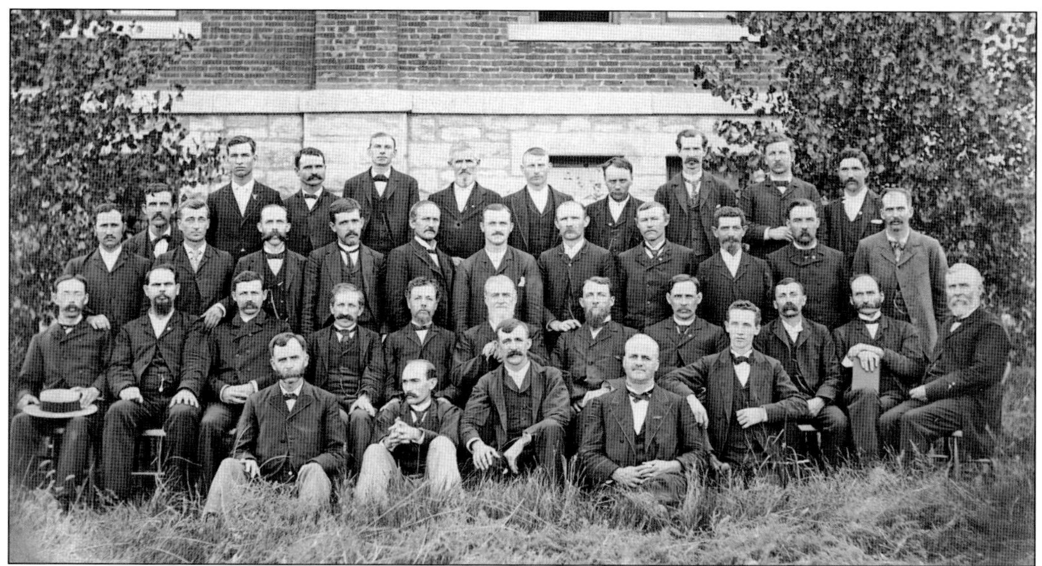

In the early 1890s, the Summer School of Theology began at Kansas Wesleyan University. This 10-day course typically met the last week of August or the first week of September. The sessions were specifically designed for instruction and spiritual refreshment. Those in attendance included pastors, bishops, and theology professors.

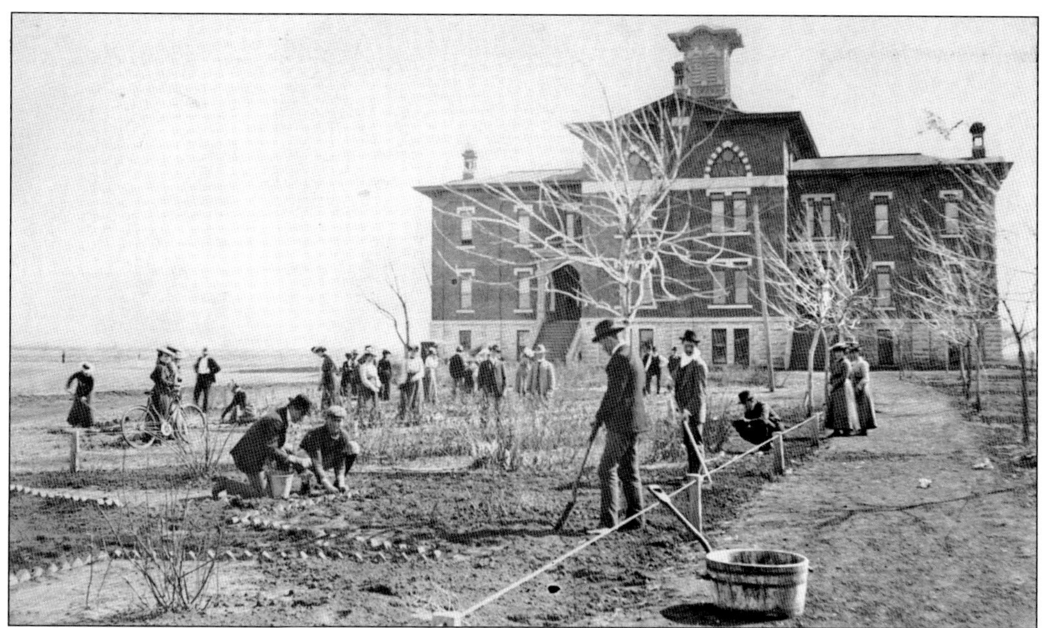

In the first academic year, two literary societies were formed, Periclean for men and Athenaeum for ladies. The Pericleans disbanded after five years and became the Delphians. In 1892, the men organized the Philharmonic, which later became the Ionians. The ladies organized the Zetagathean in 1899. These literary societies held social events and oratory contests. As early as 1888, Arbor Day was observed to take care of the campus's grounds, and students planted 160 trees. On Arbor Day, 1899, students were dismissed early to participate in campus beautification. Pictured above is Arbor Day 1902. Around 1914, the Delphians established a lapel pin in the shape of their emblem, an anchor. Pictured below is the annual oratorical contest on the third floor of Lockwood Hall; the Delphian and Athenaeum Societies are seated in a boat that represented the societies' emblems of the anchor and the fleur-de-lis around 1914.

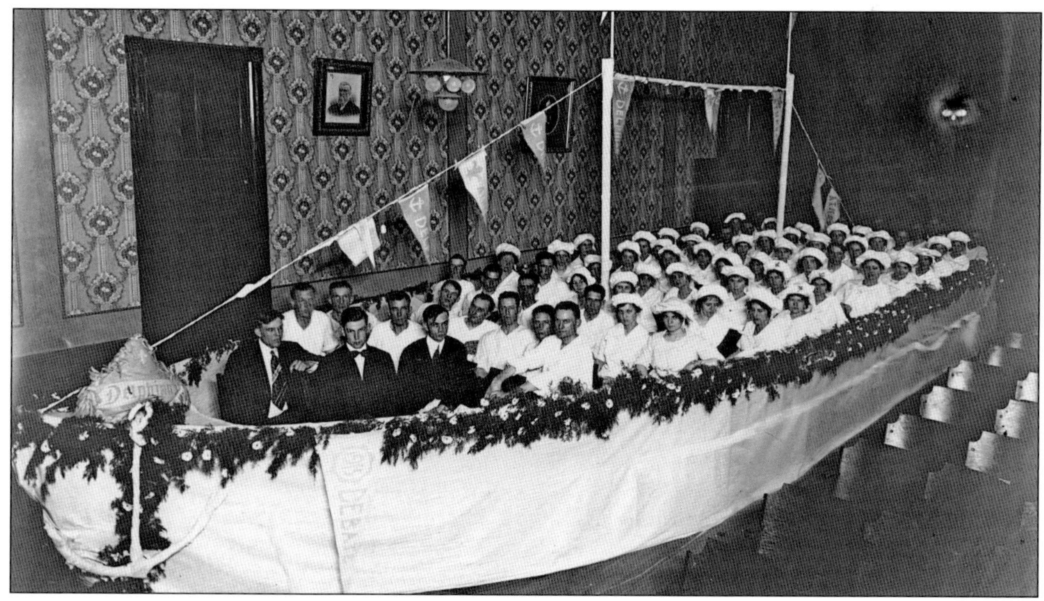

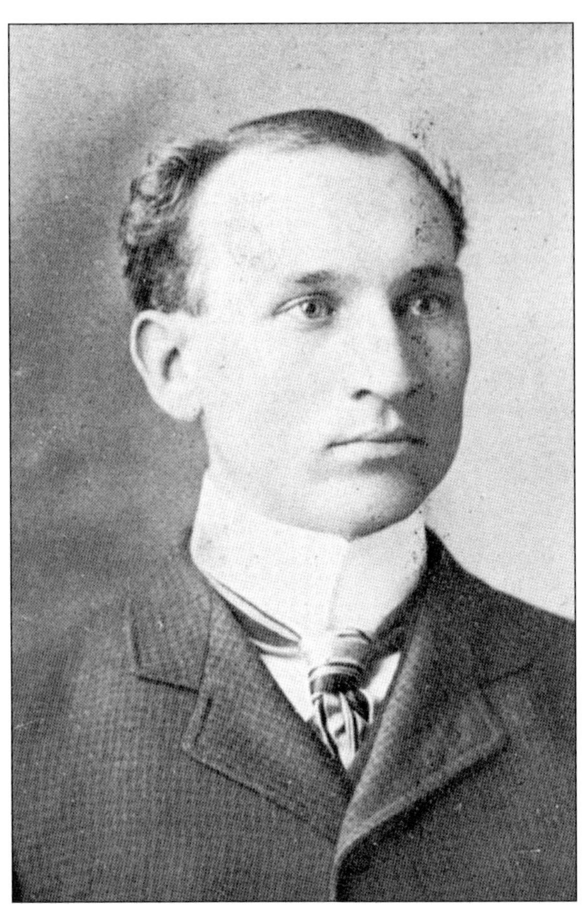

George Kleihege, class of 1902, was editor-in-chief of the *Advance*. In his senior year, he won the inter-society oratorical contest for the Delphians. His speech, "A Plea for Peace," was followed by his opponent Ionian, Charles W. Smith. The contest was close, but judges Thomas Bond, George Crissman, and Charles Burch decided on Kleihege's delivery. In 1912, Kleihege ran on the Socialist ticket for governor of Kansas.

On Arbor Day 1903, the Delphians and Athenaeums updated their associations' plots. Among the work completed was the addition of rose and lilac bushes. Lilac bushes have a special significance to the campus community, because lilacs became a vital part symbol of Lilac Fete. Pictured are the plots of the Ionian, Delphian, Zetagathean, and Athenaeum around 1904.

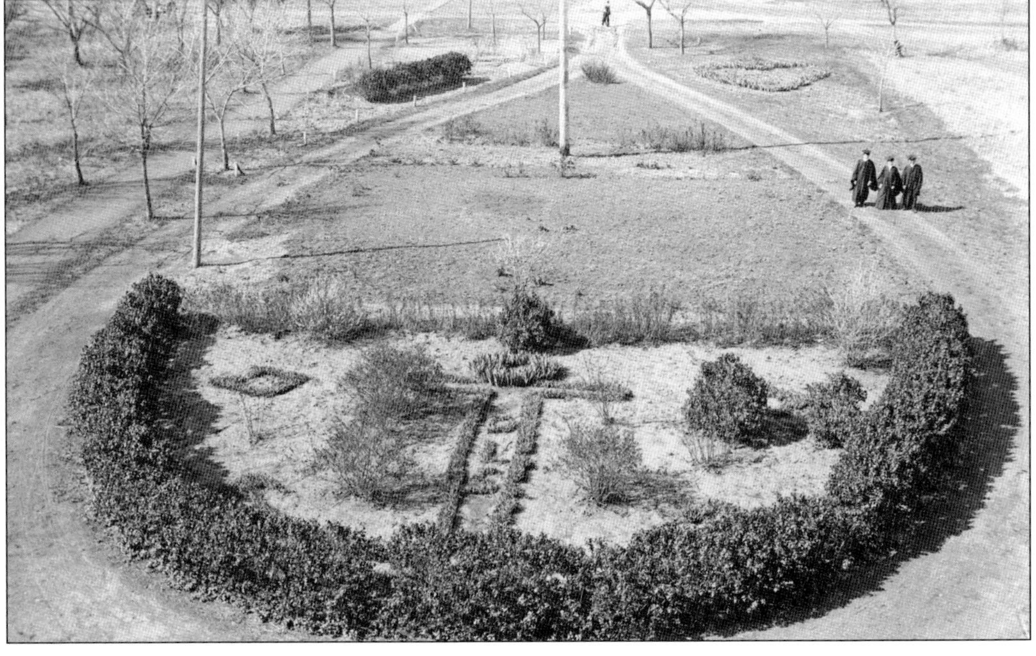

The Roach Home, located at the corner of Santa Fe and Claflin Avenues, was a gift from Pres. Thomas Roach and his wife, Angeline. After his presidency, Roach donated both funds to erect the home and adjoining lots, totaling $7,500. Thereafter, the house served as the university president's residence. It contained 10 rooms, a sleeping porch, an attic, and a large oak stairway lighted by mosaic windows.

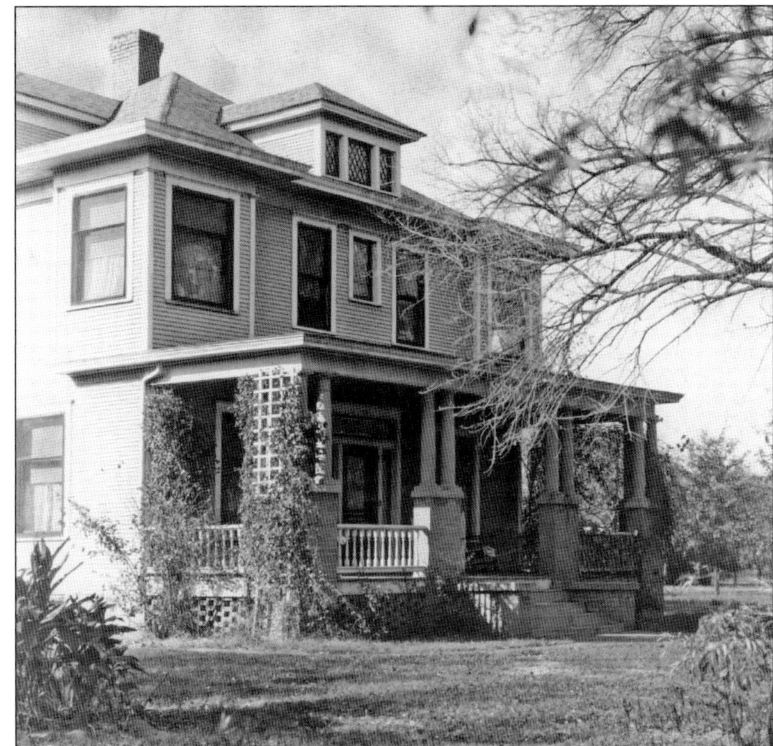

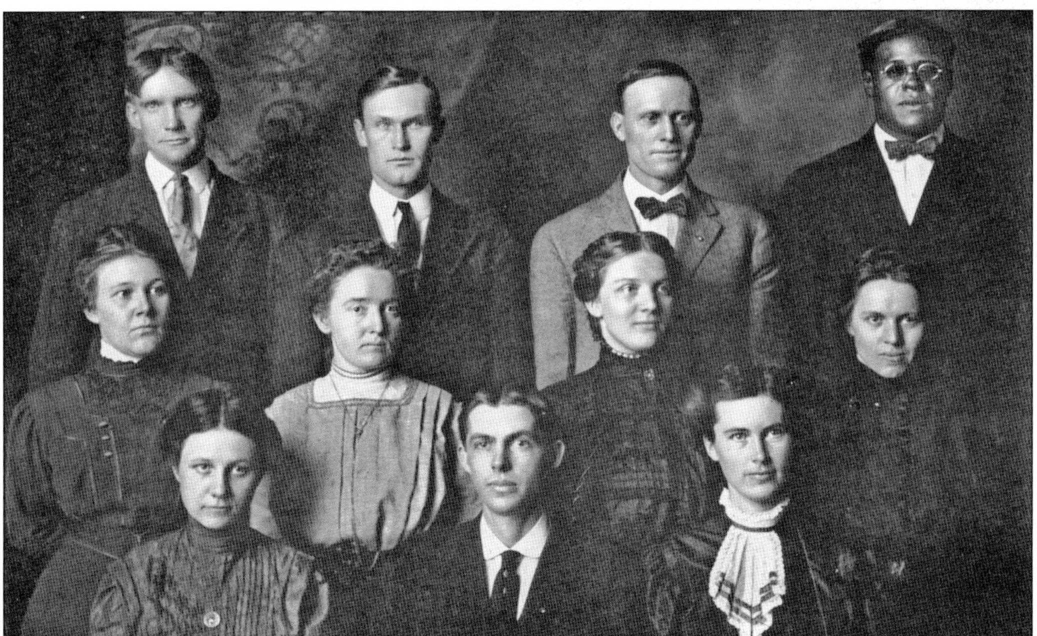

The 1911 junior normal class met during the Student Pedagogical Club, in which students discussed future goals. Powers G. Porter (third row, far right) voiced his goals and added "my aspiration is to be a second Booker T." Porter became an inspiring African American leader in education in the Kansas communities of Atchison, Olathe, and Salina. In 1922, he became the first principal of the Dunbar School in Salina.

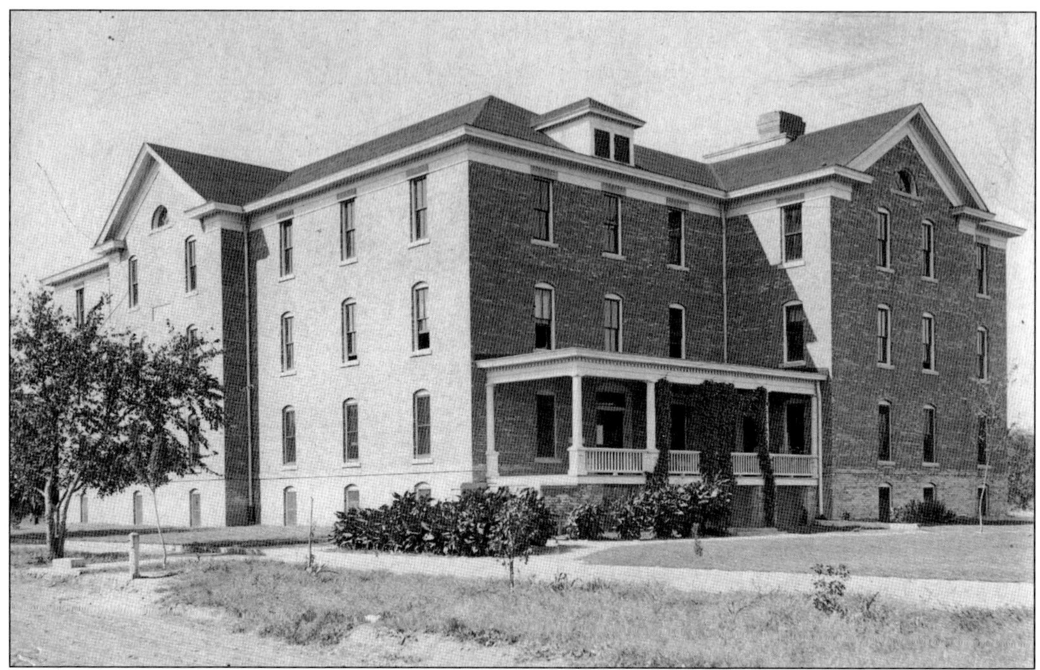

In 1904, Schuyler Hall, named in honor of Aaron Schuyler, was the first dormitory erected on campus. This four-story building included a kitchen, laundry, music hall, and meeting rooms. Inside the dormitory, students ate in Kemble Dining Hall, which served 300. The dining hall was made possible by a generous donation from trustee Fortunatus Dulancy Kemble of Long Island, Kansas.

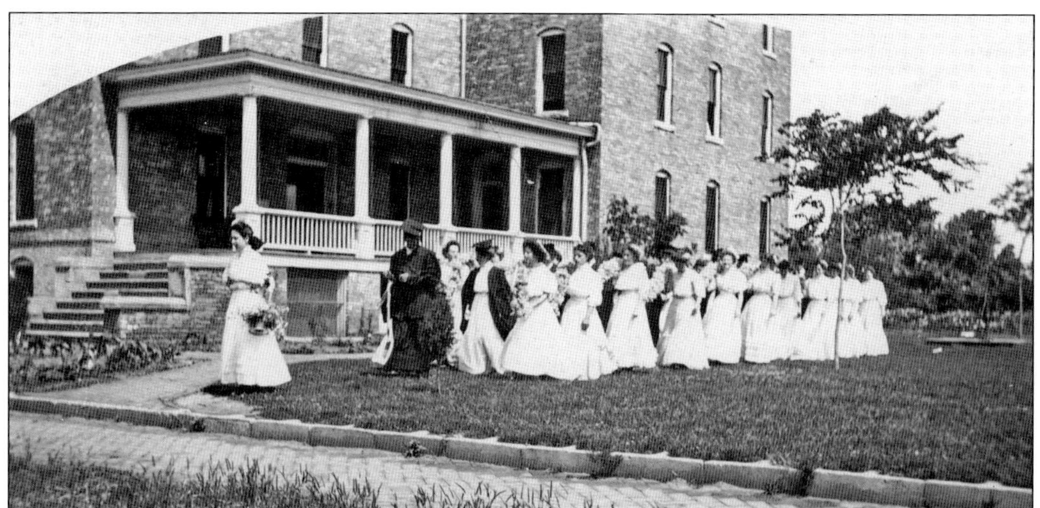

In June 1909, a large crowd witnessed the senior normal class planting ivy on the campus grounds. The senior class marched to Schuyler Hall, planted the ivy, and then proceeded to the chapel for a program where Winnifred Young read a paper, "A Glance at the Past," and Grace Boddy read on the topic "A Glimpse of the Future." That evening, graduation exercises were held in the university chapel.

Caroline Matson began her preparatory education at the Kansas State Teachers College and Baker University. While teaching and serving on the administration for Salina's city schools, she attended summer classes at the University of Chicago and Harvard. She then earned her degree from Kansas Wesleyan and joined the faculty in 1906. Matson was an integral part of the campus and served in multiple positions, from professor to dean of women.

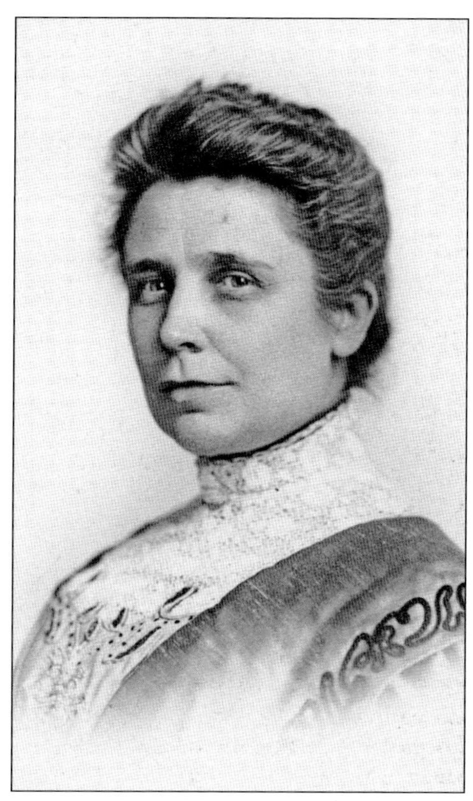

Dr. Wilbur F. Hoyt was instrumental in securing the Peate telescope, the first university observatory in the state. On the morning of June 5, 1902, the observatory was dedicated during commencement exercises in which Dr. Aaron Schuyler provided a lecture on the topic of astronomy. For 25¢, members of the public had the opportunity to view the stars. In 1910, the observatory was demolished to make room for King Gymnasium.

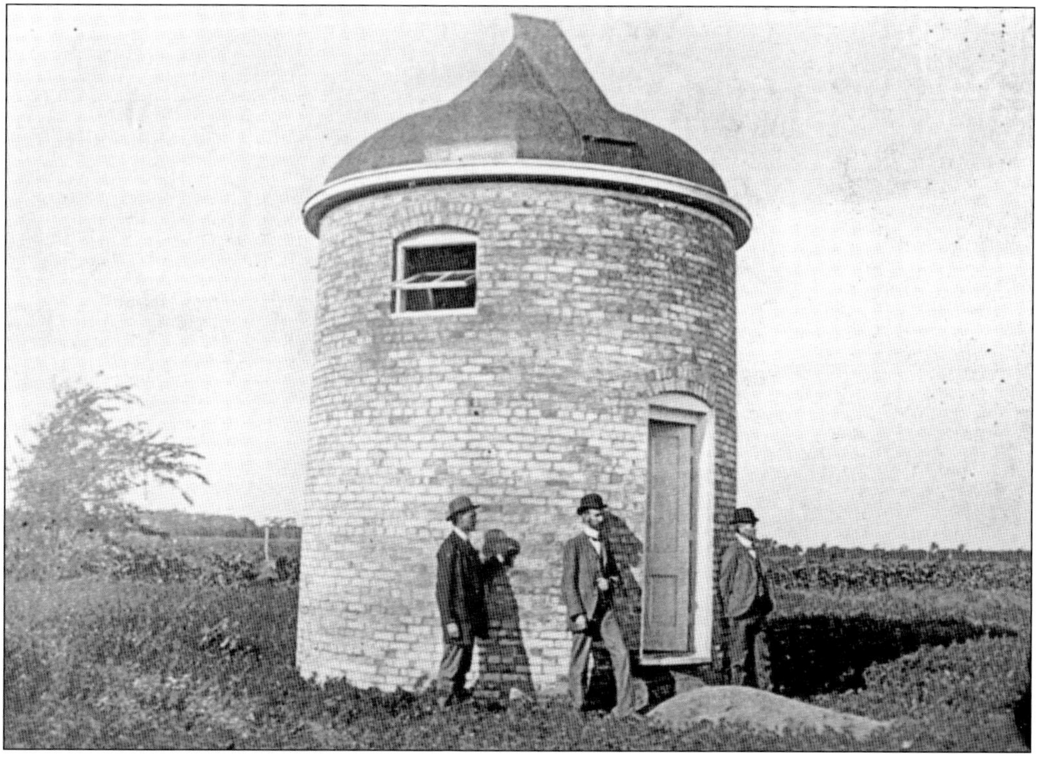

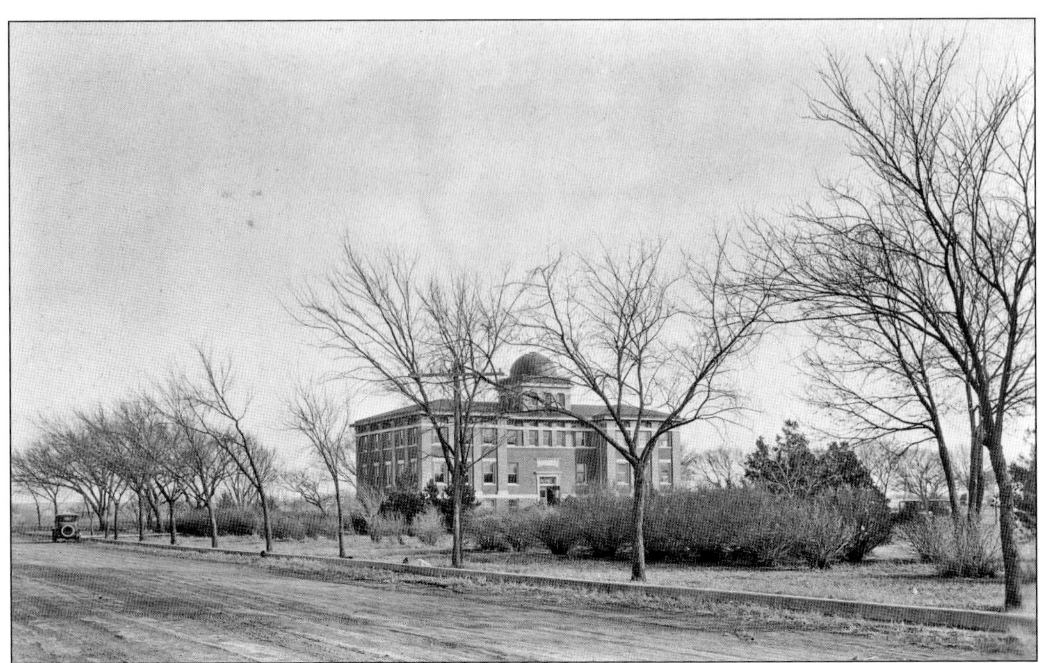

In 1906, excitement spread on campus when Pres. Thomas Roach received a letter from James Bertain, secretary to Andrew Carnegie, informing the university that $25,000 would be allocated for the purpose of building a science hall, dependent on the university raising another $25,000. By December 1908, construction had started, with the basement and concrete for the first floor complete. The architecture of the building was a combination of Greek Revival and modified Renaissance Revival. Construction included brick and reinforced concrete, and fireproofing measures were implemented. A fireproof building was extremely important, as Salina Normal University closed due to a tragic fire in 1904. The cornerstone was laid on November 17, 1908. Mary Linden Johnson of Great Bend, Kansas, donated $1,000 towards equipment. This building highlighted a need to make many improvements to the campus, including water and sewer lines.

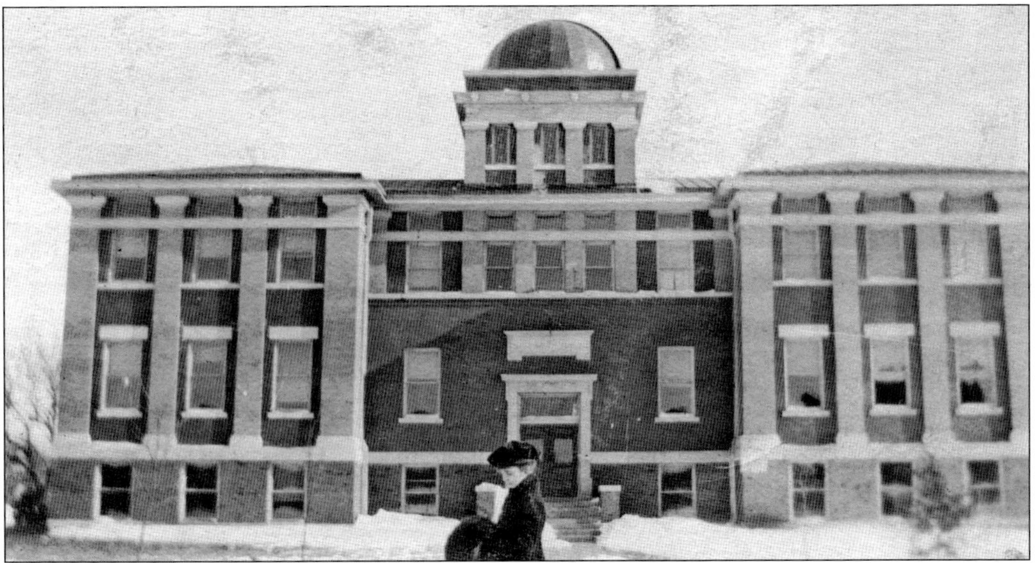

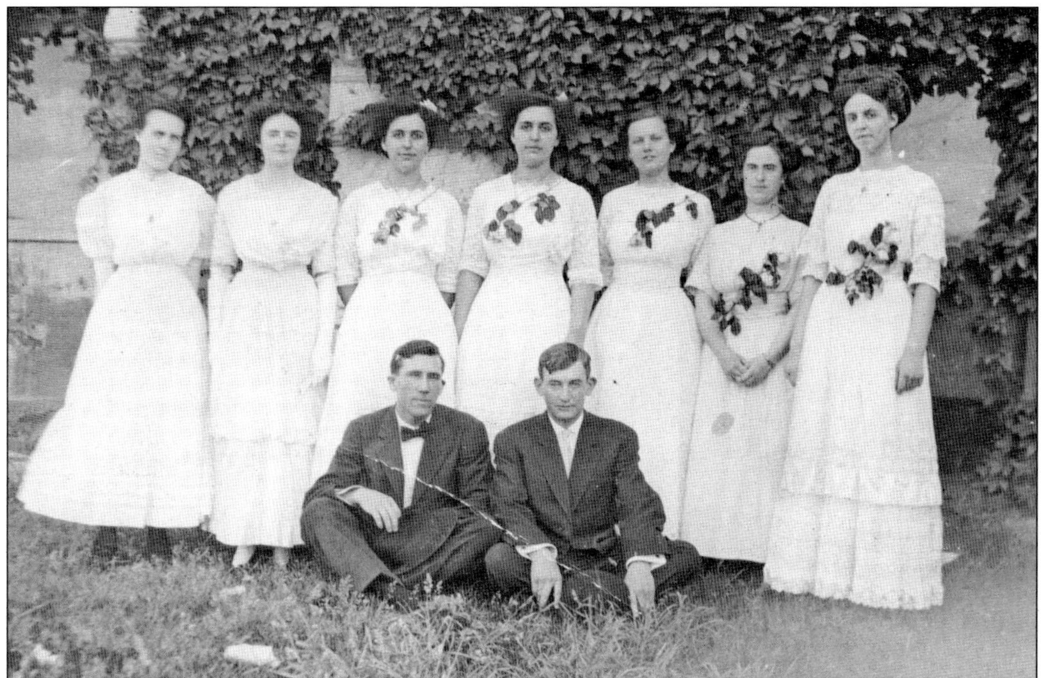

The Athenaeum and Delphian Societies often joined together to host social events. On a cold October morning in 1911, members of these societies hosted a breakfast for new students. At 5:00 a.m., they gathered at Prof. Clayton J. Page's orchard southeast of town. Throughout the morning, students enjoyed conversation while frying ham and roasting apples over the campfire. Members of the two societies are pictured around 1911.

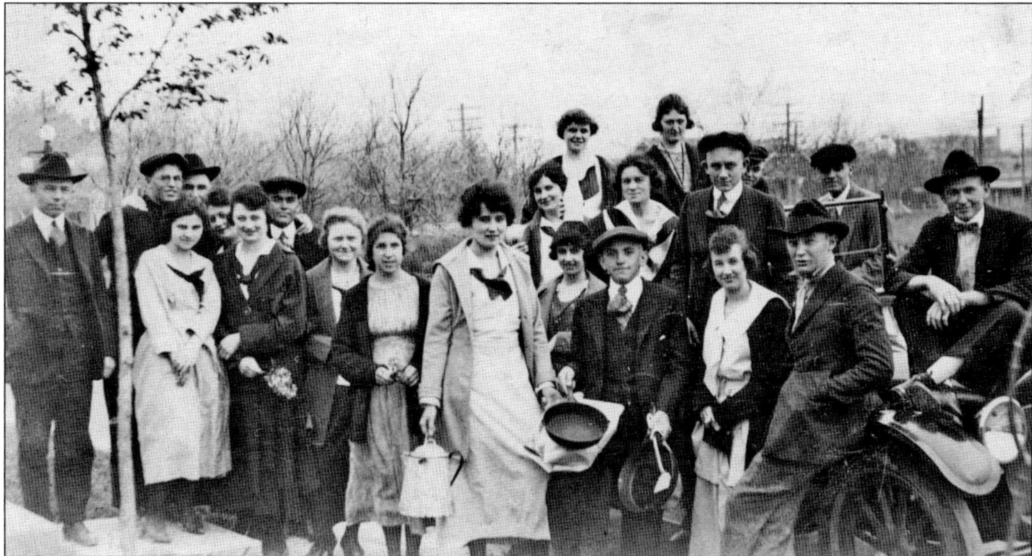

In the early 1920s, rising early to cook breakfast over the campfire became a traditional fun outing for students. Students frequently hiked to White's Ford for an early breakfast for different events. Another favorite spot was Upper Mill, where students would travel on the Coyote Motor Boat. Most noted for the routine early morning breakfasts were girls of Schuyler Hall and the Athenaeum Society.

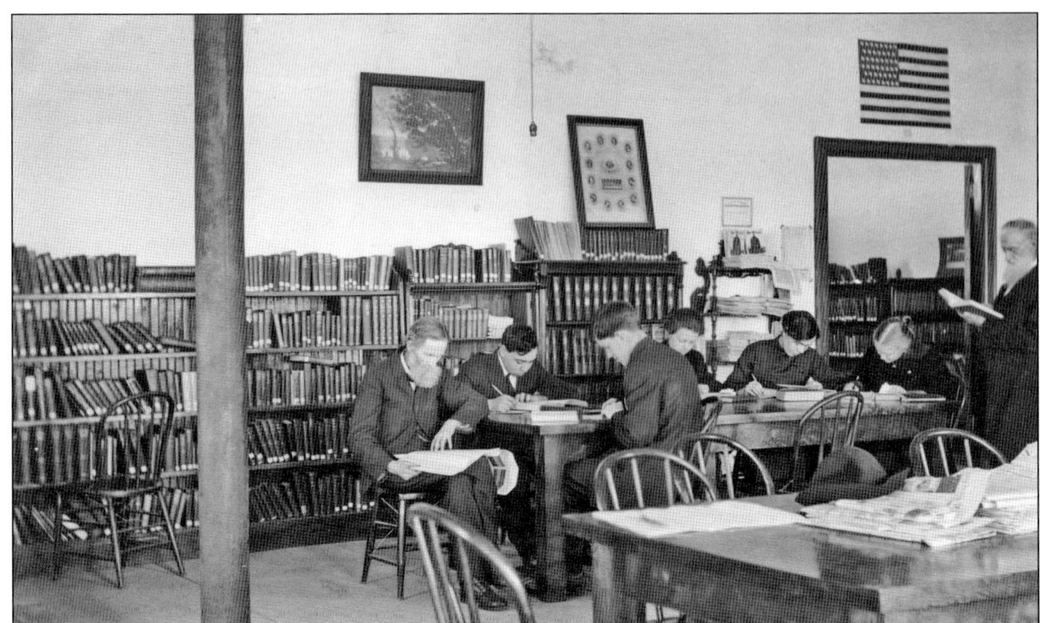

The library, located inside Carnegie Science Hall, acquired over 12,000 volumes by 1915. The acquisitions of the personal libraries of Aaron Schuyler and local Salina founder Col. William Addison Phillips added to the depth of academic material. Schuyler (seated left) and Rev. Milton Stolz (standing, far right) are pictured with students in the library around 1910.

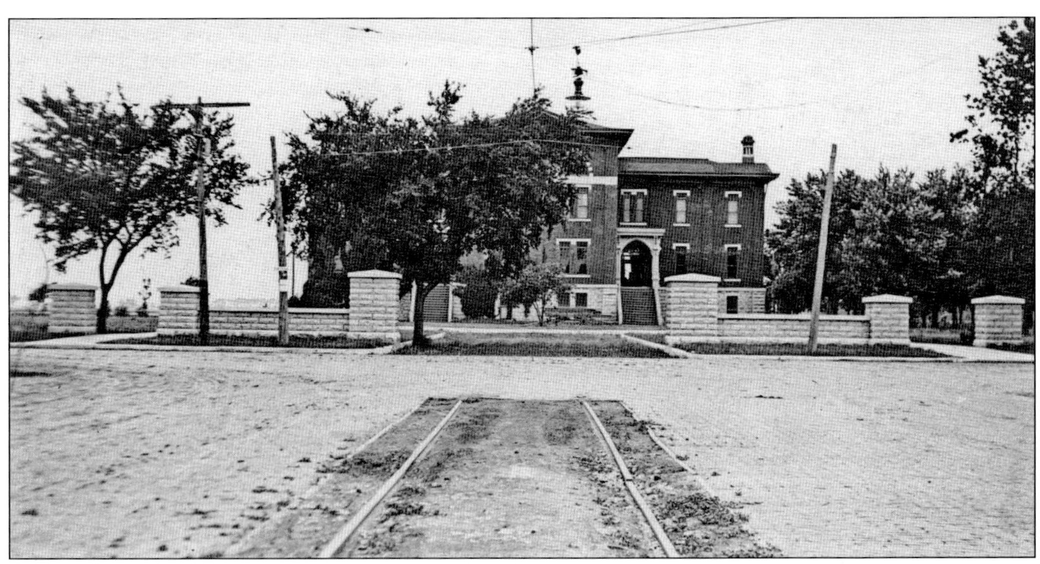

After 30 years, the lone building had company and the prairie field began to fade away. The university founders' foresight created a rhythm for future development. Pres. Robert P. Smith was a philanthropist who pledged his brain, body, and soul to ensure university ideals. He strongly believed college instilled an appreciation of life's values. A year prior to his exit, he established the first official Founder's Day on February 17, 1914.

Two

Building a Campus

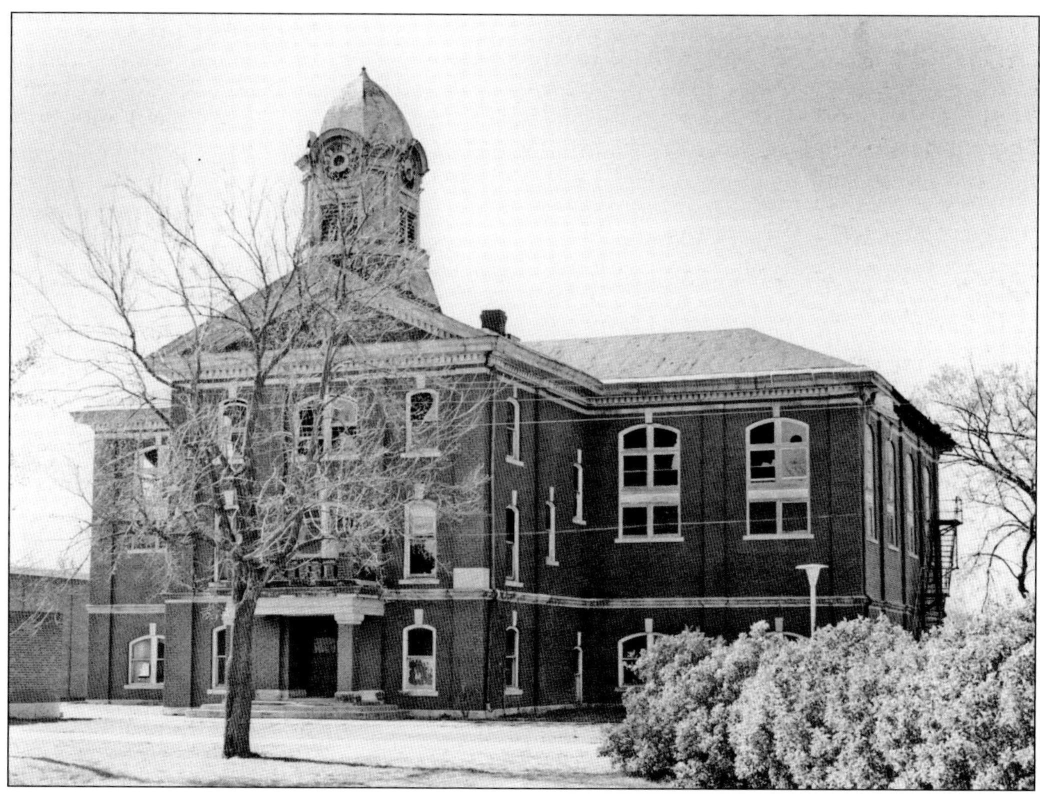

By 1914, plans were under way for a campus gymnasium. Albert King led the planning process. He visited and compared other university facilities to ensure Kansas Wesleyan's gymnasium would be the best athletic facility. In October 1915, Dr. Abram Winegardner Harris, president of Northwestern University, spoke at the cornerstone ceremony. Harris mentioned that gymnasiums in higher education were a relatively new concept that promoted an age of health.

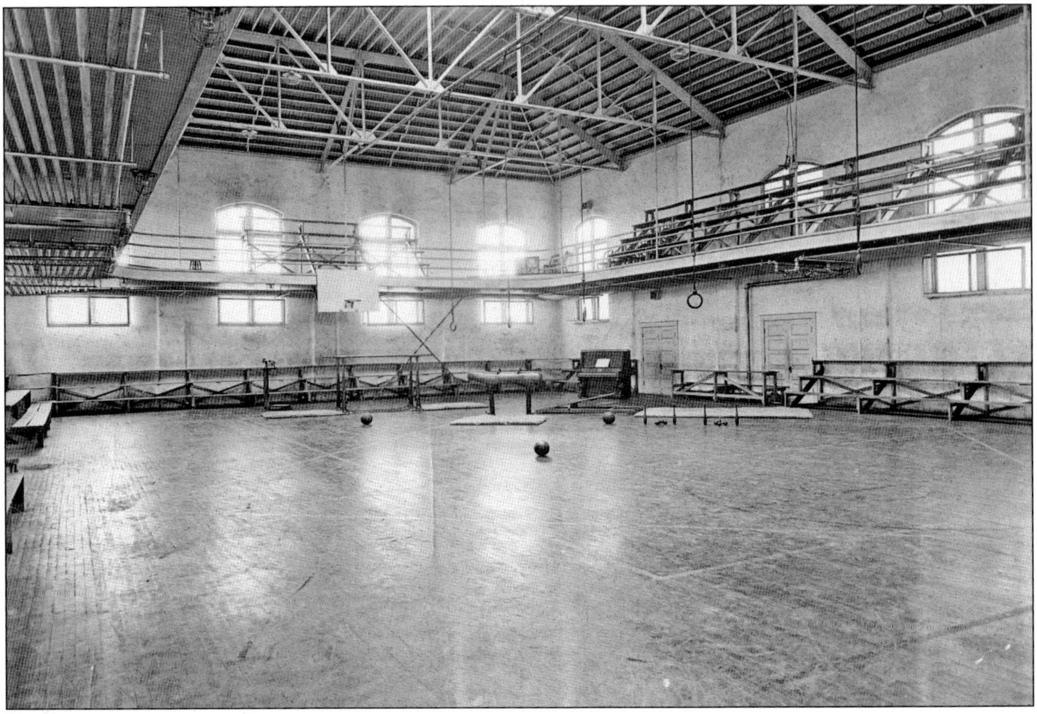

King Gymnasium opened in 1916. The interior included a 58-foot-long basketball court, an 18-by-40-foot swimming pool ranging from four to eight feet deep, offices for athletic staff, and YMCA meeting rooms. A unique feature of the period was the addition of 15 private showers for women. The class of 1915 added an exterior electric clock that weighed 350 pounds.

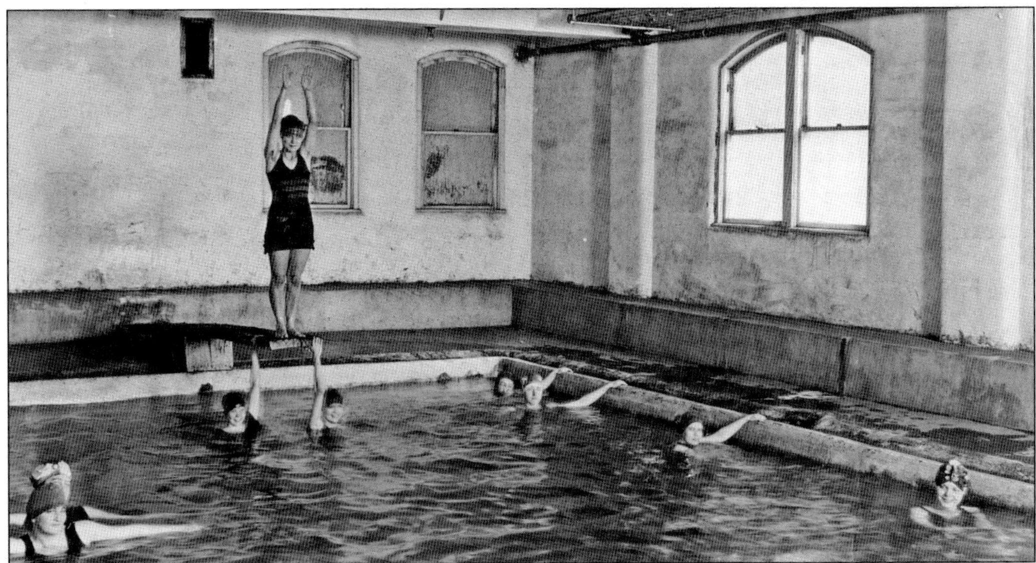

The university pool was a popular site on campus. In the summer of 1916, an average of 120 women swam daily. In November 1917, the pool was repainted with four coats of glistening white paint. By 1921, crowds grew too large and scheduled swim times were implemented. The popularity of the YMCA and Kansas Wesleyan pools served as a catalyst for the development of a public pool in Salina.

From 1915 to 1918, Pres. John Harmon (right) became known for evangelical ministry and crowd-drawing topics of life, war, and patriotism. In March 1917, Harmon, alongside Rev. Alexander Bennett and alumnus Col. Fred R. Fitzpatrick, led a patriotic service featuring the Kinemacolor moving picture *Nathan Hale*. Harmon's son John Jr. and coach William "Bill" Floyd Ragle, class of 1916, both served in World War I and were members of Salina's Company M.

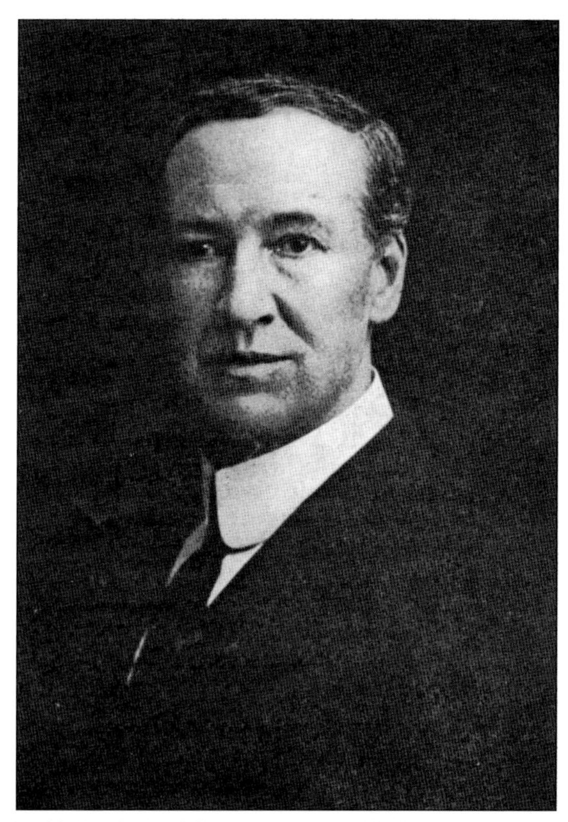

On October 1, 1918, a crowd watched acting president Albert King raise the flag and Howell's band play "The Star-Spangled Banner." Speeches were given by William Heusner, Edward Heslop, alumnus Charles Burch, and Gen. Peyton C. March of the War Department. Kansas Wesleyan was one of 10 Kansas universities that hosted Student Army Training Corps. The spacious, well-equipped Kemble Dining Hall was swiftly turned into a mess hall.

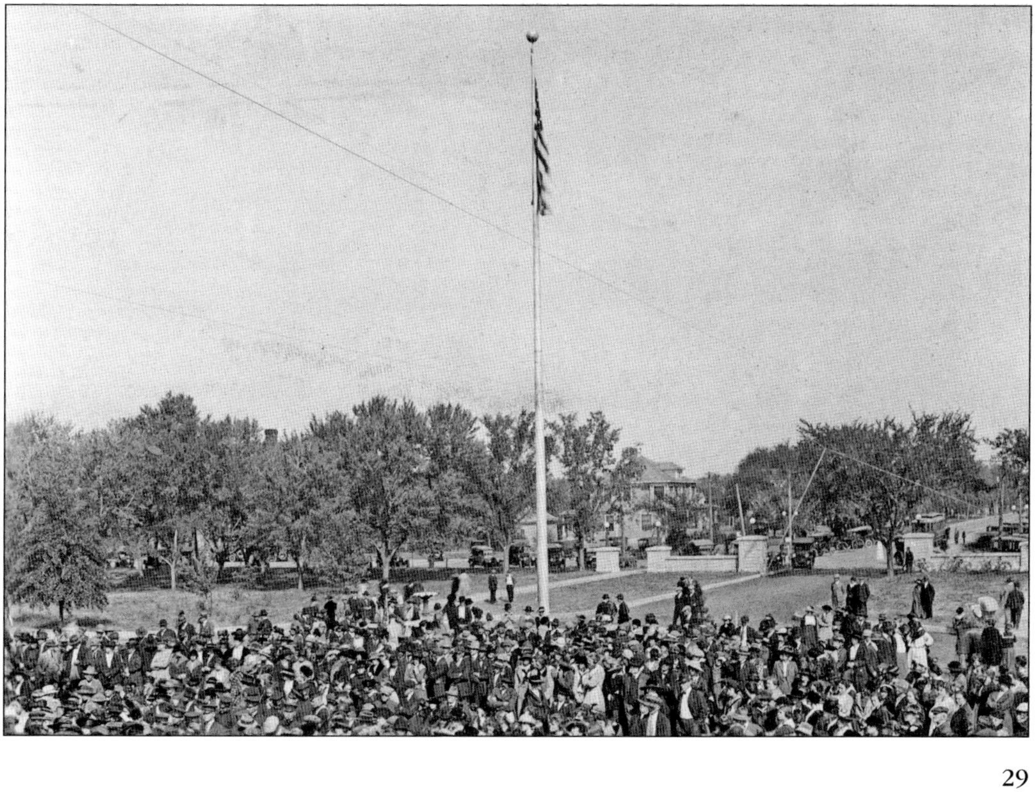

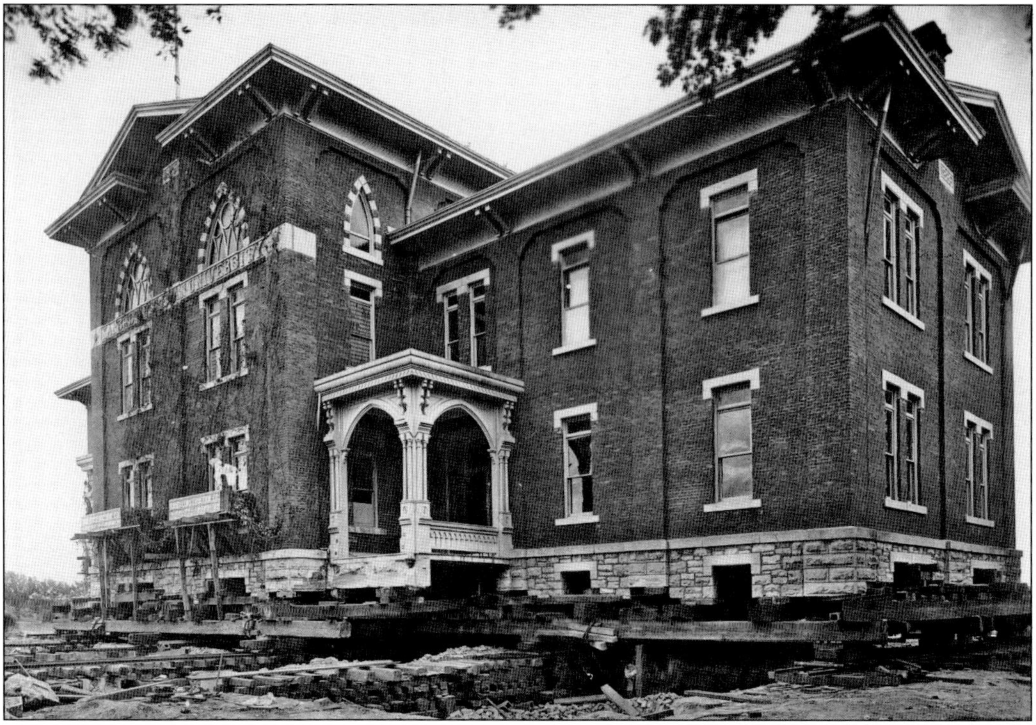

In preparation for a new administration building, the existing building was moved in 1921. The building was carefully moved south and west 40 feet per day for 550 feet. A rededication ceremony was held on June 6, 1922, in honor of Rev. John Hughes Lockwood, and the building became known as Lockwood Hall. It was used primarily for art and music classrooms and was razed in 1959.

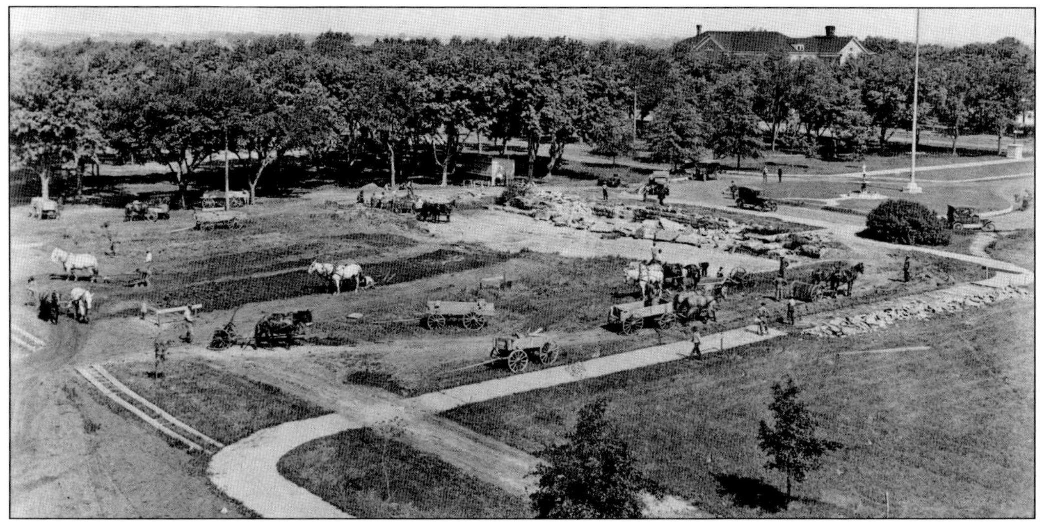

In 1922, excavation began for the Hall of Pioneers, which remained under construction for eight years. Meanwhile, Robert Grafton painted the mural *The Coming of the Pioneers* for Sams Chapel, which was made possible by Laura Clubb. Kansas City–area Methodist bishop Ernest Lynn Waldorf spoke at the dedication ceremony on the school's anniversary, September 15, 1930. He noted his words would be brief but of "mighty import."

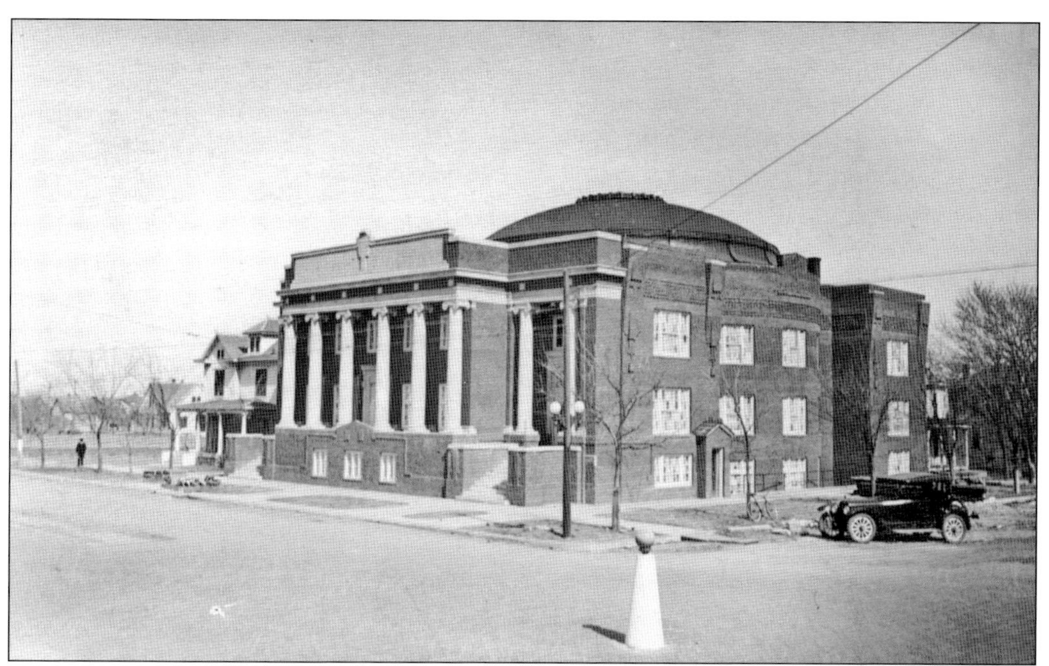

From 1909 to 1917, the University Methodist Church held services inside the administration building's chapel. In 1917, construction started on the Greek Revival old-rose brick and algorile stone church at the northeast corner of Santa Fe and Claflin Avenues. In January 1918, a dedicatory cantata, *The Prodigal Son*, was delivered under the direction of Grace Nason-King. The first year, the church temporarily closed due to an influenza quarantine.

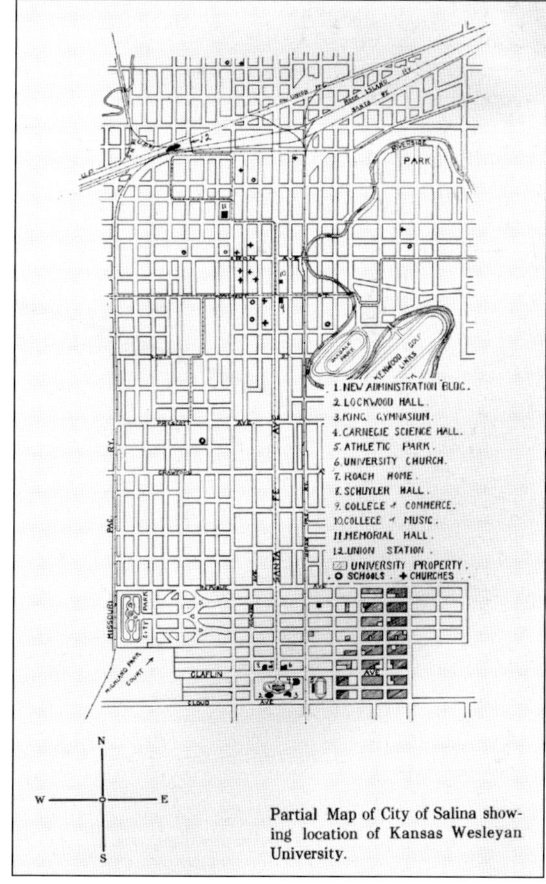

Partial Map of City of Salina showing location of Kansas Wesleyan University.

This c. 1923 campus map features the city of Salina, because the music and business colleges were located downtown. It indicates locations on the main campus including the new administration building, later named Pioneer Hall. For many years, the campus remained the southern city boundary. In 1930, the *Advance* sponsored a contest to select a name for south Salina. One of the proposed names was Wesliville.

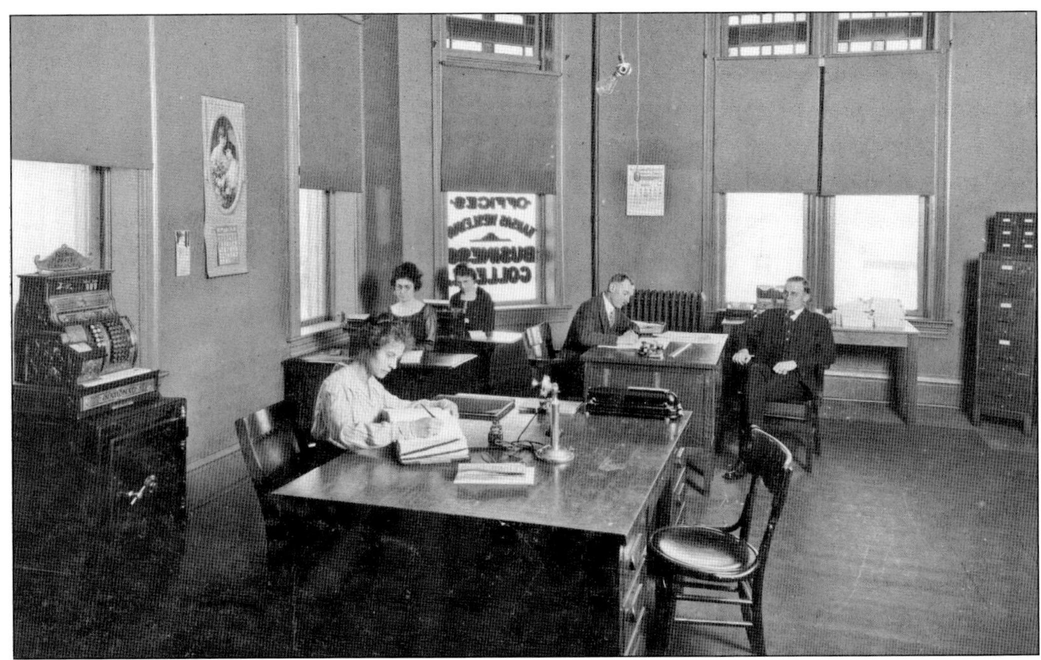

By the 1920s, the Kansas Wesleyan Business College evolved into the Kansas Wesleyan College of Commerce. The university was comprised of three colleges. The College of Liberal Arts was located on the main campus, while the College of Commerce and College of Music were located downtown. Over the years, the business courses included stenography, telegraphy, and eventually executive business skills. The school was well known in the Midwest for its notable curriculum and dedication to excellence. As the university's academic goals shifted, instructor Perry Brown purchased the business school in 1933, changing the name to Perry Brown Business College. Following suit, longtime athletic director Alexander Brown Mackie purchased half the business school in 1938, creating the Brown-Mackie School of Business. The school became Brown Mackie College, with 26 schools across the nation, which are set to close by 2018.

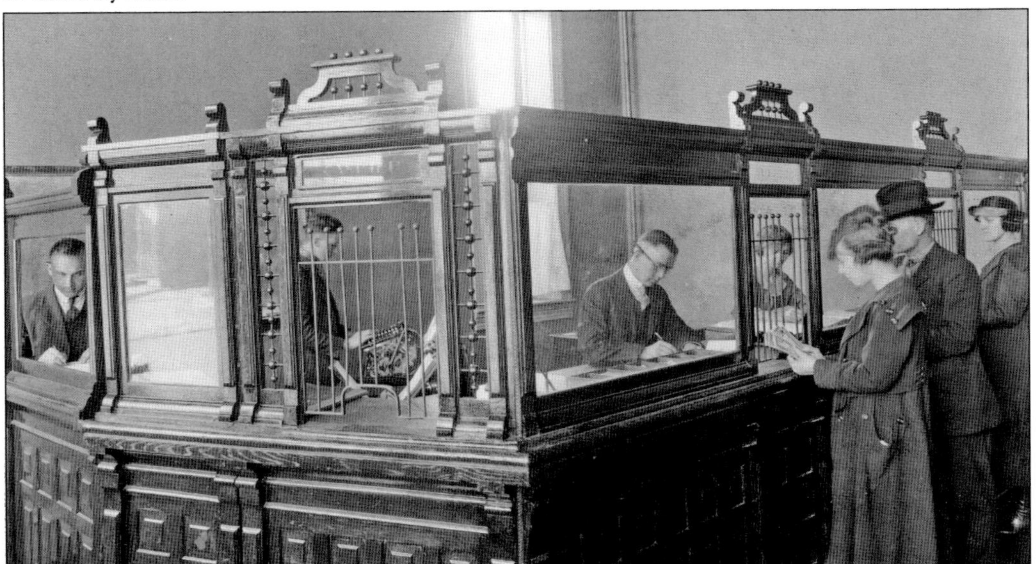

Earl Corder Sams's exorbitant generosity to the university impacted campus growth. Sams served on the board of trustees as well as many other philanthropic interests. In 1907, he began as a sales clerk in the first J.C. Penney Store in Kemmerer, Wyoming. A decade later, Sams was elected chairman of the J.C. Penney Company. Sams (left) is pictured with Pres. Larkin Bowers around 1925.

The Roach home (foreground) served as the president's residence through the 1960s. D. Arthur Zook was the last president to reside in the home. Schuyler Hall (background) was a women's dormitory until 1951, when Pfeiffer Hall was built. Schuyler Hall became a men's dormitory and was used until it was torn down in 1966 to make room for new dormitories, Wilson Hall and Wesley Hall.

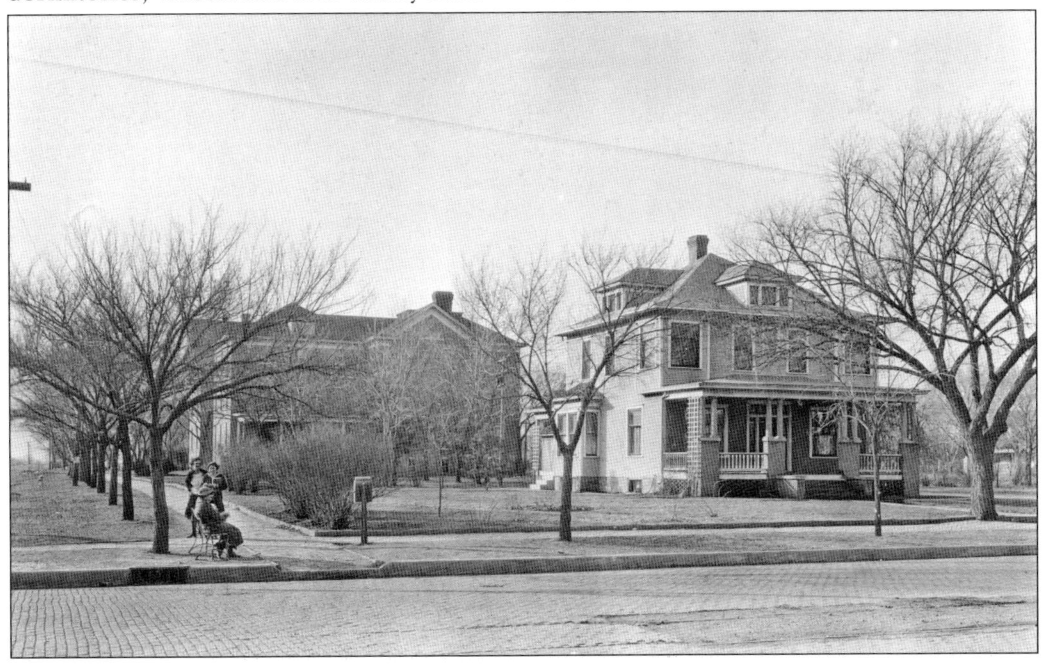

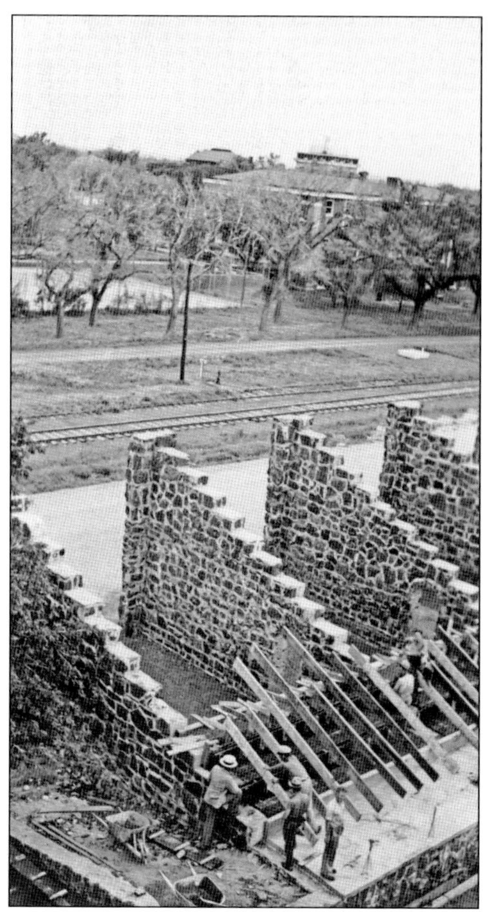

By the fall of 1938, plans for a new stadium project were under way. The stadium was built as a National Youth Administration project, a branch of the Works Progress Administration. The stone used was a native sandstone hand-quarried from a farm five miles west of Salina. Construction workers prepared the stones by hand and mortared them into place. Several challenges occurred during the construction process, including a delay in the delivery of materials. This also caused the planned eight-foot rock wall around the athletic field to not be built. The stadium was named in honor of Glenn L. Martin, an aviation pioneer who attended the Kansas Wesleyan Business College. On September 21, 1940, the Coyotes faced off against the Sterling College Warriors in the 2,200-seat Glenn L. Martin Stadium. The Coyotes won 14-0.

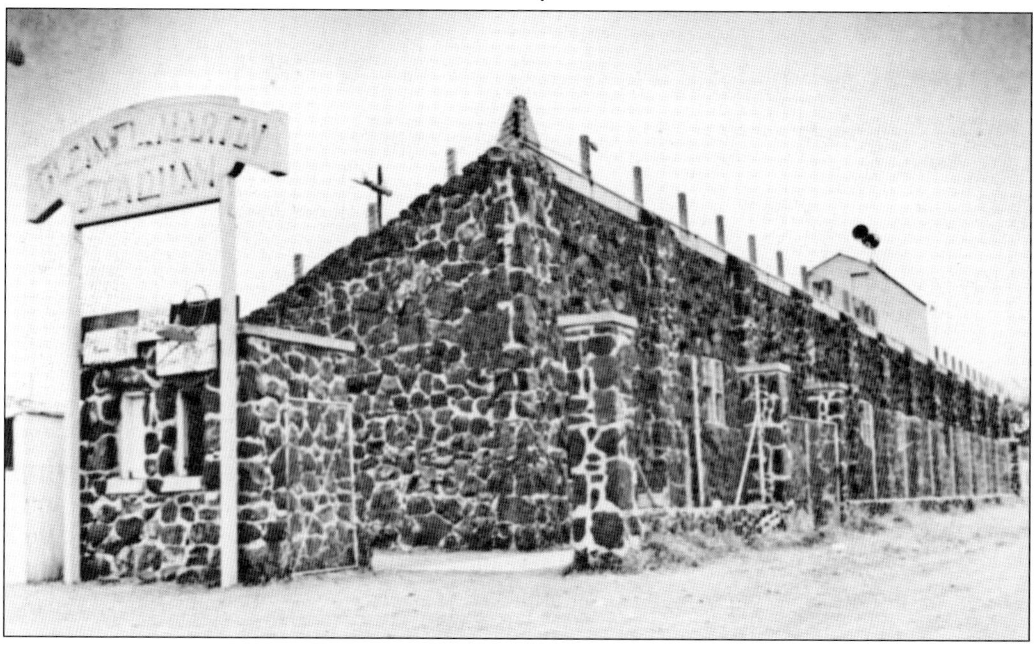

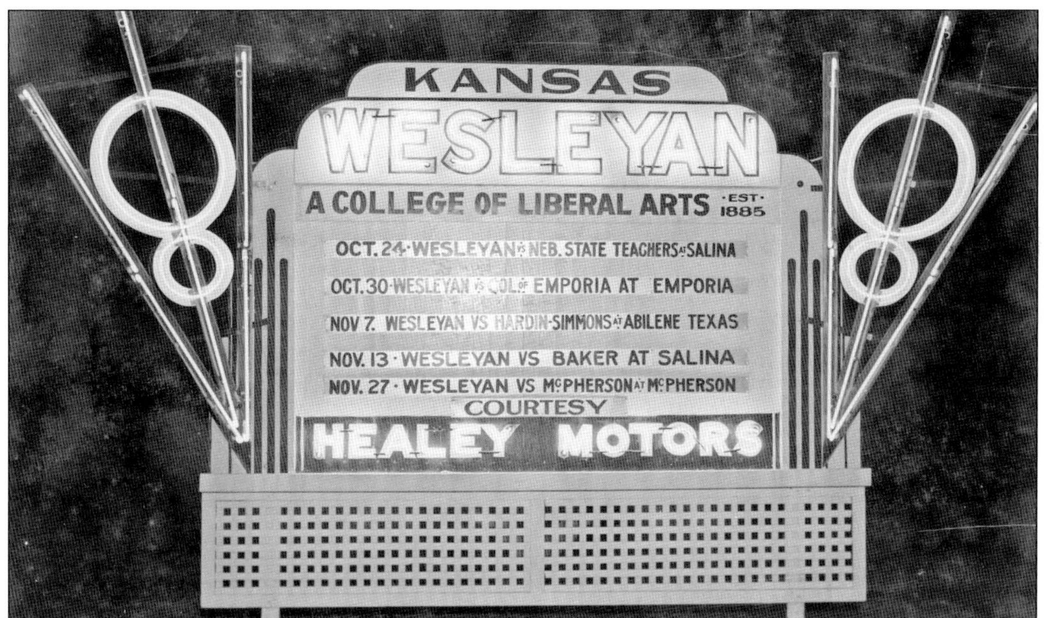

The university sign sponsored by Healey Motors advertised "courses in step with the times," including business, fine arts, science, and aviation. By November 1939, the university received approval from the federal flying program at the Civil Aeronautics Authority to move forward with the pilot training program. Dawson Air Service was contracted to implement the aviation program. Pictured here, the opposite side of the sign features the 1936 football schedule.

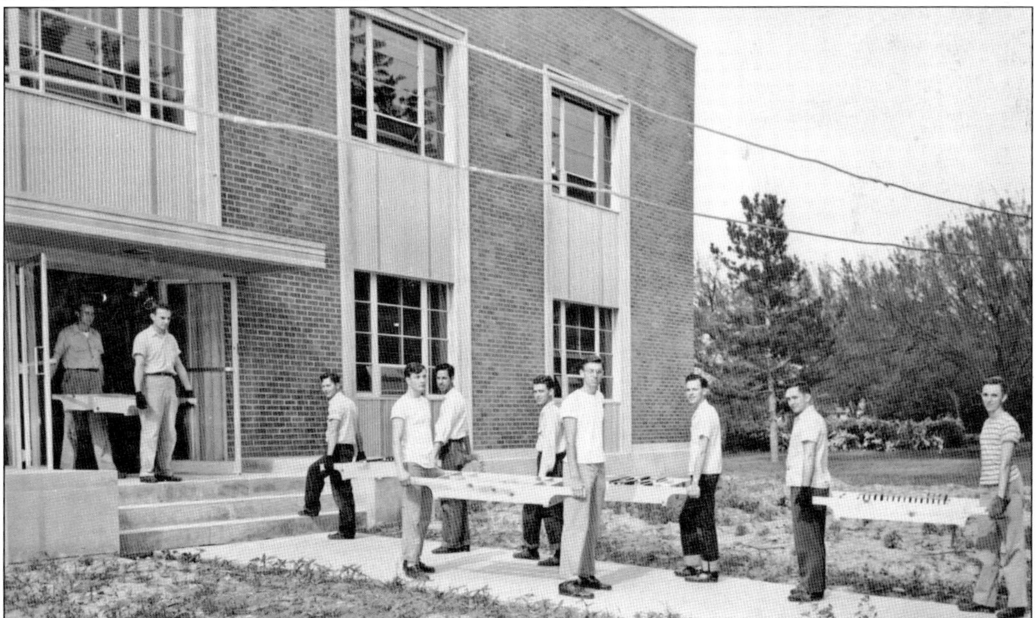

Pres. Herbert Root initiated a "Committee of 100" fundraising campaign to raise $100,000 for a new library. Memorial Library was dedicated in June 1949 to veterans from the student body and alumni, especially those who paid the ultimate sacrifice. Ruth Wyatt was the first librarian to oversee the building and its holdings. Here, students assist with moving materials into Memorial Library.

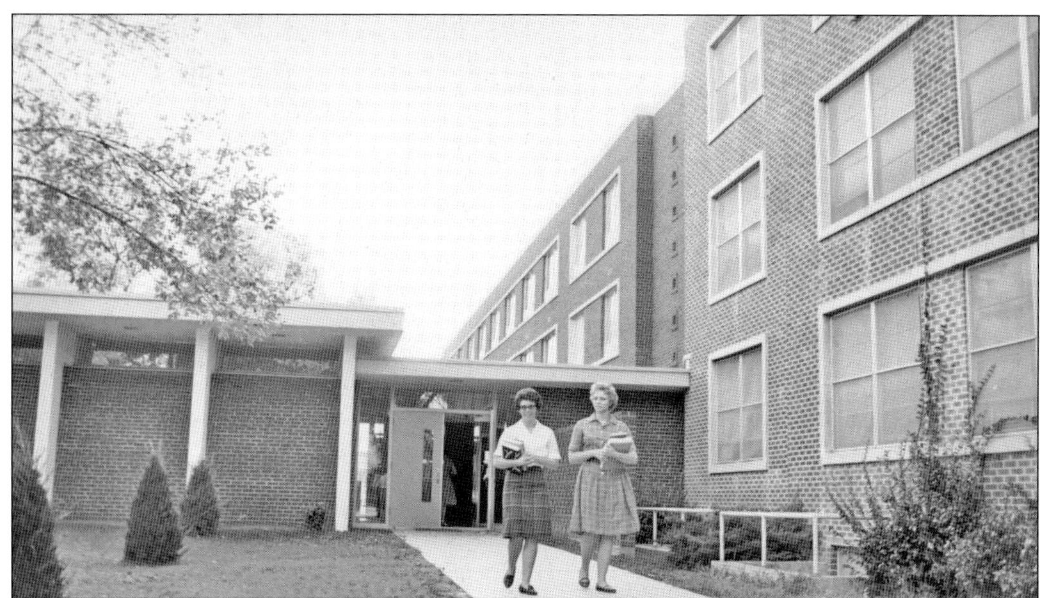

In the fall of 1951, a new women's dormitory, Annie Marner Pfeiffer Hall, opened. The rooms included solid oak furniture paired with bright and modern decor in four color schemes. The residents enjoyed the luxury of modern conveniences. The dormitory included Stewart Dining Hall, a new addition for the campus. In 1963, the Christina Shriwise Dining Hall was created. The former women's dormitory, Schuyler Hall, became a men's dormitory.

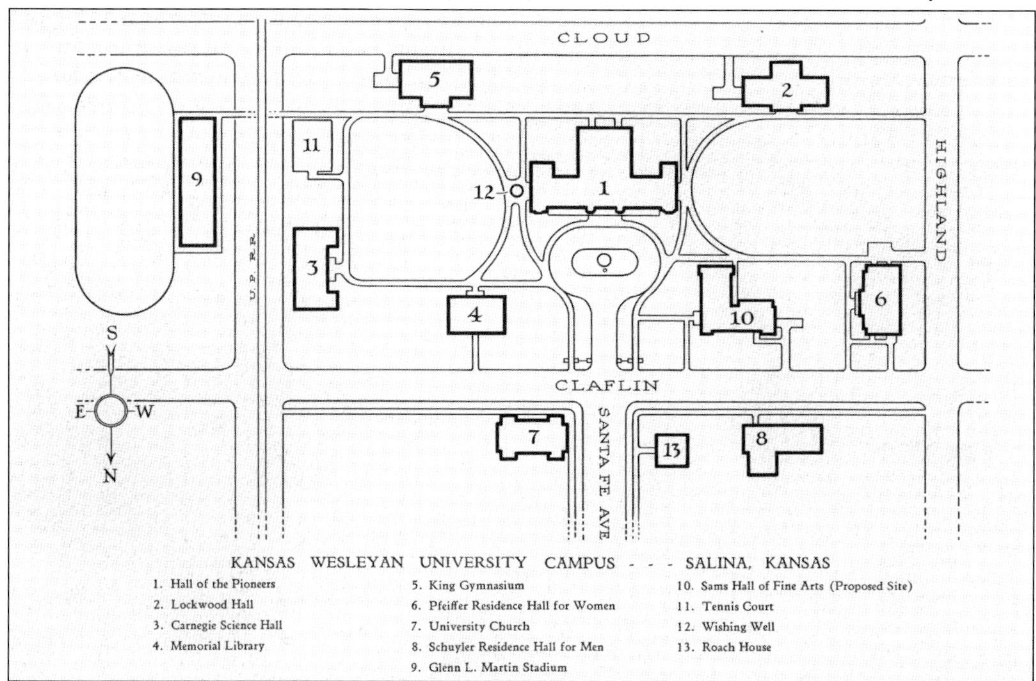

This c. 1950 campus map illustrates how campus growth dictated needs for expansion and how the university campus developed over the first 65 years. The proposed footprint of the Earl C. Sams Fine Arts Building is outlined. It also shows the shift in dormitory assignments as Pfeiffer Hall was built for women and the men transitioned to occupy Schuyler Hall.

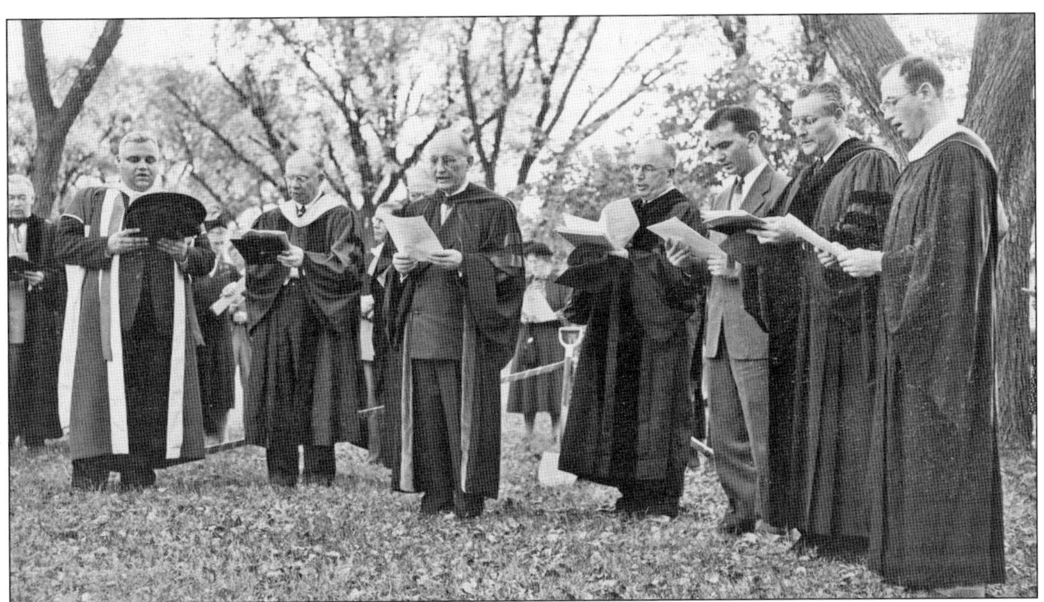

On November 14, 1951, the ground-breaking ceremony for the Sams Fine Arts Building was held in conjunction with a special convocation. Pres. Stanley Trickett (above, far left; below, holding cornerstone) led the ceremony. The building was made possible through generous donations from Earl Corder Sams and Leila Sudendorf Rearwin. This was an exciting time for Division of Fine Arts faculty. Harry Huber led the Division of Fine Arts with music professors Arthur Custer, George Brown, and Edward Schiller, speech and theater professor Lilybelle Lewin Carlisle, and art professor Edna Tuttle. This provided adequate space for fine arts students to study art, dramatics, music, and speech. During commencement weekend in 1952, Sams's daughters Gladys Porter and Camille Virginia Lightner attended the cornerstone ceremony. Construction was completed by Johnson Brothers Construction Company.

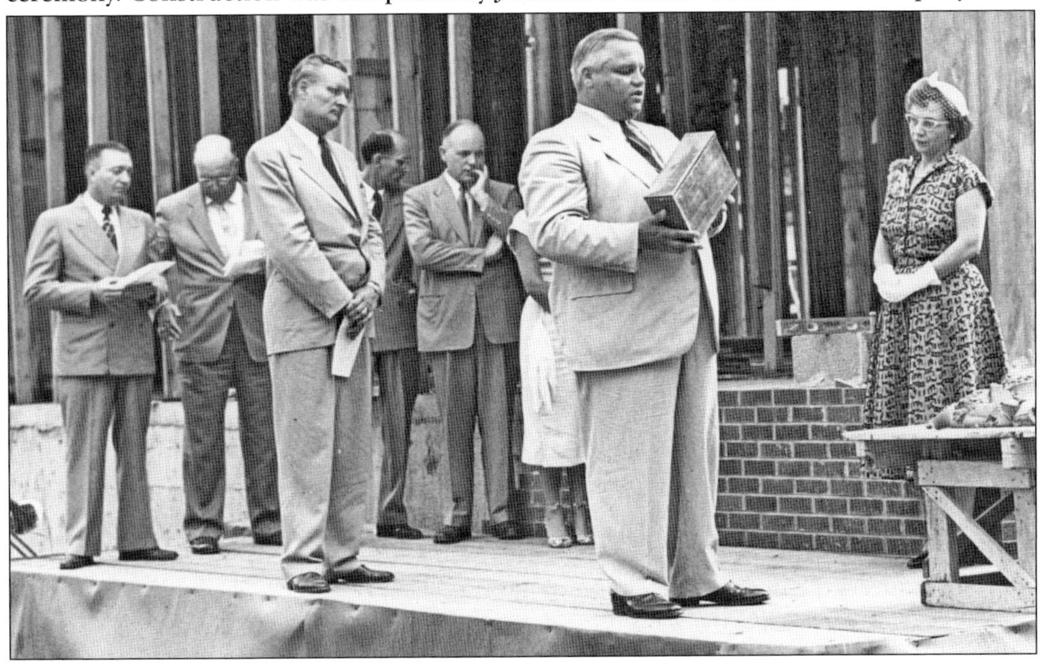

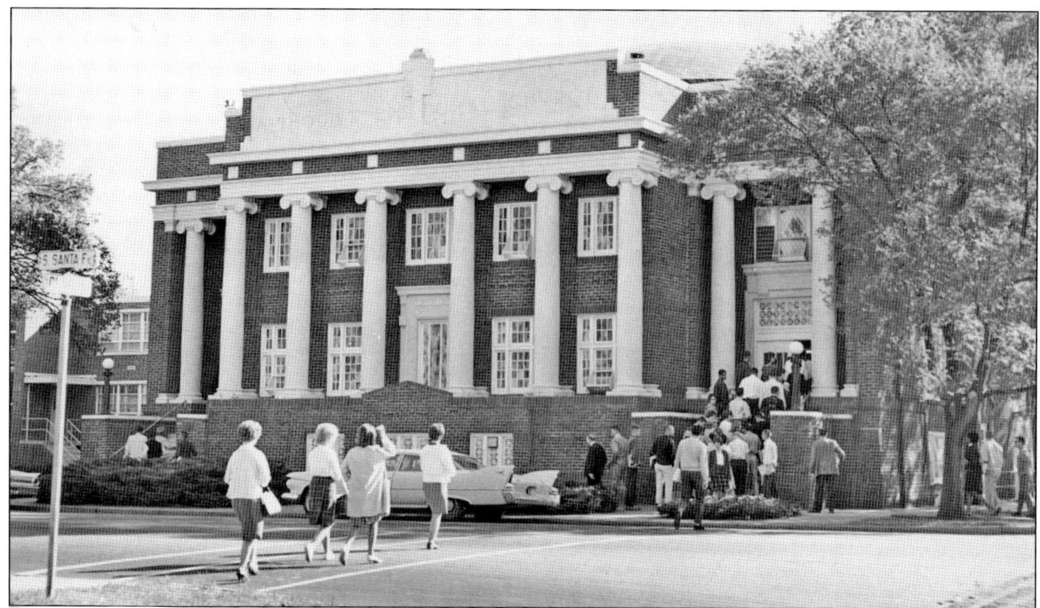

The University United Methodist Church is positioned across from the gateway to the campus. The church has remained connected through involvement in university and community activities. Inspiring interior architecture and windows have continued to provide a welcoming atmosphere for the faculty, students, and congregation. Religious life on campus was closely tied to the Methodist student movement, which included a freshman whistle walk and semester retreats.

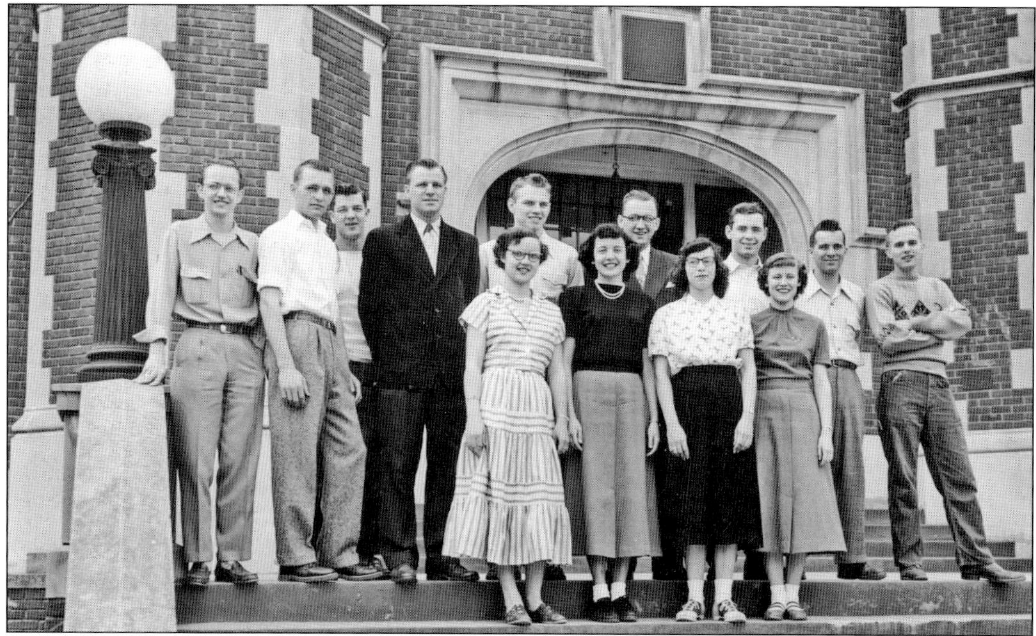

The Hall of Pioneers, also known as Pioneer Hall, was completed in 1930. The building continues to serve today as the campus administrative hub. Since its construction, Pioneer Hall has served as the iconic building on campus and beautifully caps the south end of Santa Fe Avenue. Shown here are second-generation students around 1951.

Three

Carrying the Vision Forward

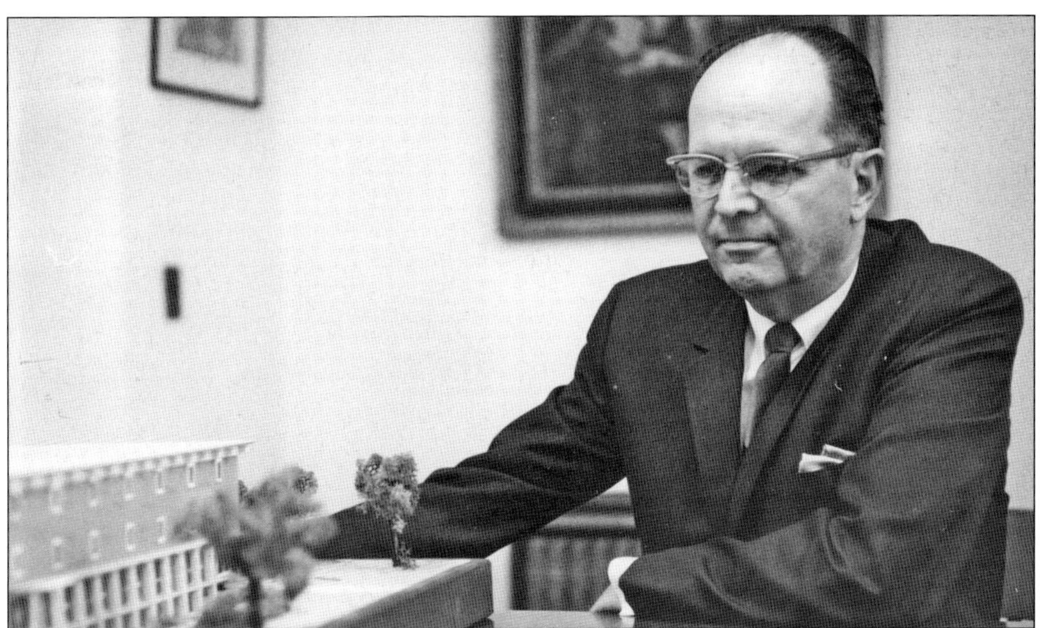

D. Arthur Zook assumed the presidency during difficult times, but in his first decade, enrollment doubled and the school achieved accreditation. During his inauguration message, he outlined three principles to govern educational institutions: service to the whole human family, institutional character, and honest self-evaluation that beacons the light of one's intrinsic value to society. According to trustee Whitley Austin, Zook was a healing force for Kansas Wesleyan.

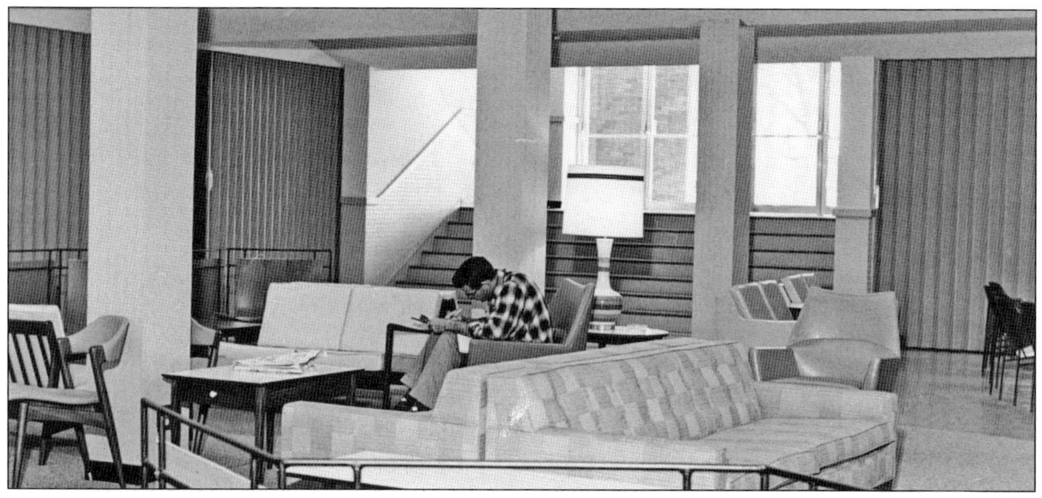

In October 1959, the university had cause to celebrate the achievements of the last decade. Over 250 people gathered for the ribbon-cutting for McAdams Student Center in the basement of Pioneer Hall. Pres. D. Arthur Zook, Salina mayor Don McCune, student council president Doug Supernaw, and trustee Murray Wilson (namesake of Wilson Hall) officially opened the new space where students enjoyed the lounge and snack bar. The space was furnished with contemporary pieces in hues of gray, blue, green, and orange chosen by Dwight Putnam. This area also included two meeting rooms and a bookstore. Below, Dr. Albert Robinson, professor of botany, and Dr. Felix Wasserman (by the bicycle), professor of languages, are pictured in the hallway outside McAdams Student Center.

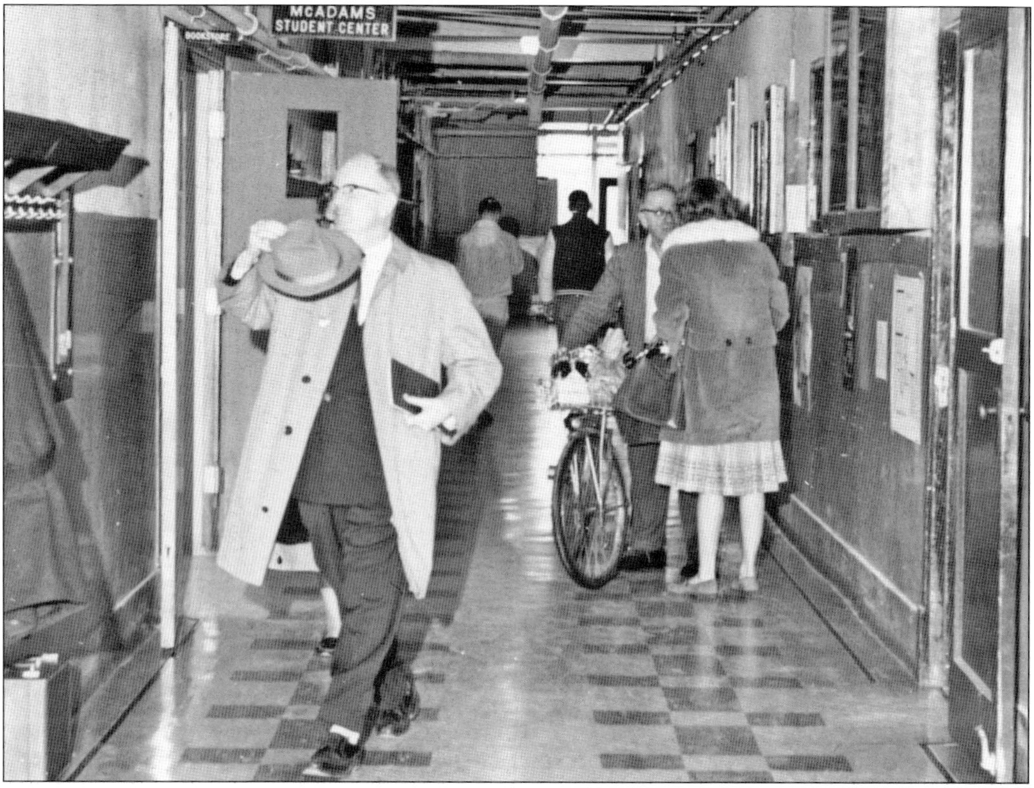

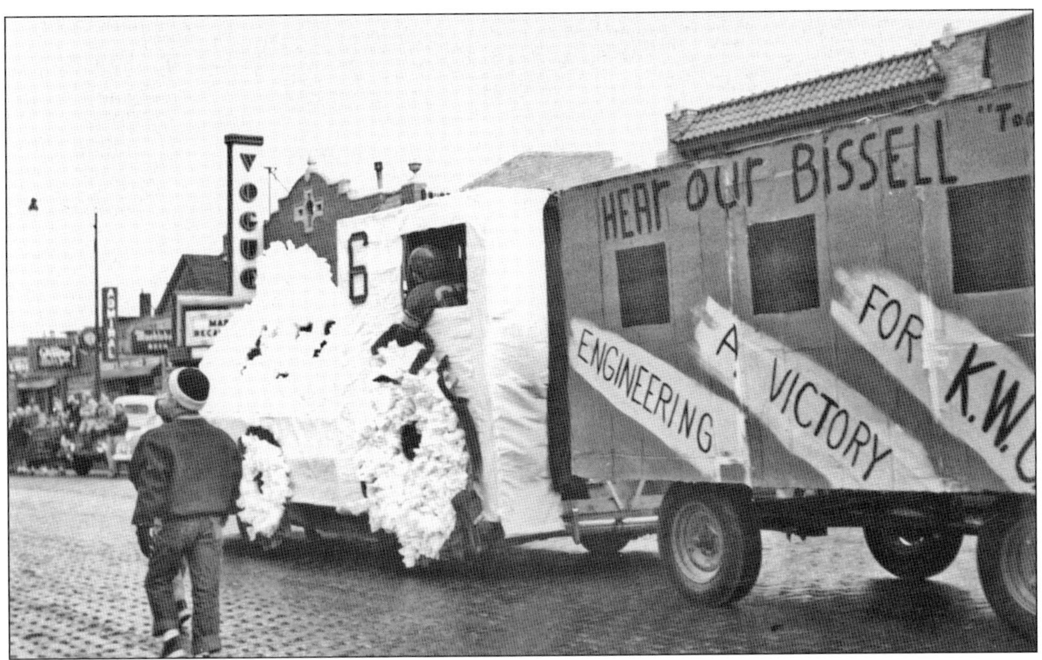

An Ohio native and a graduate of Heidelberg College, coach Gene Bissell was an inspirational force on campus for over 40 years. His care and dedication to all students made a phenomenal impact on the university community. He championed athletes, diversity, and community. The connections he made on and off campus have created an everlasting legacy. This Homecoming parade float proclaims "Hear Our Bissell, Engineering a Victory for K.W.U."

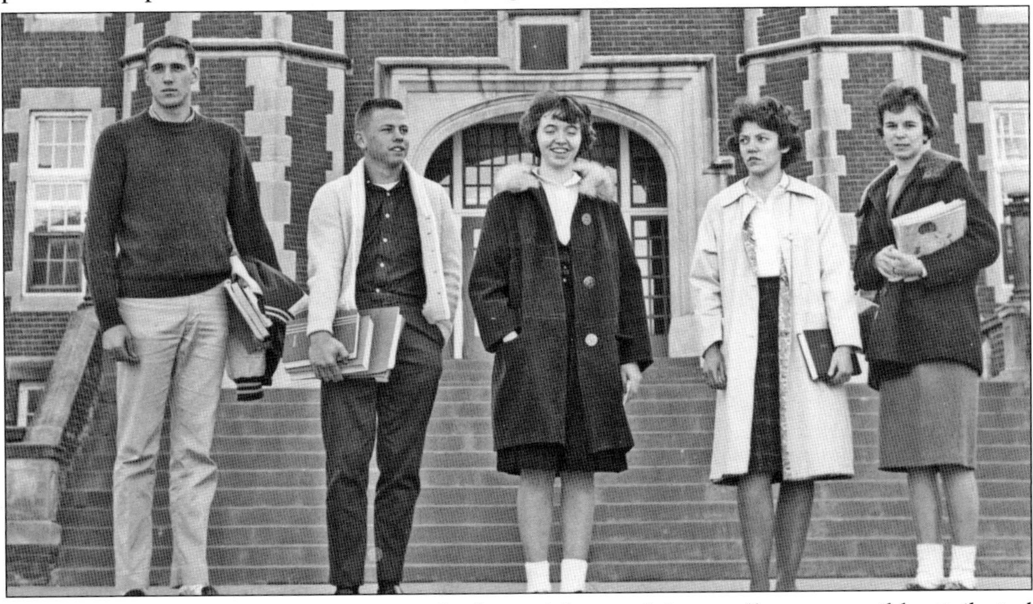

In the 1960s, the university experienced substantial growth in enrollment, possibly attributed to achieving accreditation in May 1958 from the North Central Association of Colleges. The City of Salina recognized this achievement when Mayor Harold Jaeger proclaimed November 17–24, 1958, as "Kansas Wesleyan University Week." Students on the steps of Pioneer Hall are, from left to right, Paul Peters, Gordy Gorton, Faye Alsobrooks, Sharen Atkinson, and Martha Robison.

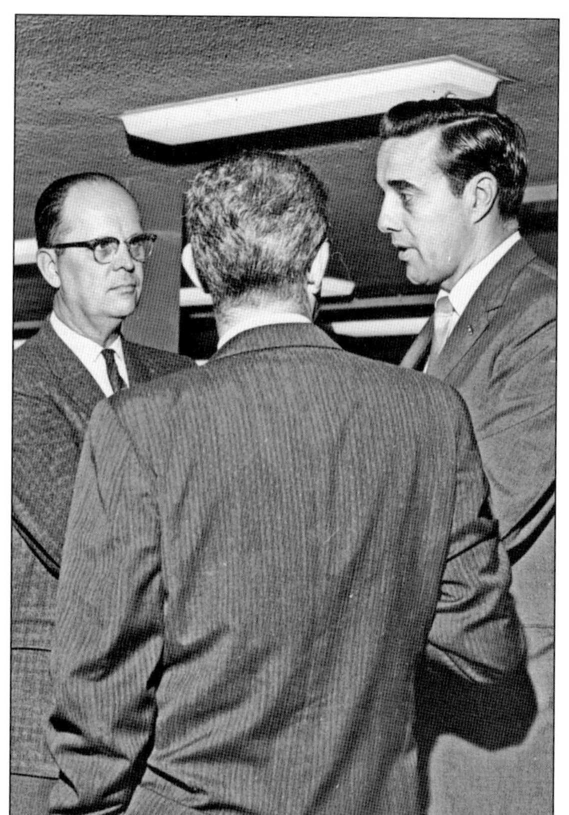

In December 1964, the Salina community held a town hall meeting to discuss the recent announcement of the closure of Schilling Air Force Base. Discussion focused on the economic impact to the community and threats to national security. Bethany College's dean Albert Zimmer and Kansas Wesleyan's president D. Arthur Zook expressed concerns about a loss of students, revenue, and educational collaboration. Pictured here are, from left to right, Zook, alumnus and administrator Lester Ruegsegger (back turned), and politician Bob Dole.

After joining the faculty in 1909, Dr. Frederick Conrad Peters retired from teaching languages in 1950 to become the alumni secretary. He was also active in the University Methodist Church and served on the Salina City Commission and as mayor. His loyalty and dedication to the university will be remembered through the Peters Science Hall. Here, Peters receives congratulations at his retirement as alumni secretary in 1962.

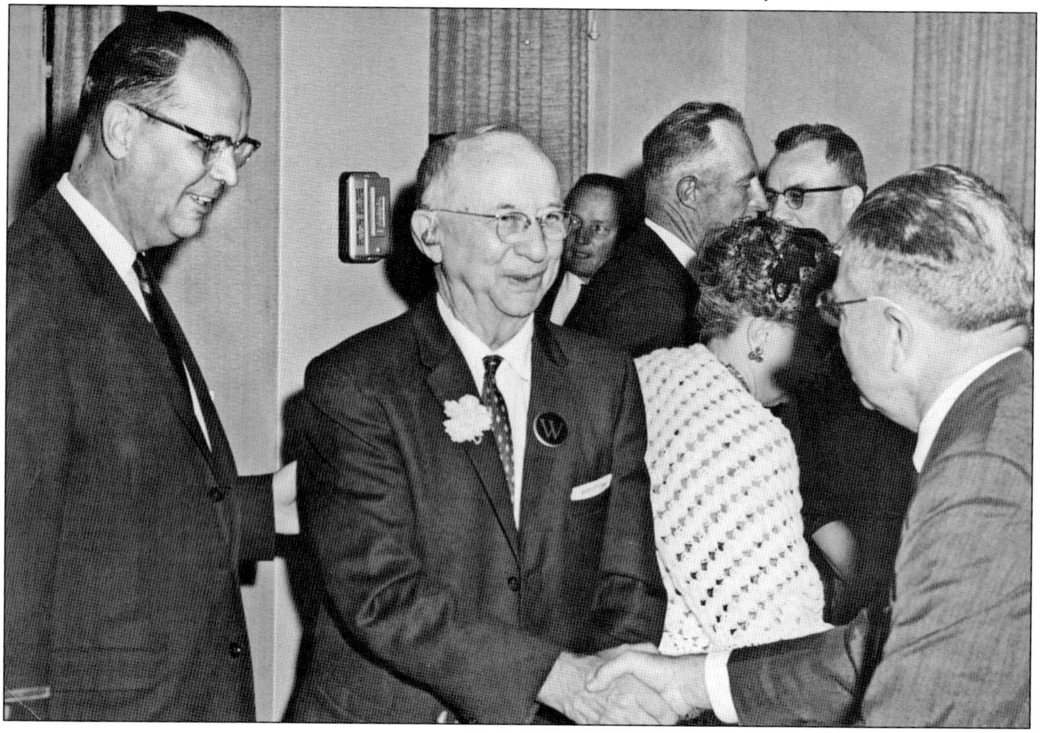

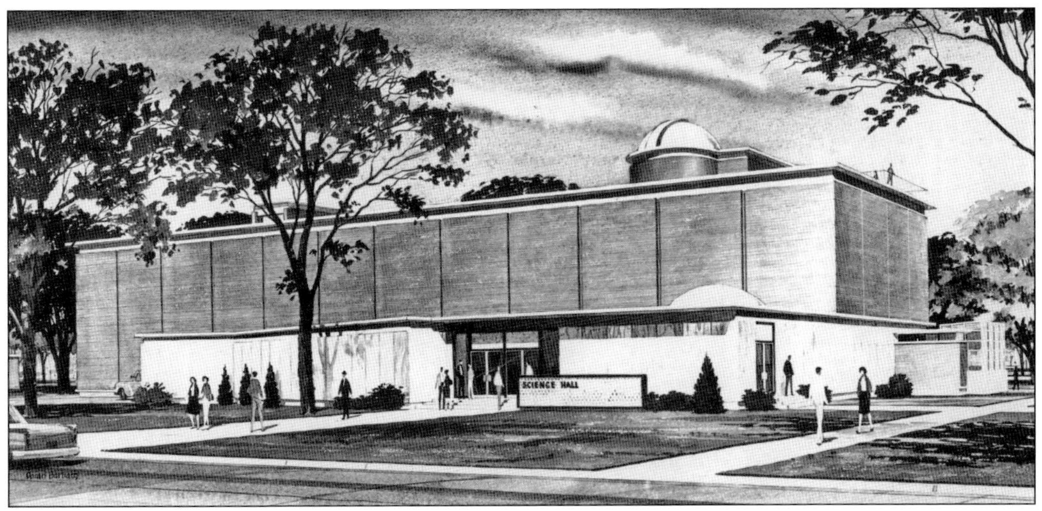

Ground breaking for the Peters Science Hall in 1967 was delayed by frozen federal funds, a problem facing other projects across the nation. Despite the interruption, President Zook remained optimistic, moving forward with the $1.5 million project, and by January 1968, the government released the funds. Prior to the ground breaking, politician Bob Dole spoke during a luncheon. A "Night around the World" celebration lit 90 candles for Frederick Conrad Peters's birthday while alumni and friends lit candles around the world. President Zook announced that the new science hall would be named in honor of Peters. In November 1969, the university celebrated, hosting an open house for the community. Above is a conceptual plan of the Peters Science Hall by Wilson Architects. Below at the ground-breaking ceremony are, from left to right, Paul Renich, George W. Richards, President Zook, and Bishop William McFerrin Stowe.

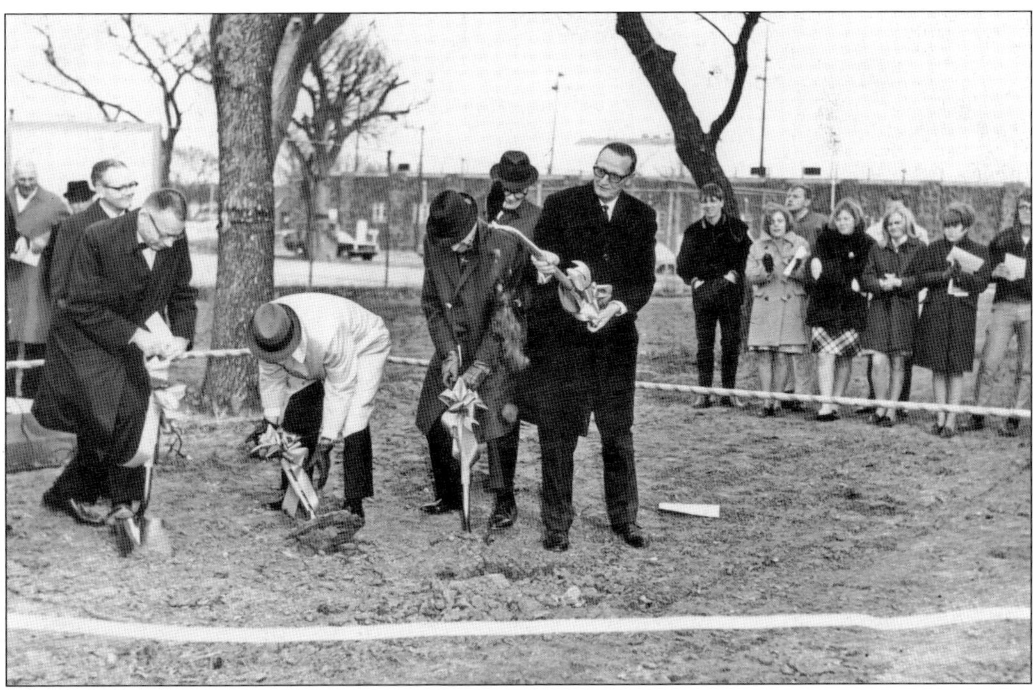

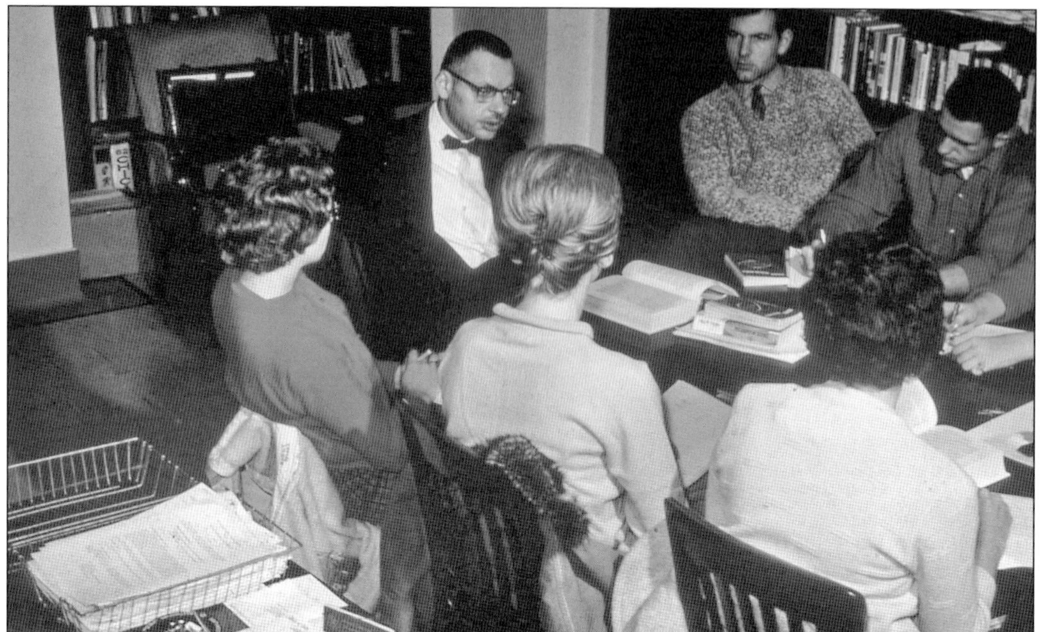

Dr. Paul Renich (pictured above with students and below with his wife, Roberta) worked diligently for 25 years in multiple capacities and was often noted for his vigorous and insightful leadership. Renich was a Bethel College graduate and earned his doctorate at the University of Kansas. In 1948, he joined the faculty as a chemistry professor, and in 1951, he became dean of students. Dean Renich demonstrated community leadership on and off campus, serving on the Salina Board of Education and National Association of Accredited Colleges of Kansas. Renich became university president in 1968. His interim successor, alumnus Rev. Clarence Fogleman, referred to Renich's quarter century of work as tireless and ultimately dedicated to progress and academic excellence. Despite his exit in 1973, Renich's legacy is an interwoven thread that continues to cultivate the university past his tenure.

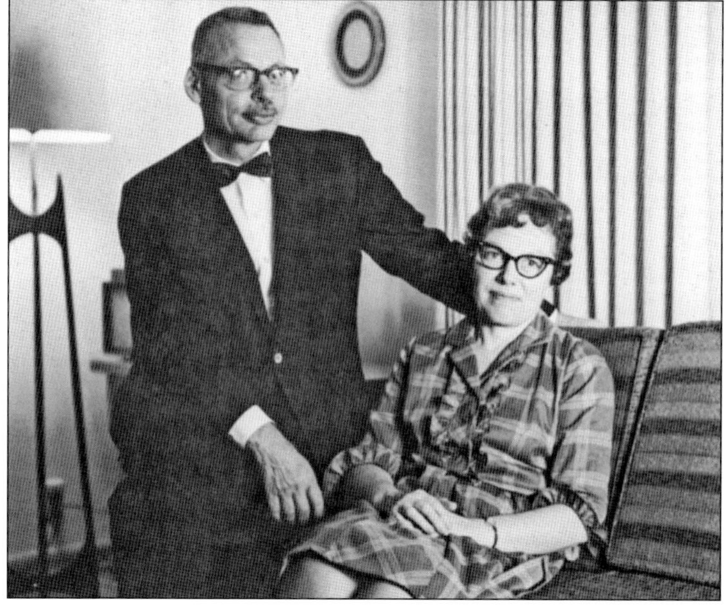

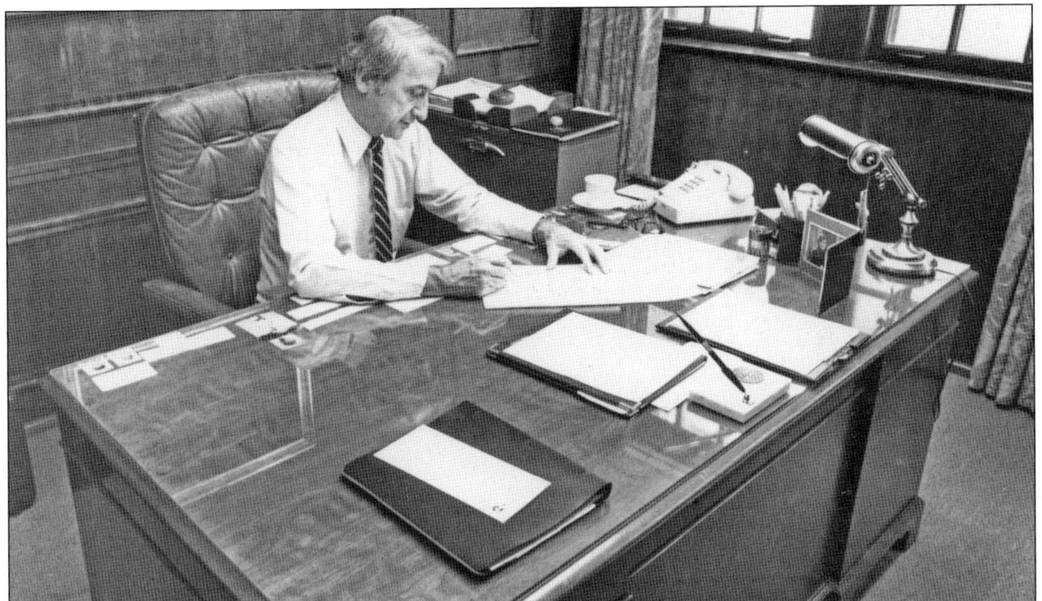

Dr. Daniel Bratton came from the University of Maryland, where he was the vice-chancellor. His inauguration corresponded with Homecoming weekend. Under President Bratton's leadership, a fundraising campaign called "Decade of Development" was launched in 1976. Many campus improvements were included in the development plan, most notably the construction of the Bob D. Muir Physical Education Center.

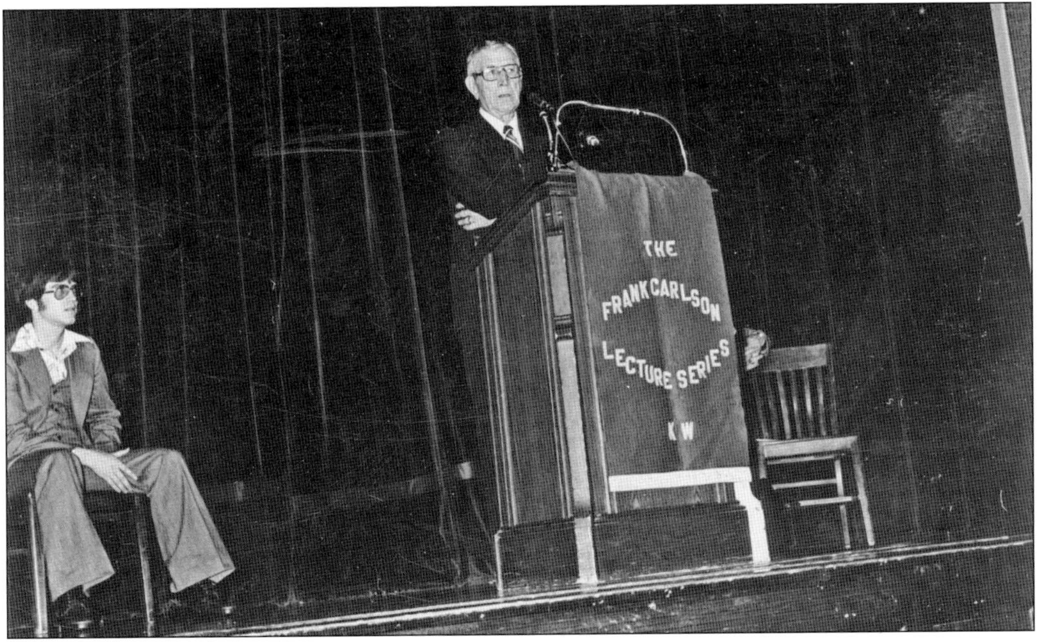

In the 1970s, the student senate–sponsored Frank Carlson Lecture Series became a successful series that featured lectures every semester from prominent national figures. The series was named in honor of US senator Frank Carlson of Concordia. The first lecture was presented in 1973 by US senator James Pearson. Here, former UCLA basketball coach John Wooden gives a lecture on "The Pyramid of Success" in Sams Chapel.

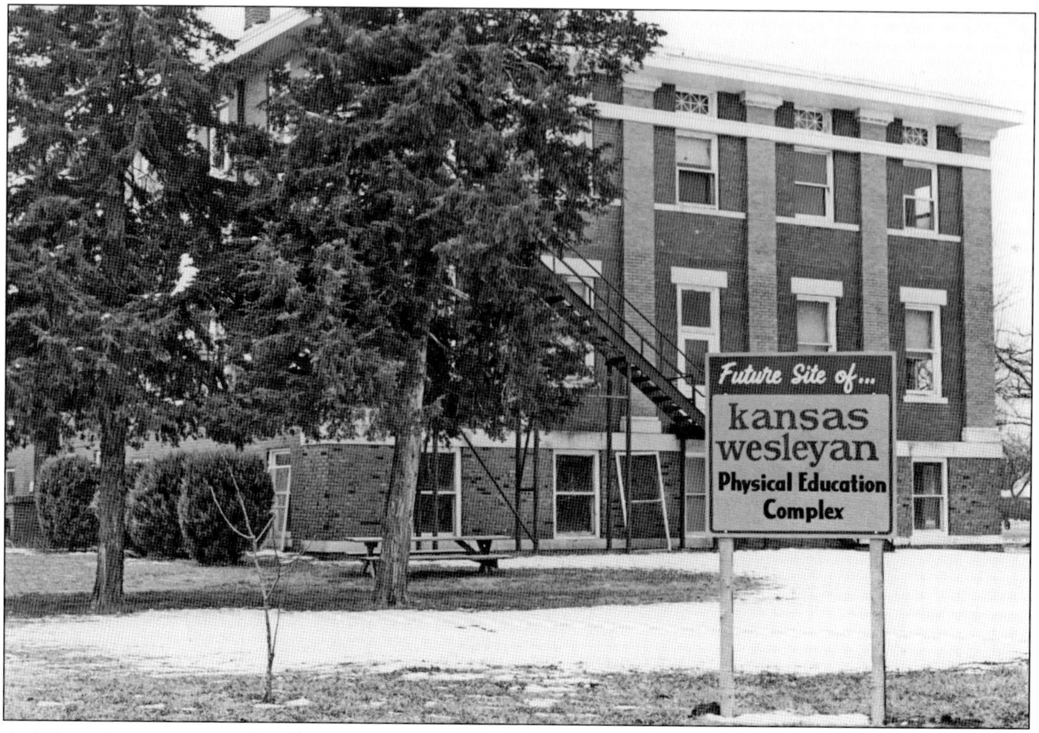

As King Gymnasium deteriorated, a new athletic facility was identified as a high priority; many games were played at other locations in Salina, including Sacred Heart High School and the Salina Bicentennial Center. With King Gymnasium unsuitable for college competition and team practices, the university decided to raze the Carnegie Science Hall and build the Bob D. Muir Physical Education Center on the corner of Fourth Street and Claflin Avenue. The center featured four locker rooms, a fitness center, training room, and coaches' offices. The seating capacity was 750. The original playing surface in Muir Gym was Tartan rubber and was replaced with a maple floor in the summer of 1996. It was the home for the Coyotes from 1981 until 2008. Below is the ribbon-cutting ceremony for Muir Gymnasium.

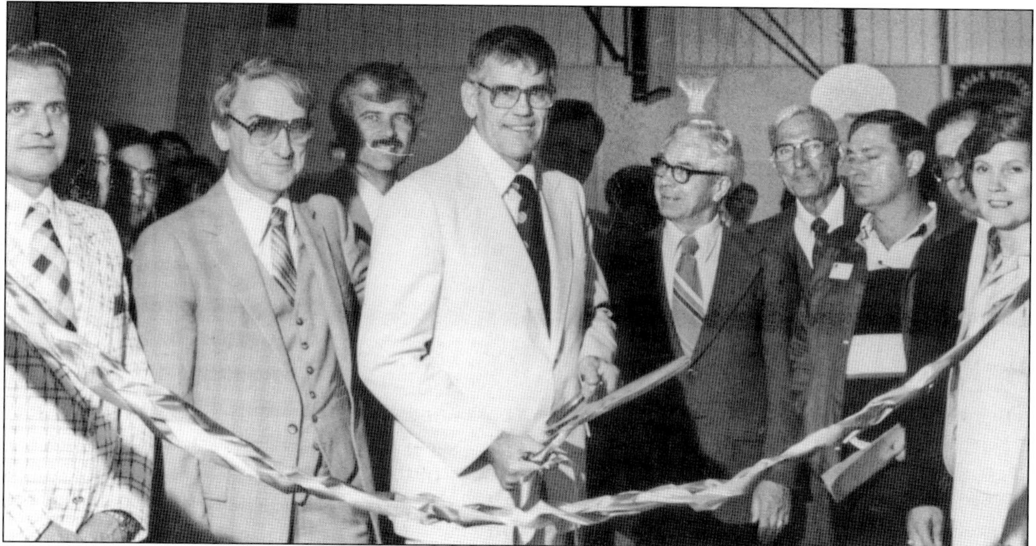

Four

ACADEMICS

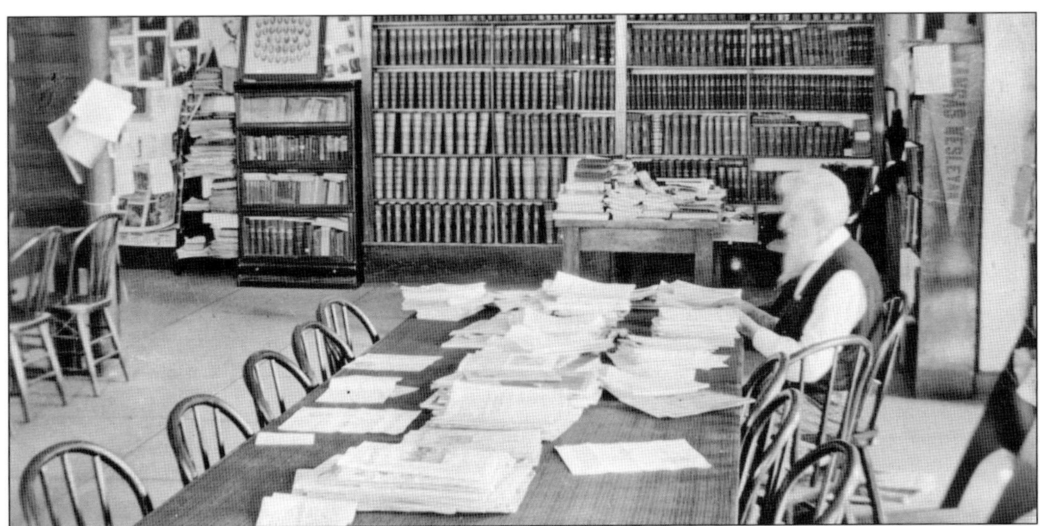

The university library grew steadily in its early years as numerous volumes were donated. After Dr. Aaron Schuyler's death, his personal library was donated to the university library. Early librarians included Jennie Smith, Linette Branham, and Dr. Milton Stolz. All worked tirelessly to organize and strengthen the library with student resources. Stolz, seated at the table in the library, was proud to acquire World Peace Foundation literature.

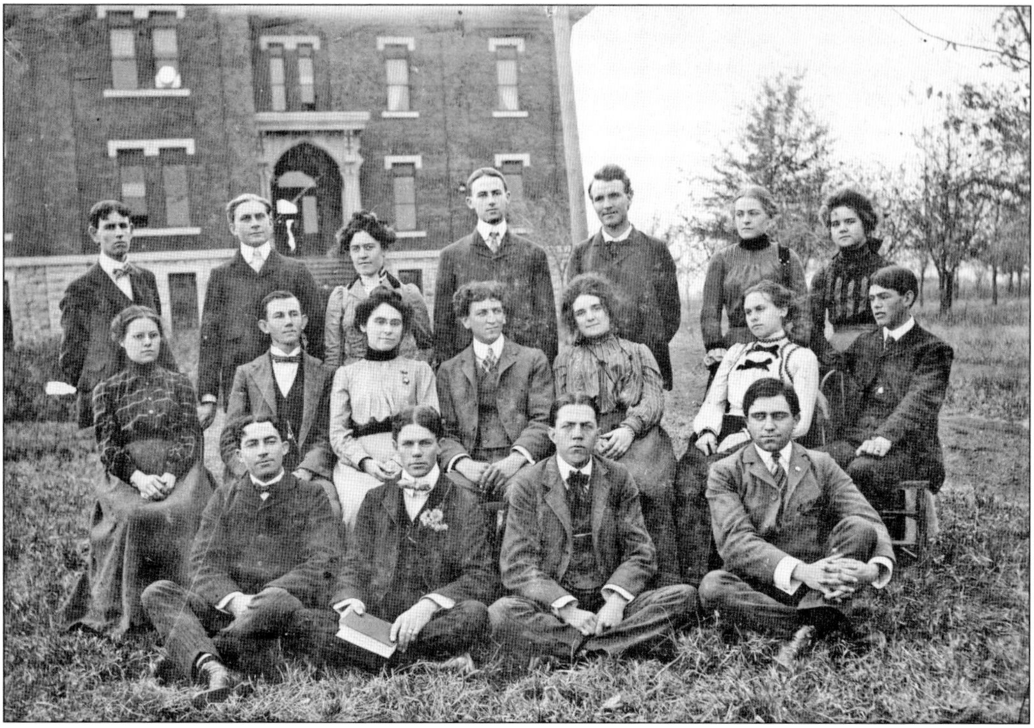

Dr. Artemus Ward, a graduate of DePauw University, taught physical sciences from the fall of 1901 to the spring of 1903. Ward replaced Dr. Frank Dean Tubbs, who departed under high criticism of his teaching methods and beliefs on science, which conflicted with leadership of the Methodist Church. Ward left Salina to pursue a directorship in the Industrial Department at Lincoln Memorial University in Harrogate, Tennessee. Professor Ward's chemistry class is pictured around 1902.

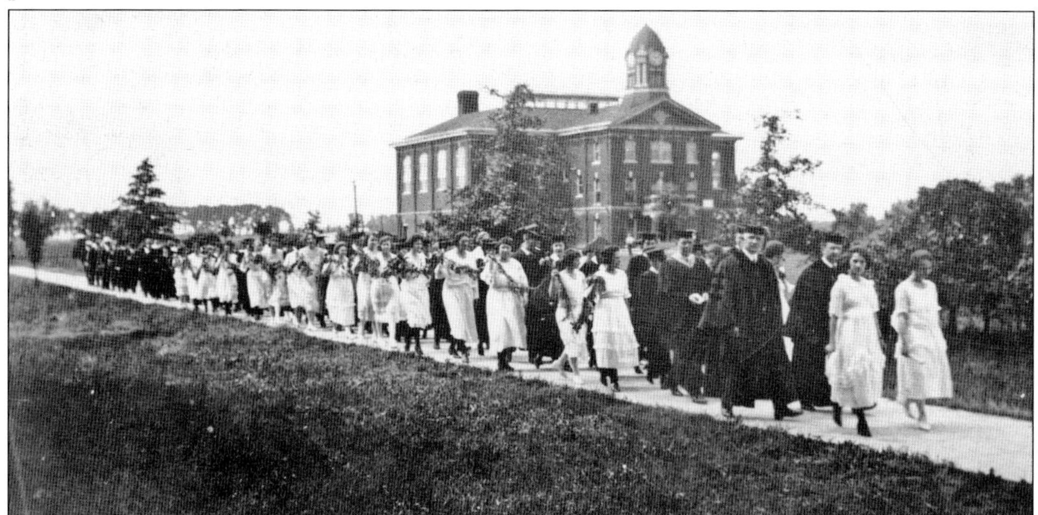

In May 1922, faculty members and trustees are led in a processional by President Bowers and two ushers, Mary Engle and Eunice Bauchop. Bowers had prepared a lecture titled "The Call of a Nation" but opted to deliver a sermon on how education can be used to draw one closer to God and how people can use their best abilities in worthwhile service in life.

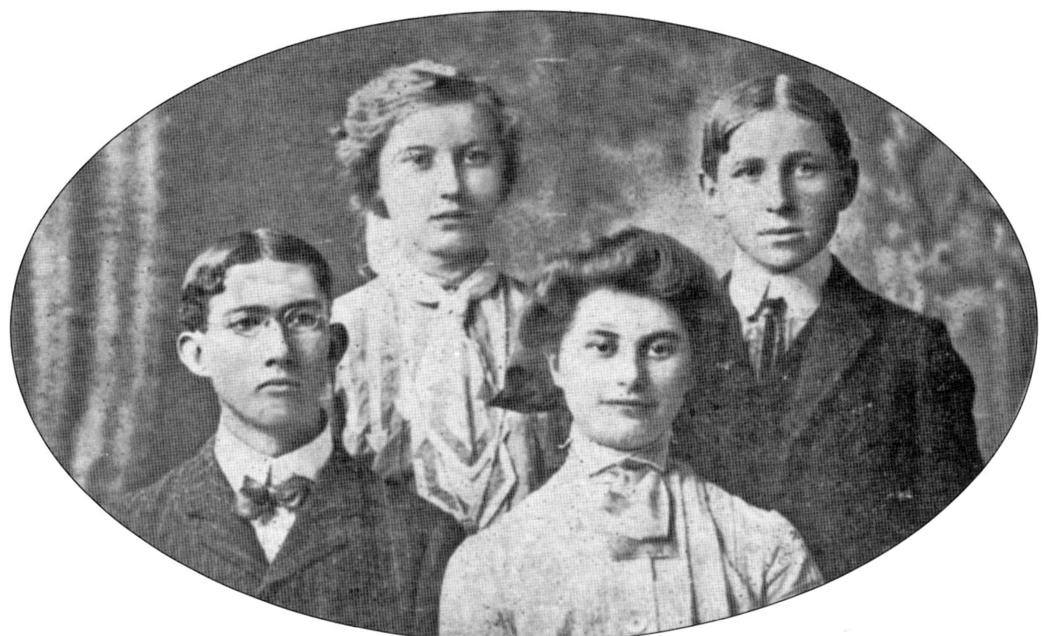

Thomas Jewell Cravens and Glenn Martin, two of Kansas Wesleyan's famous graduates, attended Salina High School. Above, 1902–1903 Salina High School sophomore class officers are, from left to right, Martin, Bernice Arner, Nina Quincy Gemmill, and Cravens. Jewell Cravens, as he was known to the Salina community, took private Greek lessons during high school from Kansas Wesleyan's ancient languages professor Ruth Belle Branham. He became a successful art critic writing as Thomas Craven and was close friends with the famous artist Thomas Hart Benton. Glenn Martin attended Kansas Wesleyan Business College and became an aviation pioneer, trustee, and benefactor to the university. Cravens (second row, far left) is pictured below with freshman classmates at Kansas Wesleyan University around 1905.

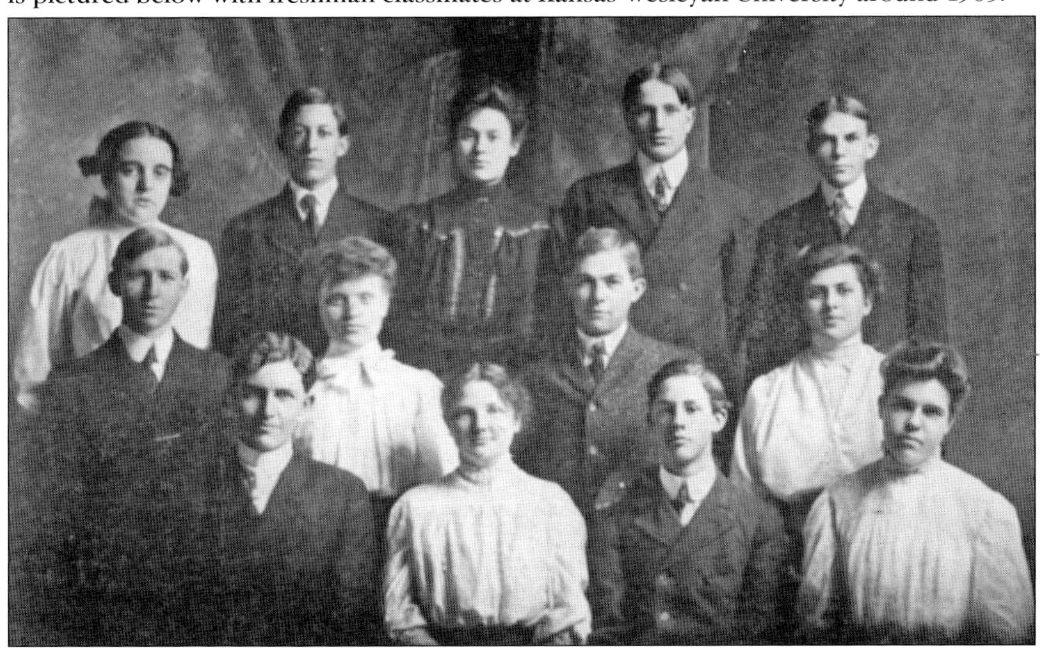

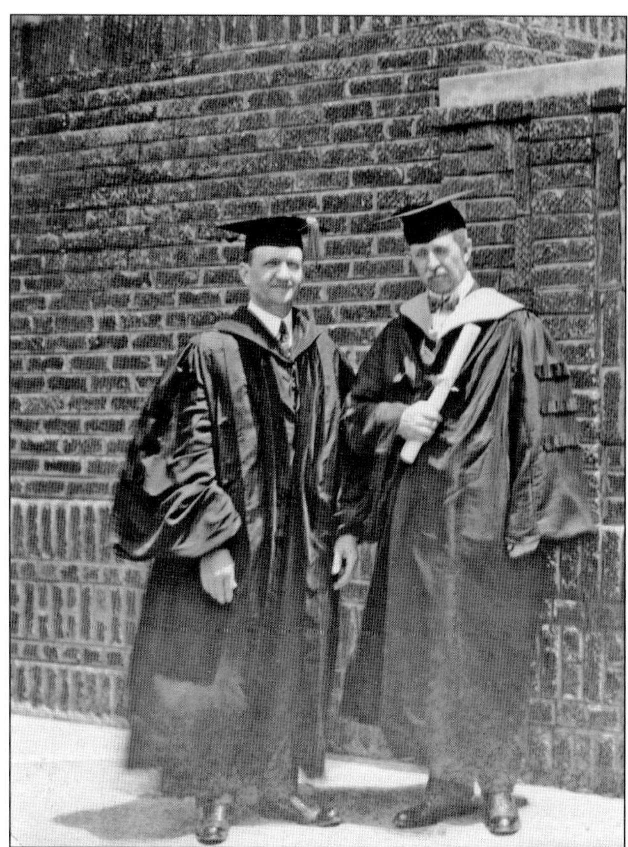

The 1925 commencement featured the largest graduating class in university history at the time and also included the second African American female graduate, Agnes Hudson. Businessman James Cash Penney, founder of J.C. Penney department store, was awarded an honorary degree. While in Salina, Penney spoke to Rotarians about life's priorities, affirming "money cannot buy peace and happiness for the soul." President Bowers (left) is pictured with Penney.

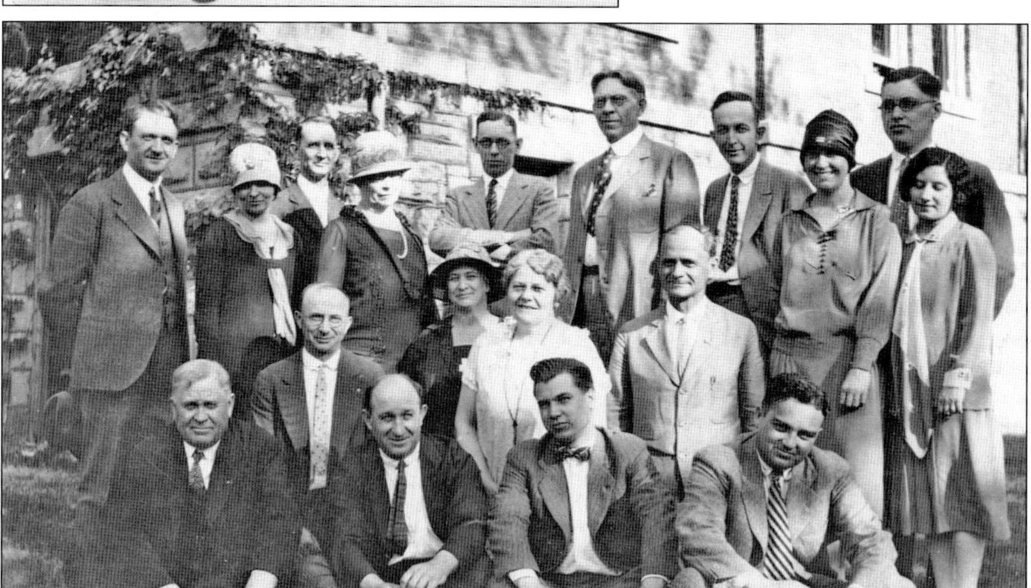

In January 1927, the Faculty Club entertained students with a variety of speeches, vocal solos, and piano duets. Frederick Conrad Peters, president of the Faculty Club, had the honor of leading the program. A reception followed in Ionian Hall at which everyone enjoyed frozen punch and wafers. President Bowers (back row, far left) is pictured with the 1926–1927 faculty.

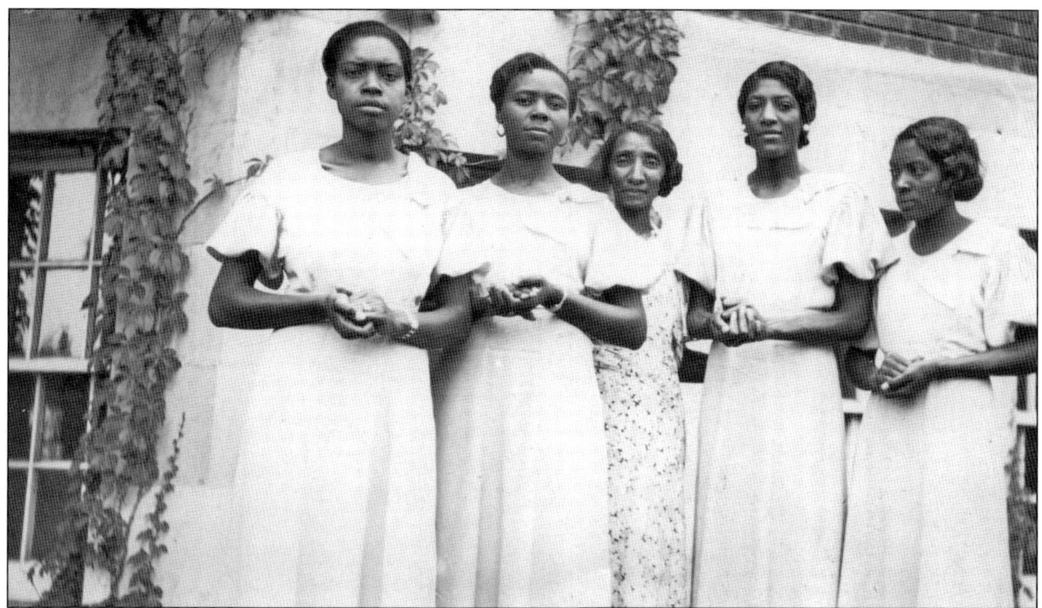

Accomplished musicians, George R. Smith College alumnae, and daughters of Rev. J. Will Jackson of Sedalia, Missouri's African Methodist Episcopal Northside Church, Minneola (fourth from left) and Violetta Willene came to teach at Dunbar School in 1925. Minneola attended Kansas Wesleyan from 1925 to 1929. Dunbar's seventh-grade girls sang "Swing Low, Sweet Chariot" for the campus YWCA. Several Dunbar teachers were alumnae, including Agnes Hudson (far right) and Bessie Green Burbridge.

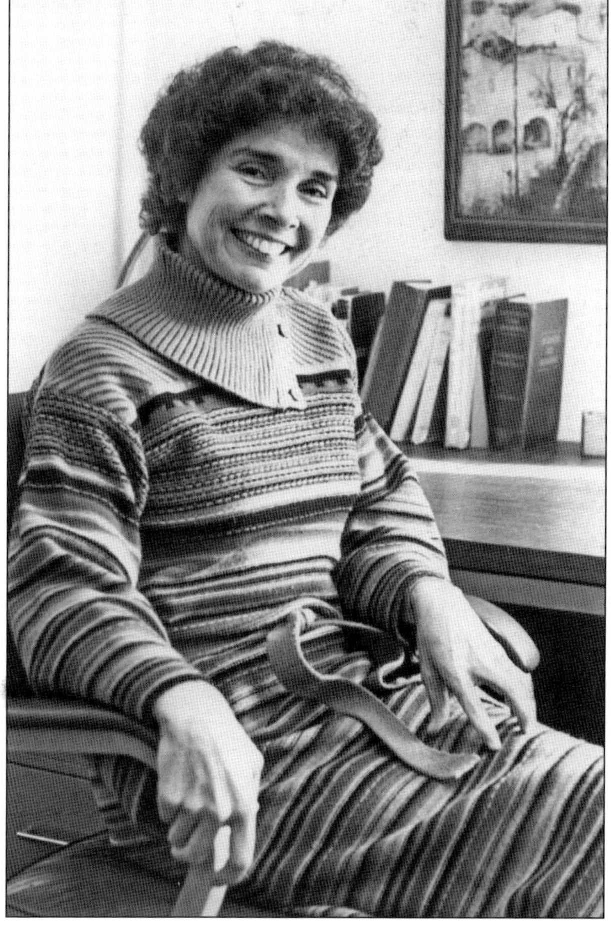

Many language professors have risen to the lectern inside Kansas Wesleyan classrooms. Among some of the best have been Ruth Belle Branham, Mary Campbell Palmer, George Hefke, Frederick Conrad Peters, and Consuelo Diaz. On Professor Diaz's office door was the Ralph Waldo Emerson quote "Nothing was ever achieved without great enthusiasm!" For over 30 years, Diaz taught with enthusiasm and inspired many students and the entire campus community.

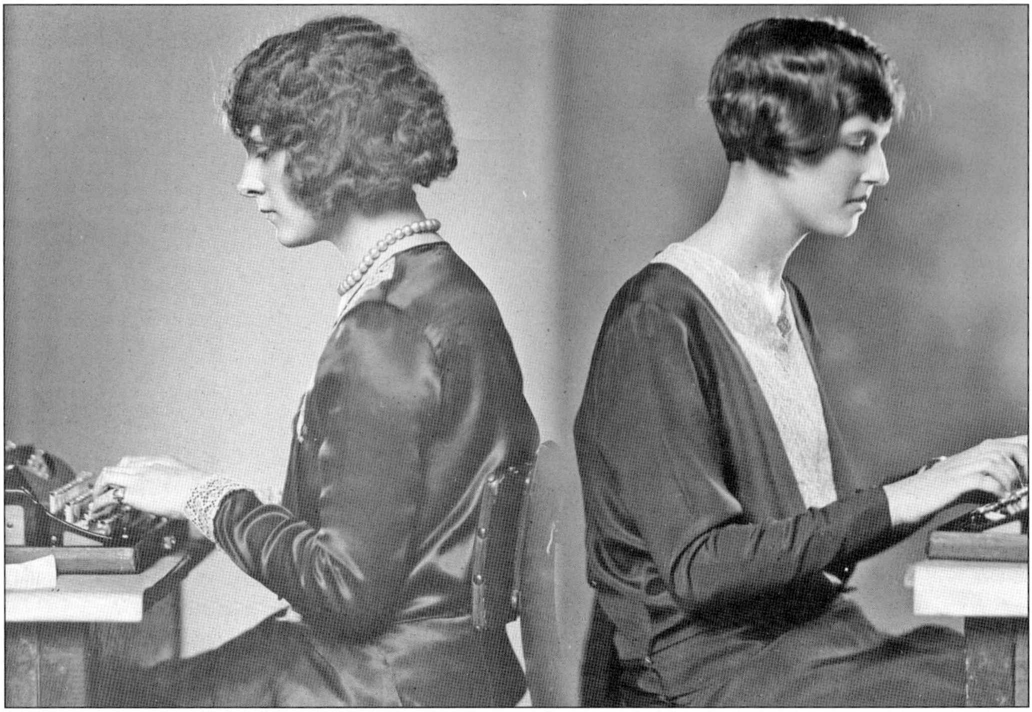

In 1929, Kansas Wesleyan Business College students Muriel Burger (above, right) and Helen Magnuson (above, left) won top honors for their typing skills. Burger ranked among the top typists in the nation: first place in the United States for the Remington Machine, second place in the United States on the L.C. Smith, and third place in the United States on the Royal typewriter. Magnuson received awards from Remington Machine and Corona brand typewriters for speed typing without error. The Kansas Wesleyan Business College prided itself on being one of the best business training schools in the Midwest. All its graduates were highly trained by skilled professionals and very likely to find job placement. Below, students learn in a classroom of the Kansas Wesleyan Business College.

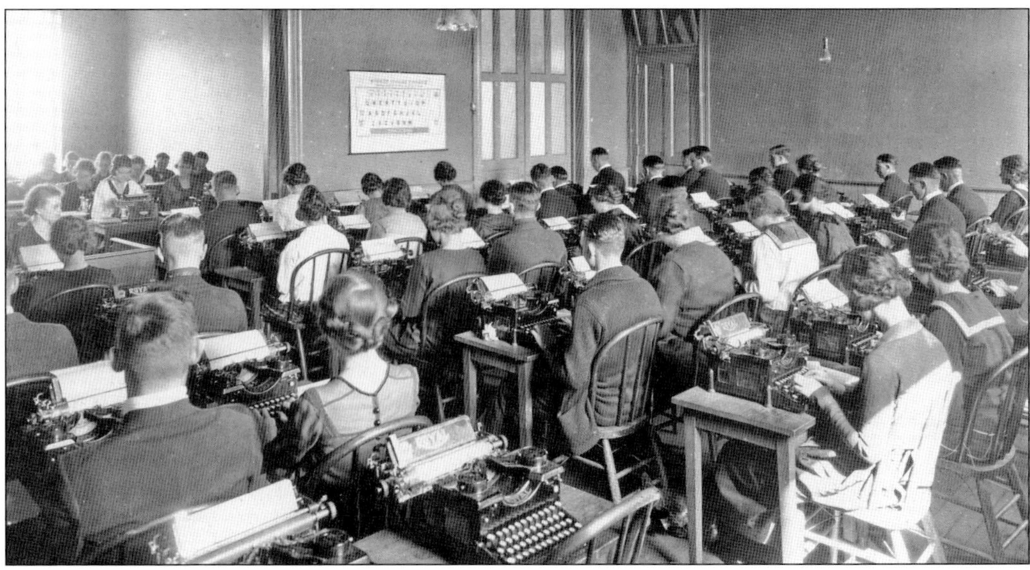

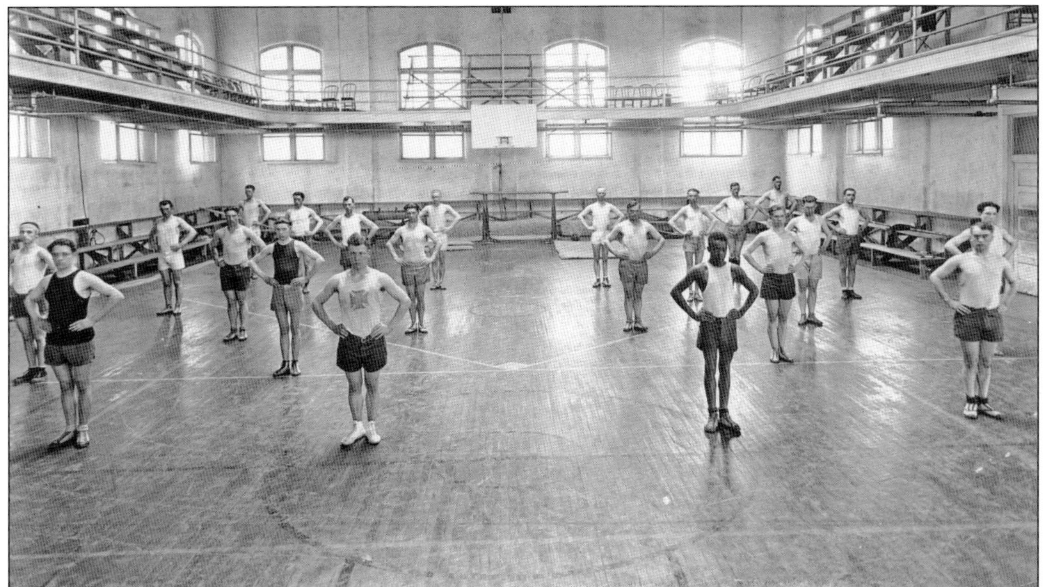

In 1902, Dr. Howard Nelson Moses became the university's physical health advisor. In 1917, George Edwards made significant changes to physical education (two years of instruction were required of all students). This prompted the hire of highly trained Ruth Karg Lipe, who had attended Chicago's American College of Physical Education, to instruct female students in 1920. Students inside King Gymnasium around 1924 include Ray Ryberg (first row, second from left) and William Jordan (second from right). All others are unidentified.

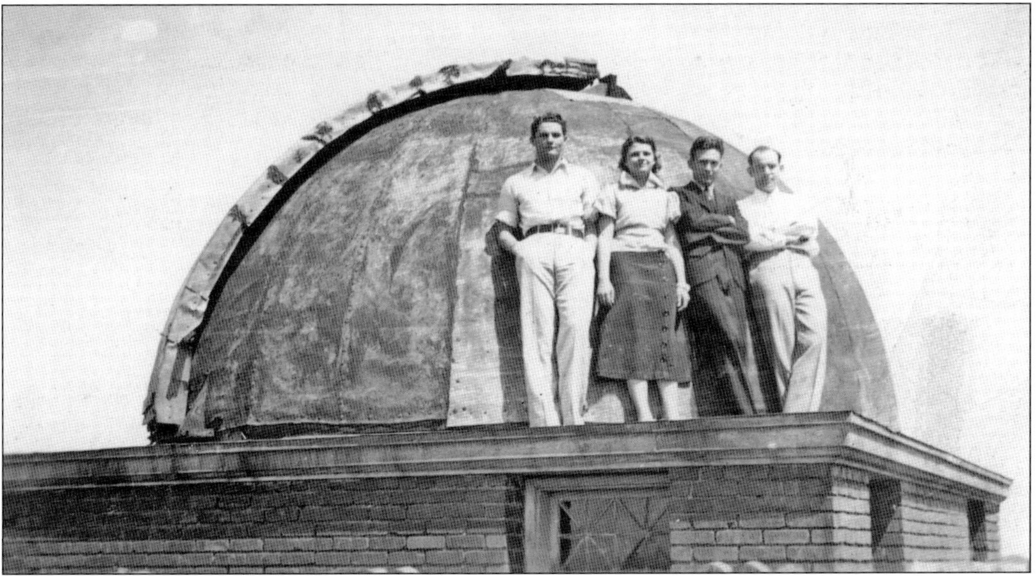

Dr. Ben F. Kimpel, religion and philosophy professor and Yale graduate, was popular due to his charming manner and philosophical attitude. He and Dale Raynesford oversaw repairs to the observatory after several years of it being nonfunctional. Pictured around 1935 are, from left to right, Sidney Smith; his wife, Frances Toll Smith; Howard Stoltenberg; and Kimpel. After Kimpel's tenure at Kansas Wesleyan, he became an accomplished author. He finished his career at Drew University.

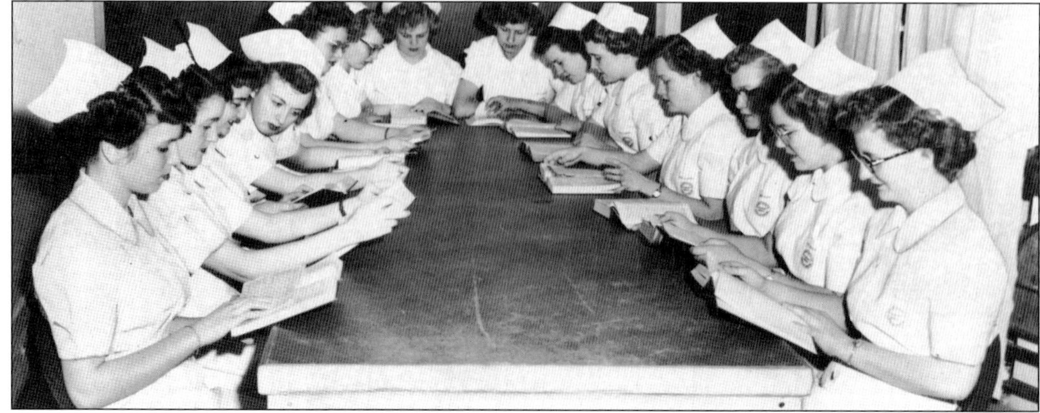

In the early 1950s, Kansas Wesleyan offered a nursing curriculum in direct cooperation with Asbury Hospital. The university offered the basic science courses necessary for students to then continue clinical training at the hospital. In 1989, the Asbury School of Nursing closed and its program merged into Kansas Wesleyan. Pictured here are nursing students around 1952.

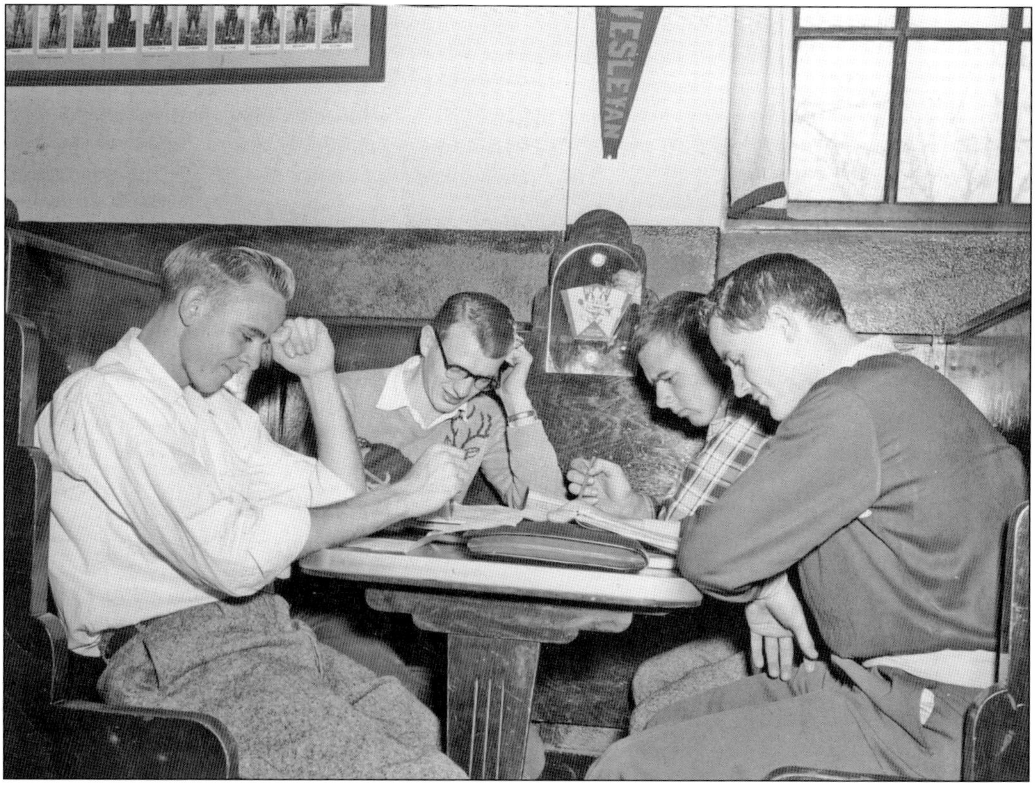

Before "Go Coyotes!" there was "Hi-Ki!" In 1896, Lawrence McKeever, the Delphians' orator, shouted, "Hi-Ki Delphi! Hi-Yi-Yo!" after winning the debate against rival Ionians. The chant transformed into "Hi-Ki Wesli, Hi-Ki Yo!" in debates with other universities. A song, "Hi-Ki Wesli," was written. In 1914, students chose between "Wesli Hi-Ki," "Hi Kiote," and "Ho Ki" for the name of the yearbook. The Hi-Ki logo is seen in the center of a booth around 1950.

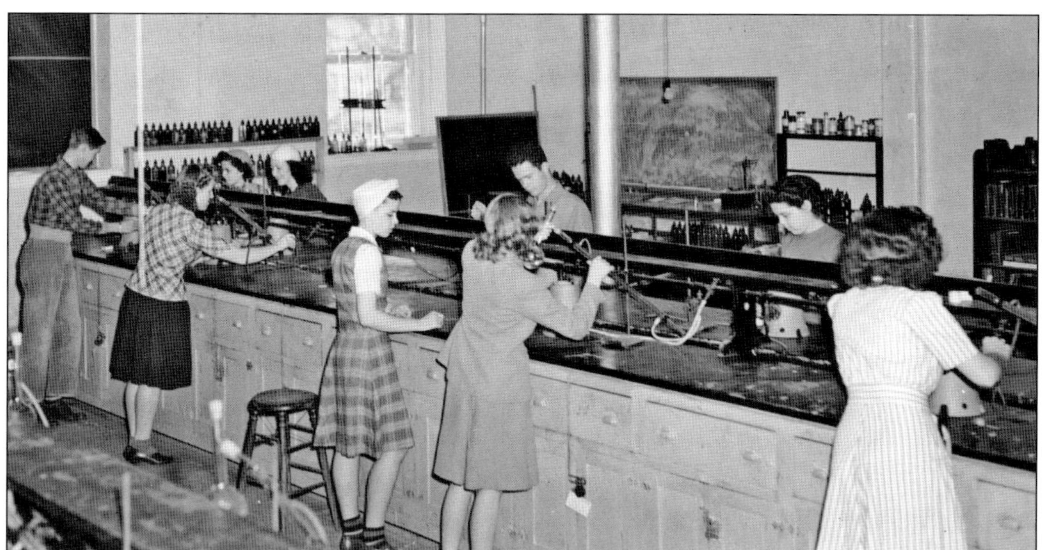

In 1939, the university received approval from the Civil Aeronautics Authority's federal flying program authorizing the pilot training program. While aviation did not become a permanent academic offering, the university partnered with the Smoky Hill Army Airfield to offer a 12-week program on both high school and college levels with special rates to military personnel. Students are pictured in the laboratory around 1945.

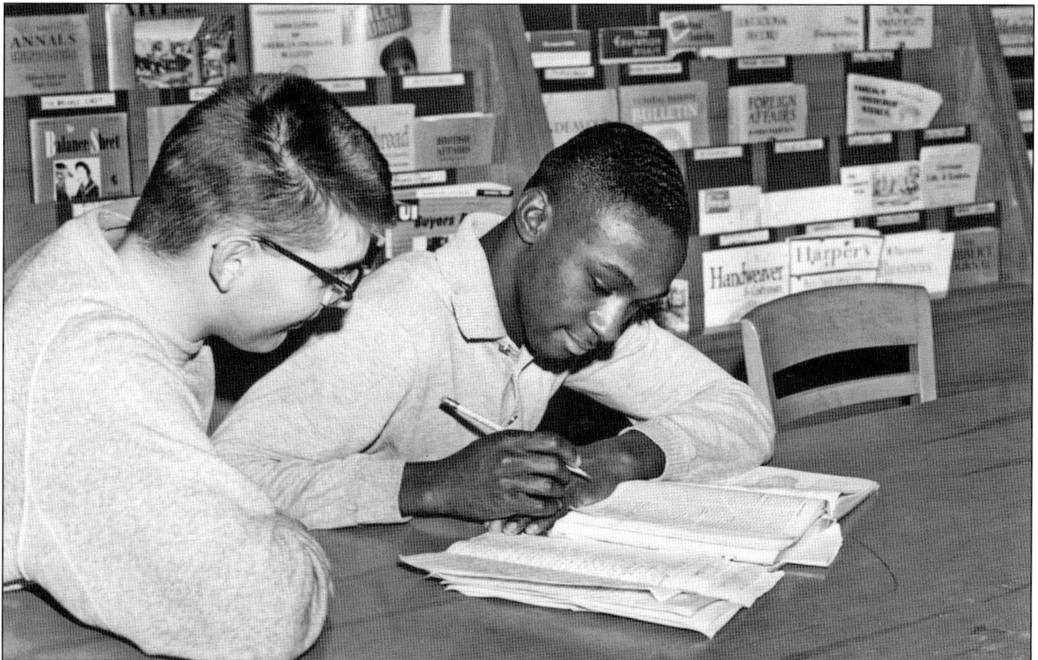

To participate in cocurricular activities, students must maintain certain levels of academic performance and progress towards graduation. Athletic eligibility guidelines were set by the National Association of Intercollegiate Athletics (NAIA), one of the first athletics governing bodies establishing nationwide eligibility requirements and emphasizing academic success while participating in athletics. Other cocurriculars may set their own eligibility guidelines for continued participation. Max Dewey (left) and Billy Toms study for exams around 1958.

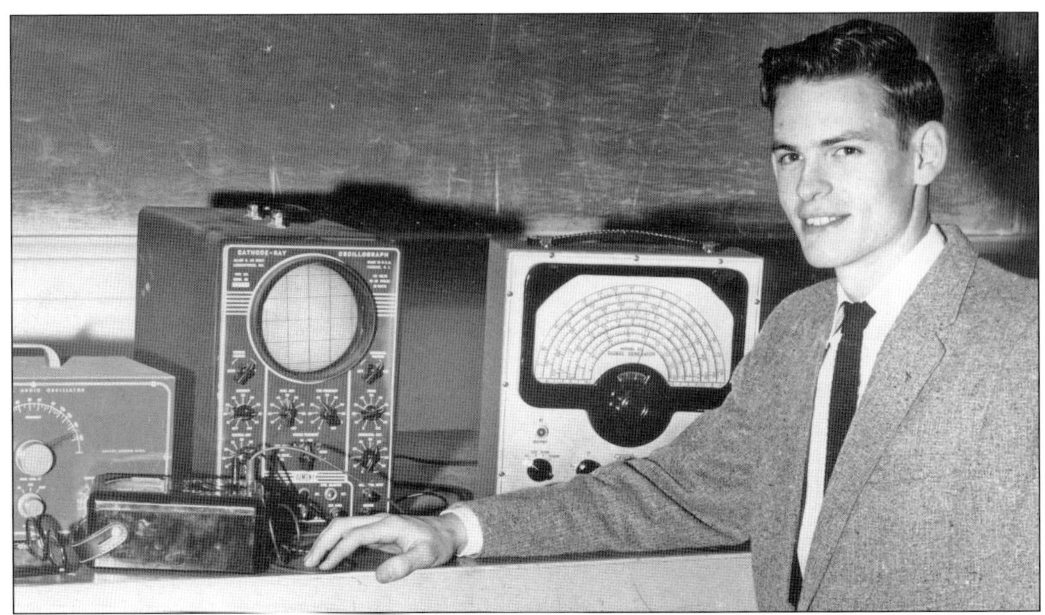

In 1958, Dr. Paul Stucky (below) resigned as an electronic researcher at the Minneapolis-Honeywell Regulator Company to join the faculty as associate physics professor. In the 1960s, the Science Division made a concerted effort to "develop a scientist with a conscience." Stucky witnessed many changes over his 26-year tenure, including the construction of Peters Science Hall, receiving funding from sources such as the National Science Foundation, and providing additional educational opportunities to students from other universities such as Kansas State University. In 1969, there was discussion of changing the university's academic focus to environmental studies. In fact, curriculum committee chair Wes Jackson, an alumnus and associate professor of biology, led the study examining the shift in focus to a proposed three divisions: environmental studies, cultural heritage, and human resources. Above is student Darrell Megli around 1960.

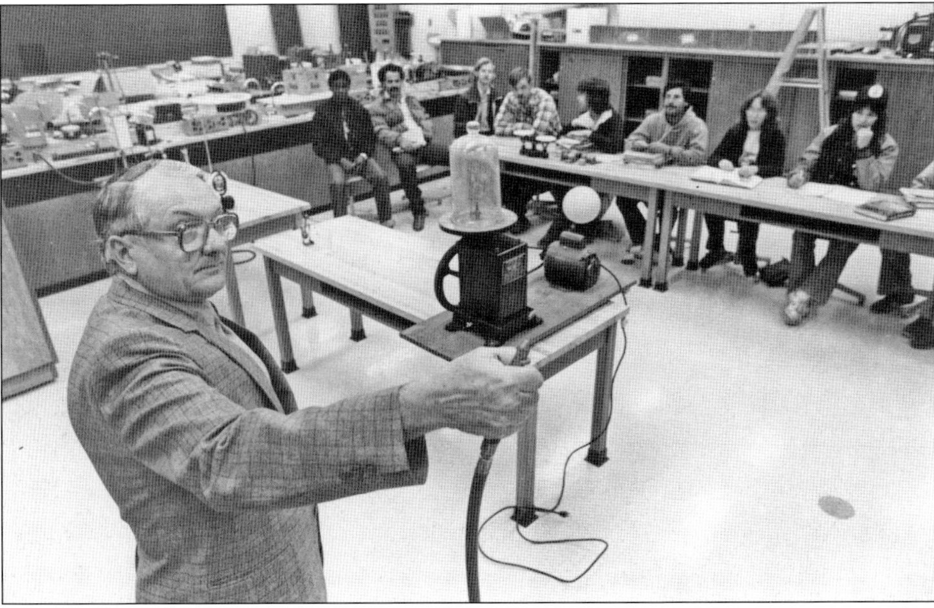

Dr. George Hefke, language professor from 1960 to 1987, focused his teaching efforts on French and Russian. During the late 1940s, he sharpened his language skills when he worked for the Bibliothèque nationale de France and the Sorbonne in Paris. He was responsible for setting up an extensive language learning laboratory. In the spring of 1965, Hefke made a $3,600 donation to the university to purchase Rheem Califone Language Laboratory equipment, which was considered state-of-the-art at the time, for the Hefke Language Laboratory. Students utilized this resource on the east wing of the third floor of Pioneer Hall. Students were required to have at least one unit of foreign language to graduate. Hefke also generously provided students with scholarships to travel abroad. At right is Diane Percival Hudson, a French and English major, around 1965.

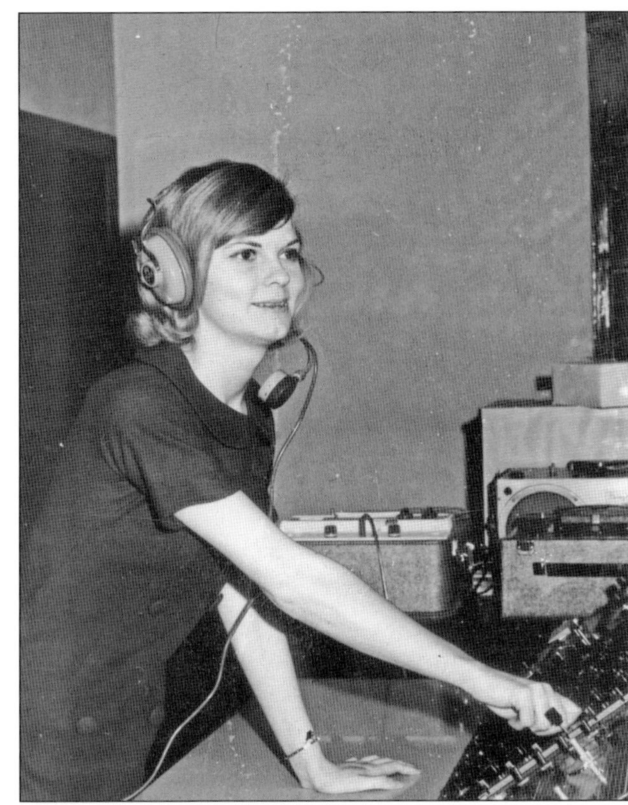

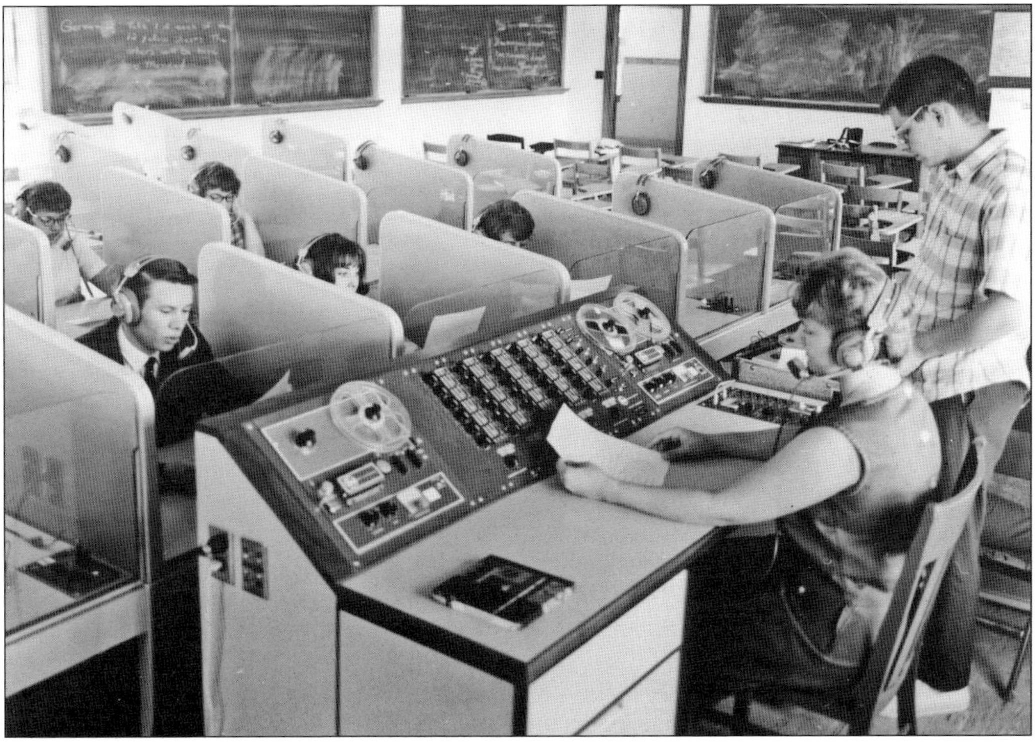

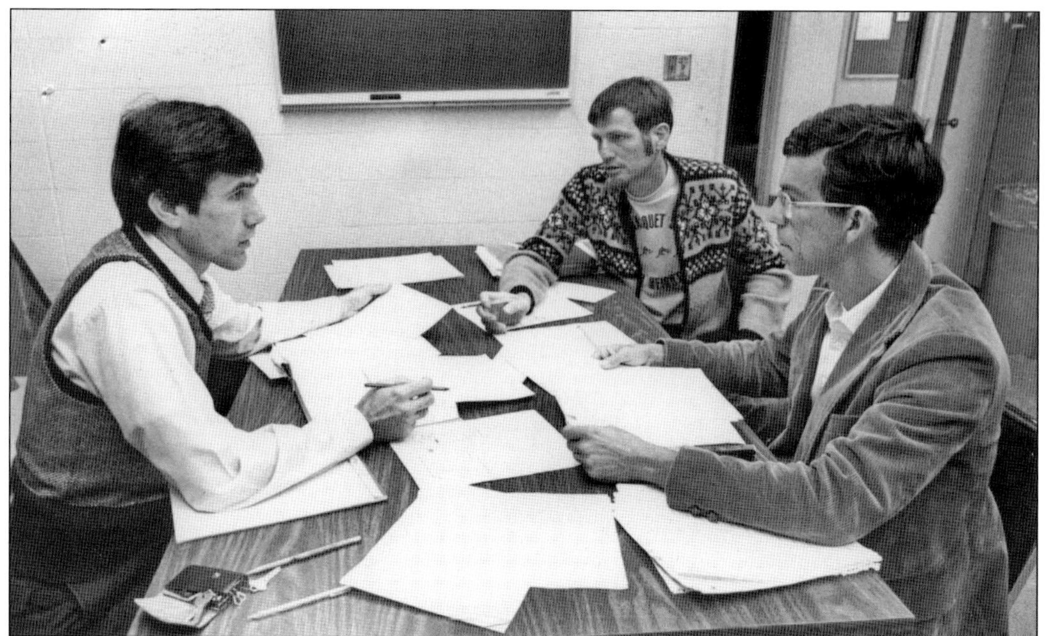

Clockwise from left, economics professor Randall Reichenbach, mathematics professor Ted Zerger, and biology professor Art Neuburger meet around 1980. Reichenbach brought his experience with the Battelle Endowment Program for Technology and Human Affairs while at the Ohio State University. In 2000, Zerger, professor emeritus, received the Distinguished Service Award in recognition of his 37-year tenure. In 2012, Neuburger was named professor emeritus after dedicating 40 years to the university's biology department.

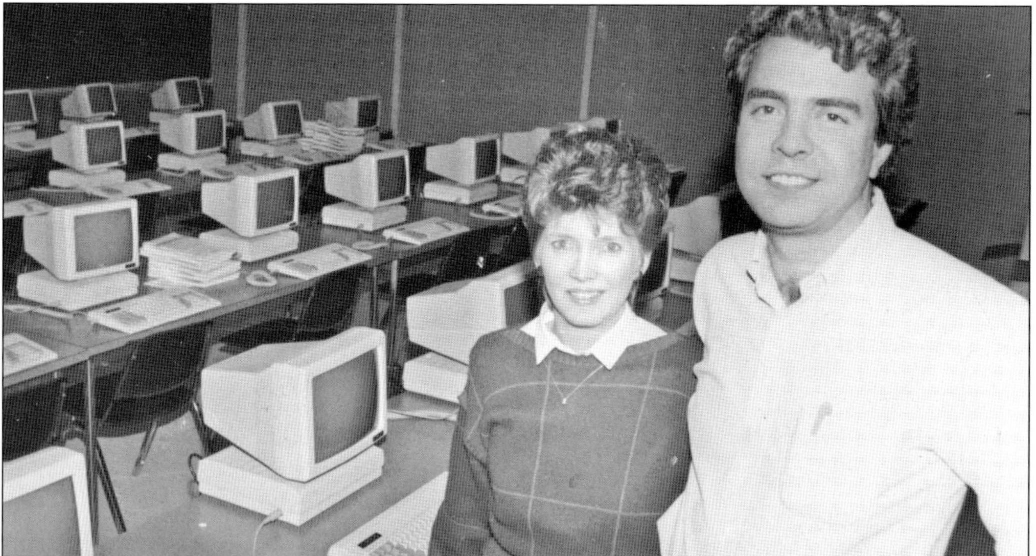

In 1981, the university offered a new major, computer science. Alumnus Thomas Duell returned to the Salina area and established Eagle Software. He was instrumental in the implementation of the new academic offering. Located on campus in Peters Science Hall, Eagle assisted in the maintenance of the university's mainframe computers and microcomputers. In 1982, Eagle Software was featured in the *Wall Street Journal* and *Businessweek*.

Five

THE WESLEYAN EXPERIENCE

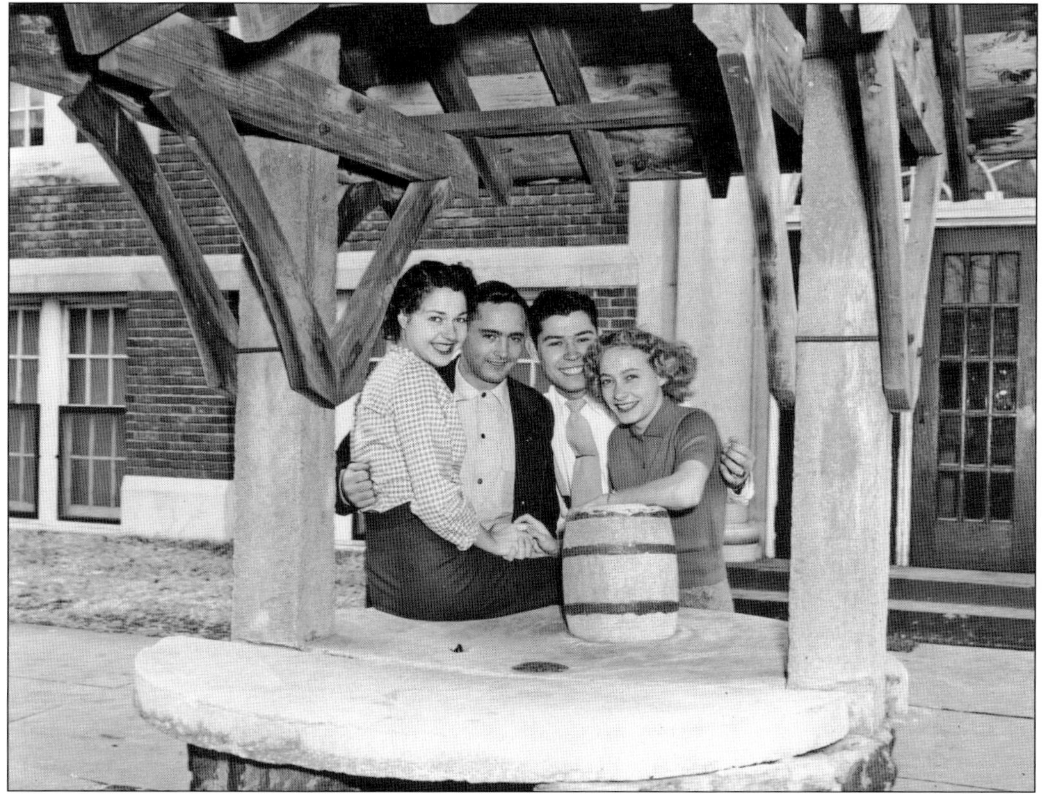

President Bowers suggested the addition of the Pioneer Well during a campus beautification project funded by James William Bean around 1928. Here, students gather around the Wishing Well, featured in a 1950s brochure. From left to right are Phyllis Poland Whitman, Robert Eades, Kenard Kelly, and Shirley Nelson Holst around 1950. Both Phyllis and Shirley were attendants for the 1950 football queen and members of Delta Kappa Chi sorority.

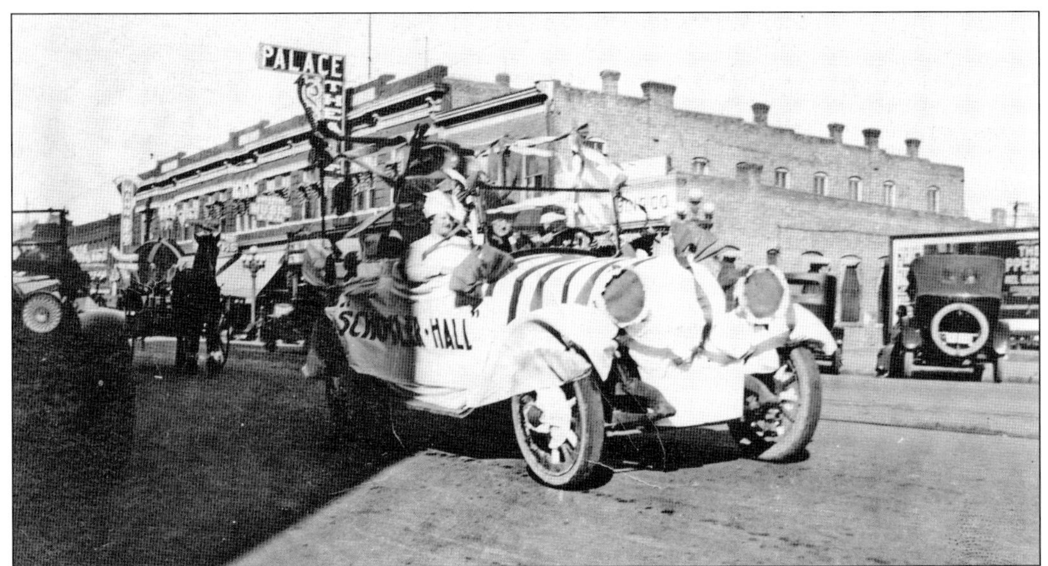

In 1920, the university launched the Victory Campaign to raise funds for a new administration building. Local businessman Winfield Watson led the fundraising effort in Salina. To kick off the campaign, a parade was organized by history professor Clarence Miller. The large procession included this Schuyler Hall float passing by the Kansas Wesleyan College of Music, housed in the second floor of the Palace Theatre on Santa Fe Avenue.

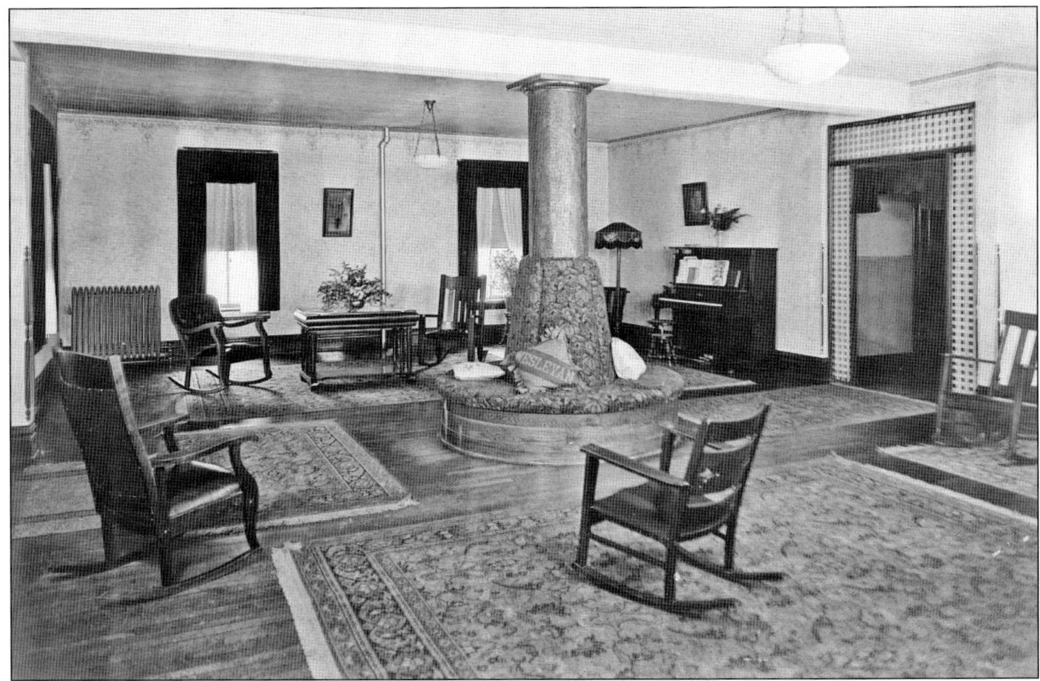

When Schuyler Hall was built, the university took pride in having one of the largest women's dormitories in the state, equipped with modern conveniences of the time. The four-story building had four parlors and rooms dedicated for music and reading. The dormitory was frequently used for Young Women's Christian Association meetings. The interior of Schuyler Hall is pictured around 1910. This lounge served as a meeting place through the late 1950s.

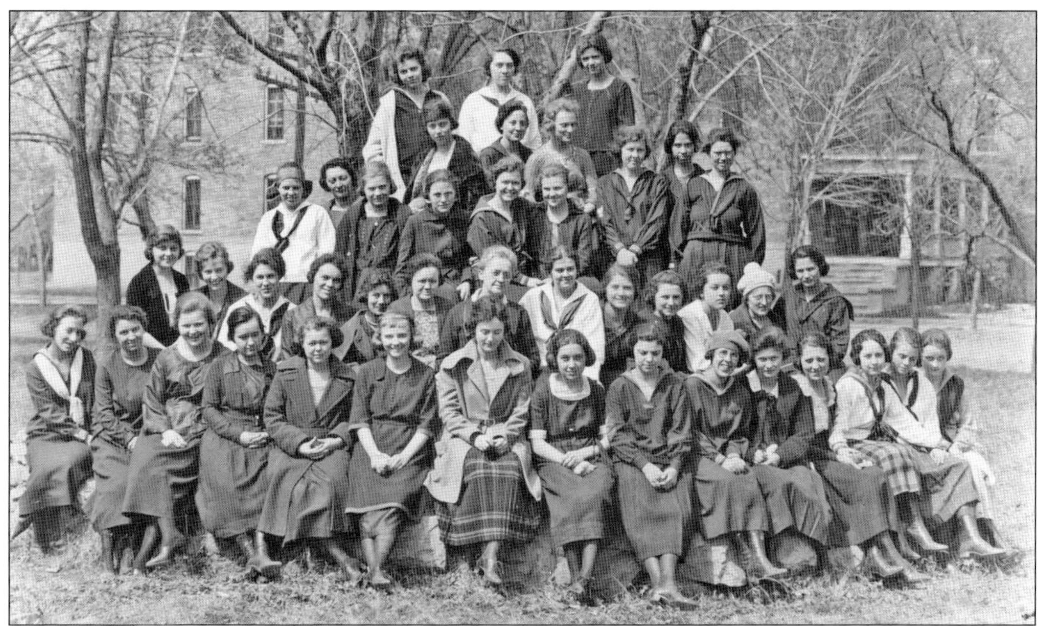

Learning and personal growth happen not only in the classroom but also in the residence halls. Pictured above are residents of Schuyler Hall around 1921. Roommates and others who resided close by provided friendships with lasting connections. New dormitories provide modern decor and features for more comfortable lifestyles, but camaraderie and opportunities for social development continue to be a lasting tradition on campuses nationwide. At Kansas Wesleyan, Greek life and other organizations provided social outlets for fellowship and development of student growth. In the 1940s and 1950s, it was typical to see students gathered in the dormitory lounge, on a Coke date in the Coyote Den, at a Greek formal, or studying in the library. Below are students in a dormitory room around 1980.

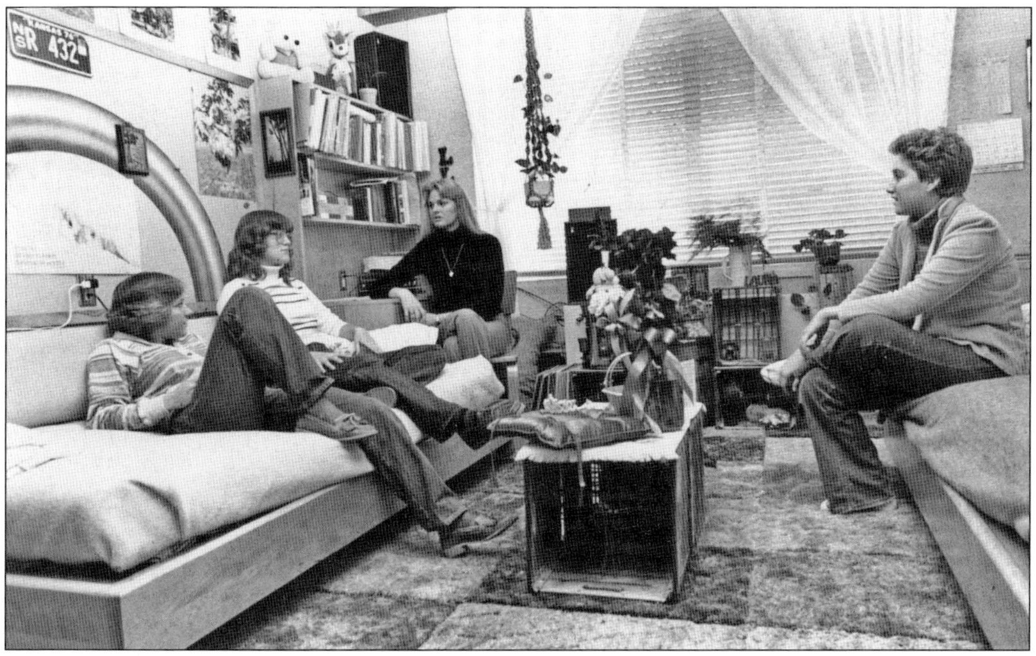

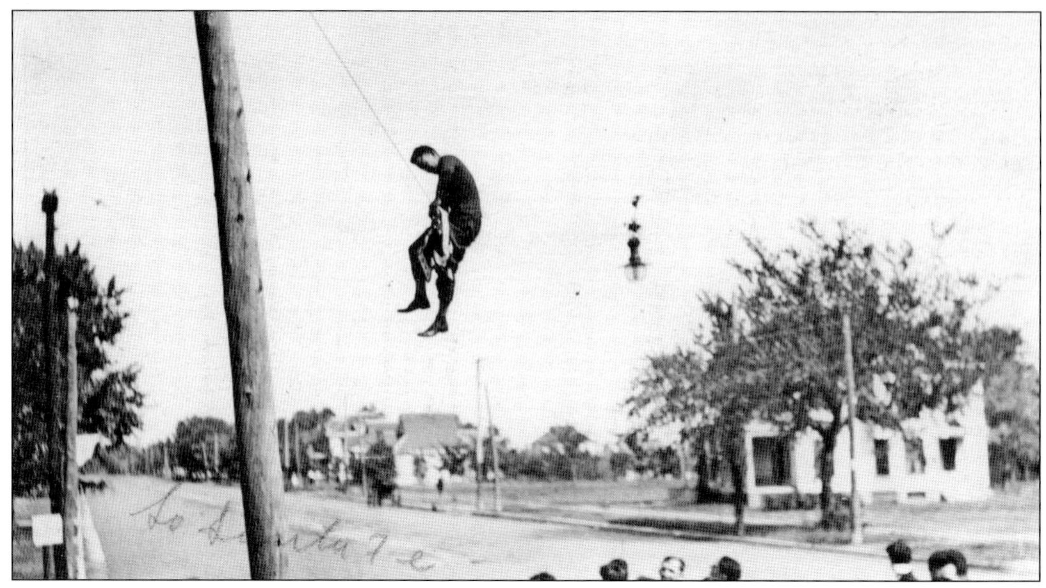

The annual Color Scrap was a tradition where groups on campus challenged one another. In the late 1890s and early 1900s, people in the community not aware of the competition thought decorated flags on houses near the Kansas Wesleyan addition were cause for alarm, indicating sickness and quarantine. The competition began between the literary societies, but later the battle became fierce between the classes. In the 1920s, all the colors were sent up a flagpole, the pole was greased, and a representative of each team climbed the pole to retrieve the flag (above). A lack of rules led to unruly behavior, which caused faculty and staff to intervene to create a more orderly competition. Below, professors Albert King (center, right) and Frederick Conrad Peters (center, left) oversee the students' quest to win the Color Scrap.

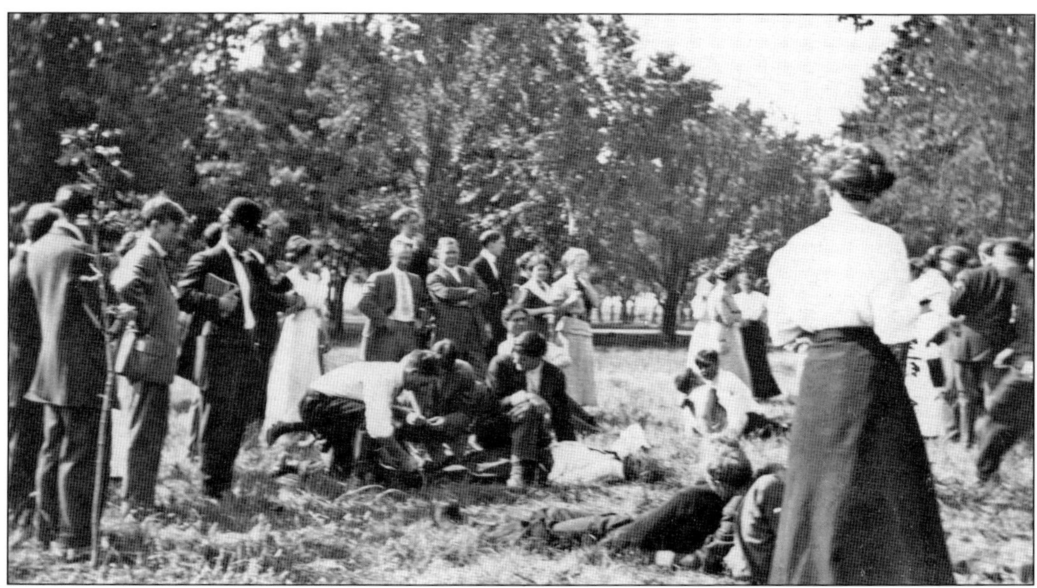

In 1909, the Zetgathean Literary Society decorated a streetcar with its colors during the annual Color Scrap. This streetcar ran from Kansas Wesleyan to the Lamer Hotel, at 201 South Santa Fe Avenue in downtown Salina. In the 1920s, it cost a nickel to ride. Female students are pictured on the Wesleyan streetcar around 1921.

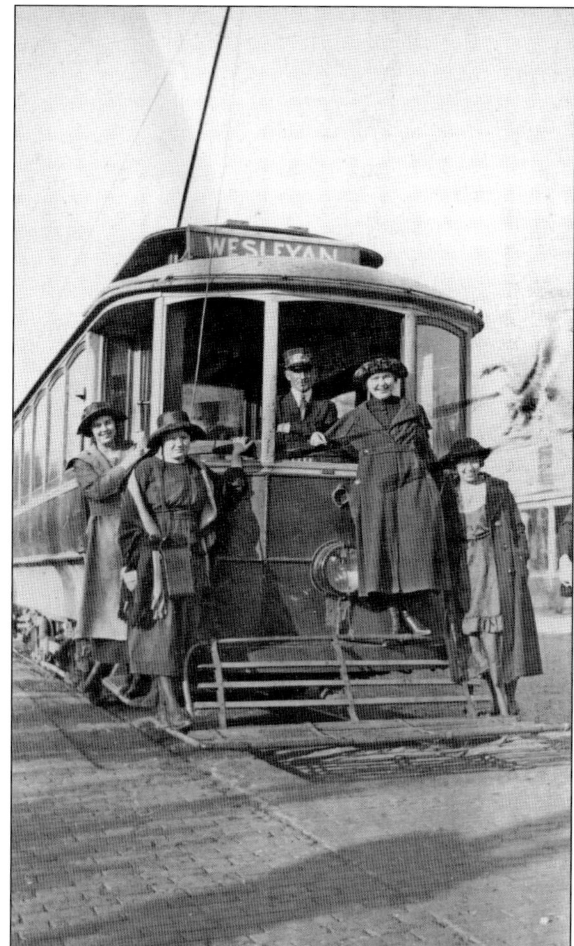

The Rainbow Club was a group dedicated to helping students feel at home and adjust to college life. The members of the club divided their duties and tasks into sections based on the colors of the rainbow. In 1930, this group was one of the most active associated with the Kansas Wesleyan Business College. Pictured are the 1928 Rainbow Club officers.

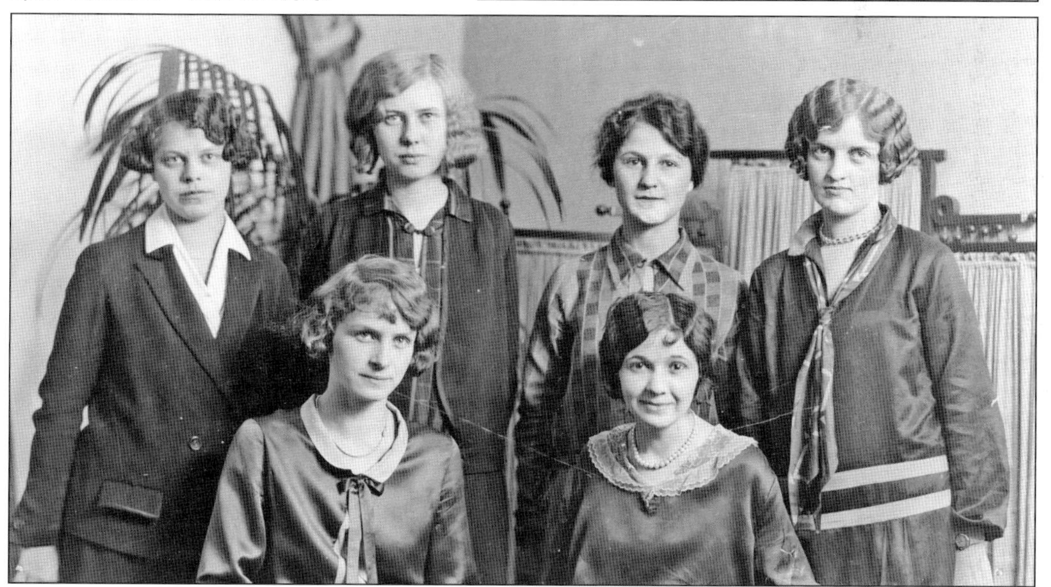

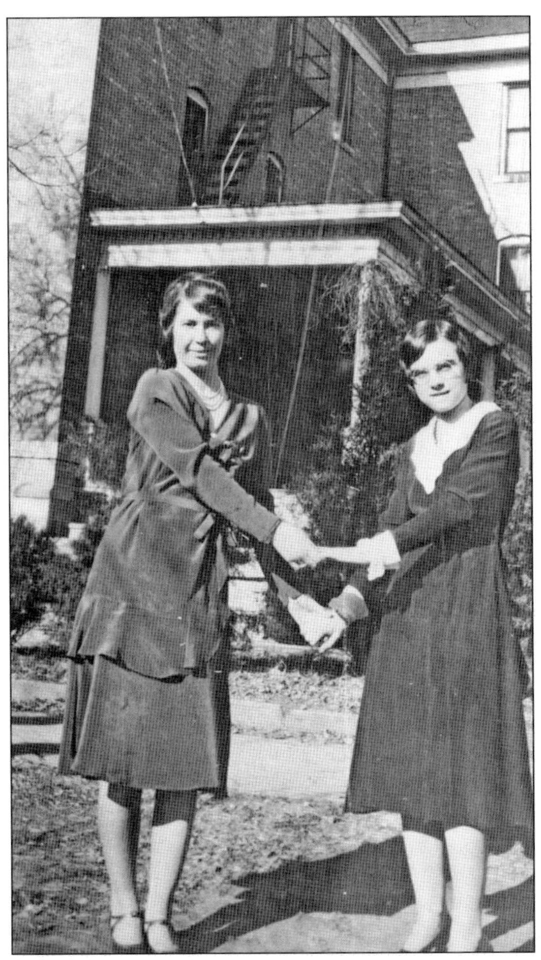

Friends Alice Shahan Hieb (left) and Gayle Anderson (right) were members of Pi Alpha Pi sorority. Gayle served on the Inter-Sorority Council, and Alice encouraged school spirit as the school's yell leader alongside Paul McNutt (below, upper left) and Thayne Coulter. This trio coordinated spirit rallies at pep chapels and athletic contests. McNutt gave up his position as yell leader to play on the football team. Pictured below, members of the Pi Alpha Pi sorority and Phi Gamma Epsilon fraternity sit on the steps of Schuyler Hall after a workday to clean up the campus around 1932.

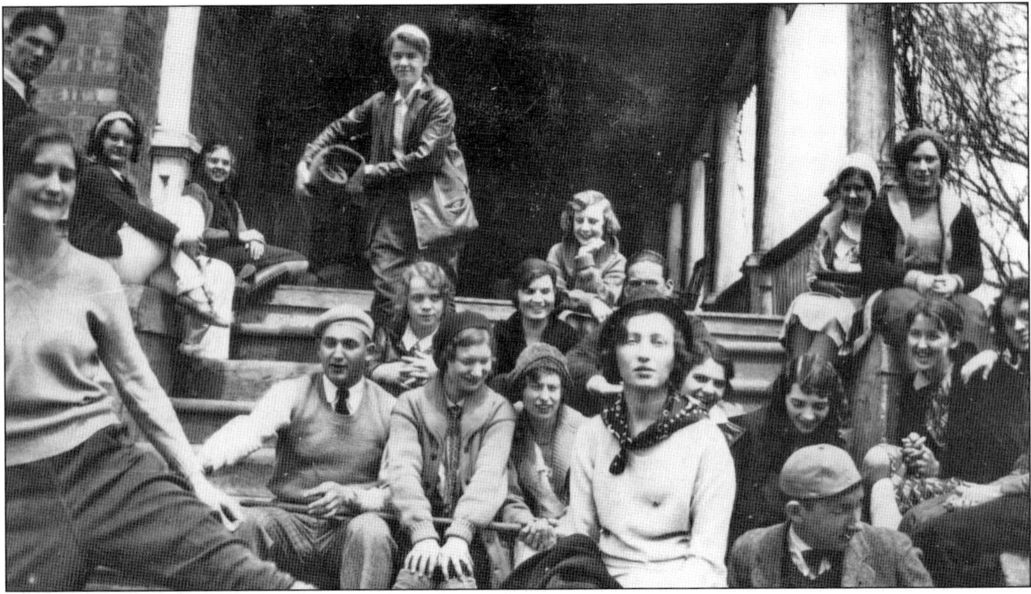

The Pi Sigma Epsilon fraternity was established in January 1928 with the colors of cerulean and maize. Prof. Frederick Conrad Peters was an honorary member. In 1948, the fraternity celebrated 20 years with a formal banquet and dance with Delta Kappa Chi, which celebrated its 25th anniversary. The dance was held at the Hotel Warren in McPherson. Pictured are members of the fraternity in 1960.

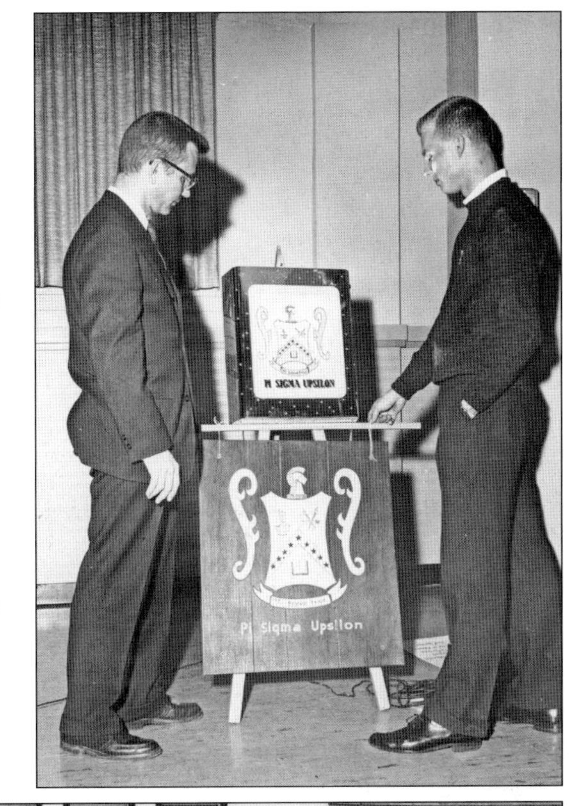

Established in 1947, the Beta Tau Omega fraternity acquired its own house by the fall of 1950, becoming the first fraternity to do since before World War II. Fraternity sponsor Capt. Jose Guzman Baldivieso, professor of Spanish, and fraternity president Joe O'Shea made the purchase of the house a reality. This fraternity was known for its community outreach efforts, including hosting a Christmas party for children in Salina.

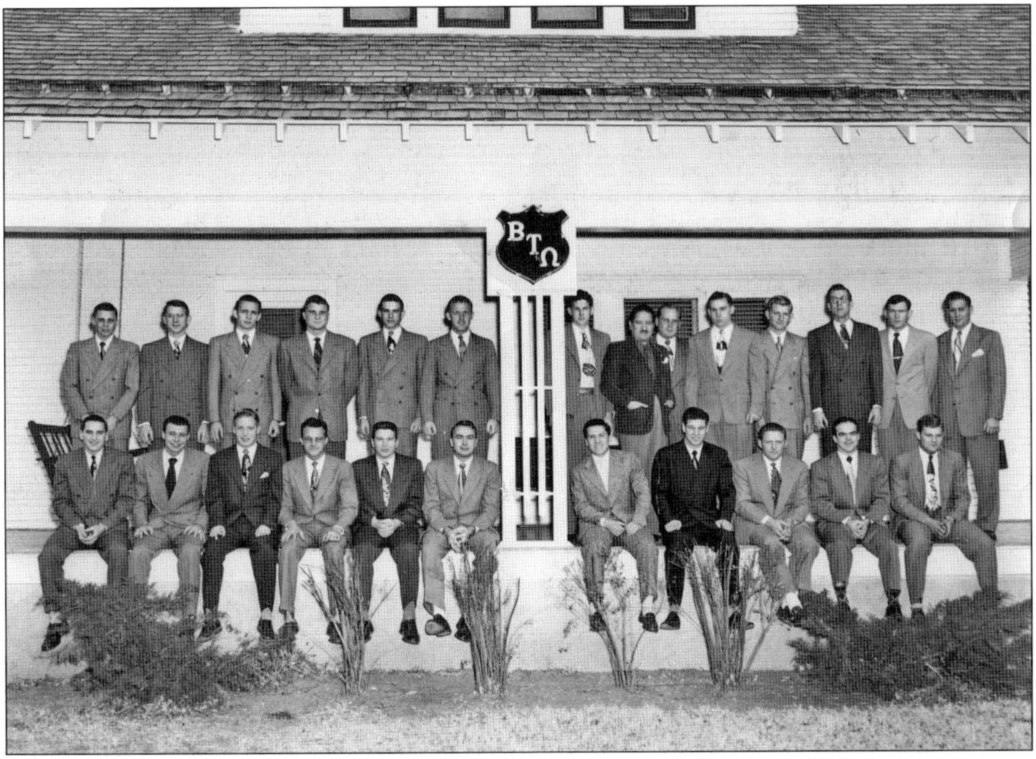

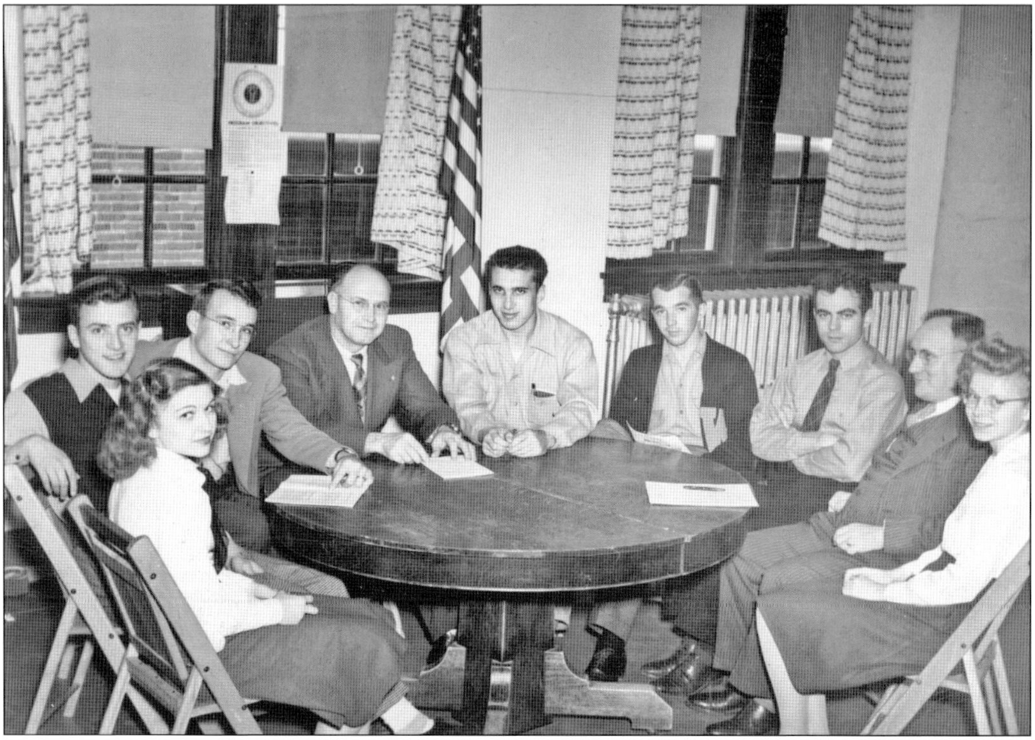

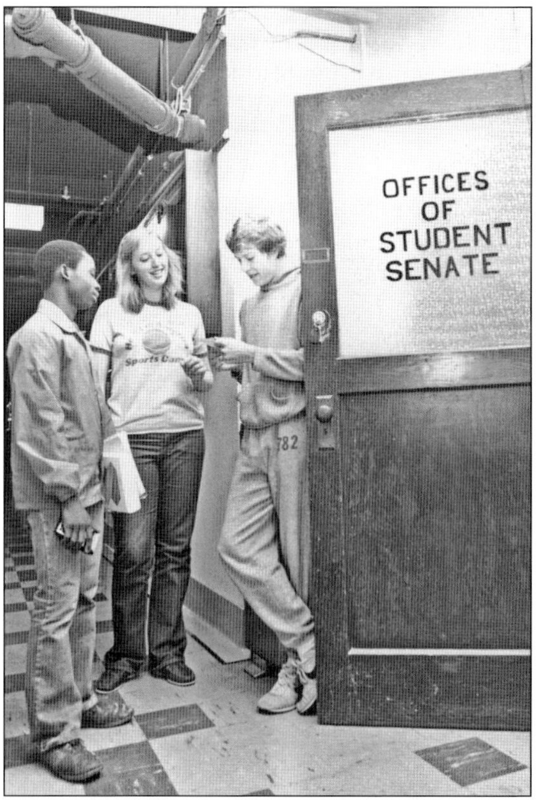

Student council leaders often met with the university dean to discuss and implement ideas on student policies. This was a group of dedicated leaders integral to policy-making and event planning on campus. The name of this group changed over the years from student council to student senate. In 1981, the student senate created a new constitution and changed its name to student congress. These dedicated and energetic students made improvements for student services and activities on campus. Above is the student council around 1948. The 1981–1982 student senate (left) includes, from left to right, William Giddens, Donna Galmbacher Carr, and Dan Winston. Galmbacher is wearing a Heart of America Sports Camp shirt. The sports camp, founded by Ken Cochran, has called the university home since 1979.

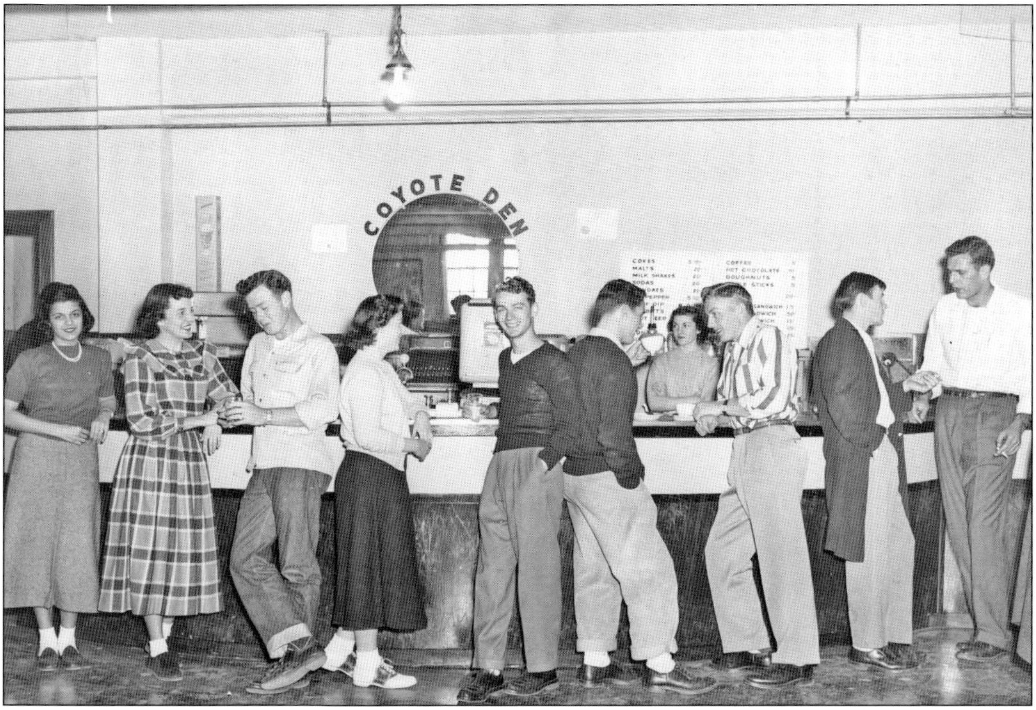

The Coyote Den was a popular place for students to socialize. Students met for snacks and Coke dates or grabbed a sandwich between classes. The Coyote Den opened in the late 1940s and a few years later was remodeled. Spanish professor Capt. Jose Guzman Baldivieso was credited with the opening and redesign of this important student life location. Students are pictured in the Coyote Den around 1950.

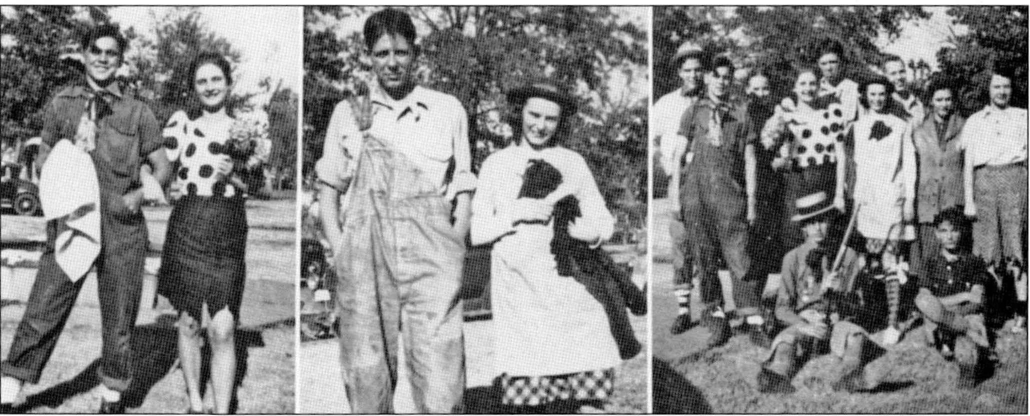

The first Sadie Hawkins Day on campus was held in 1939. It was inspired by the hillbilly comic strip *Li'l Abner*, which began in 1934. Many dressed like characters Li'l Abner and Daisy Mae. Mary Lovene Price and Wayne Ulrickson (left) were awarded best portrayal of the characters. Sadie Hawkins Day evolved into the custom of the Sadie Hawkins Dance, where females ask males for a date.

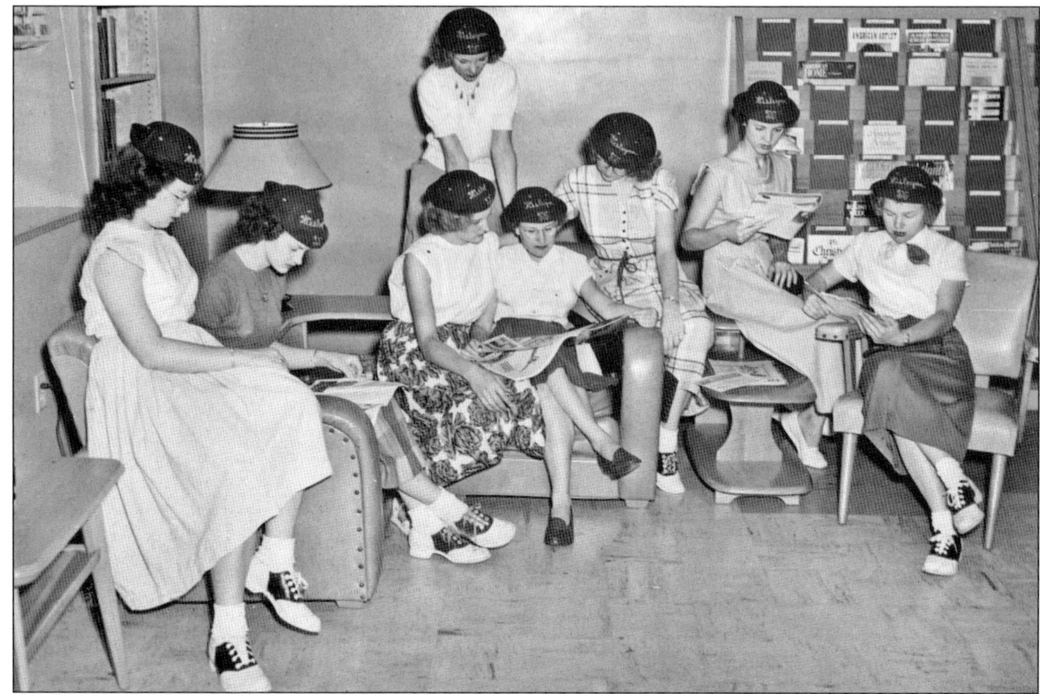

One requirement rooted in tradition was that freshmen wear beanies. The beanie was considered a memento not only identifying but also unifying the freshmen on campus. While some reflect fondly and proudly on sporting their beanie across campus, there was once opposition to this long-standing tradition. In 1920, opposition to wearing the green headgear came from the freshman class. The opposition obviously did not stand, as wearing the cap continued in future decades. The poem "Ode to a Beanie" reads, "Two fingers above the bridge of my nose. I'm a humble freshman and on my toes. Most honored sir, I'm proud to relate. My beanie is sitting both square and straight." Above, students wear beanies in the library. Below, students are pictured in Schuyler Hall after it became a men's dormitory.

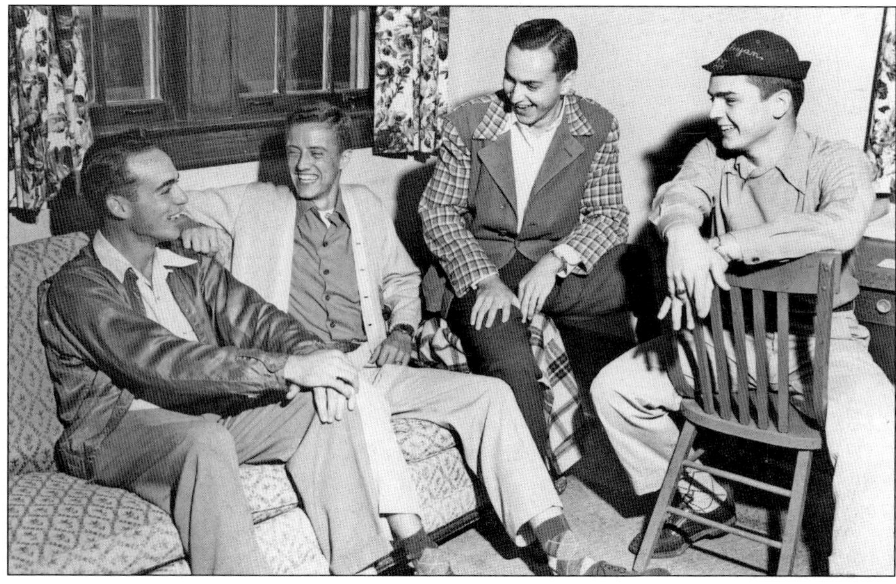

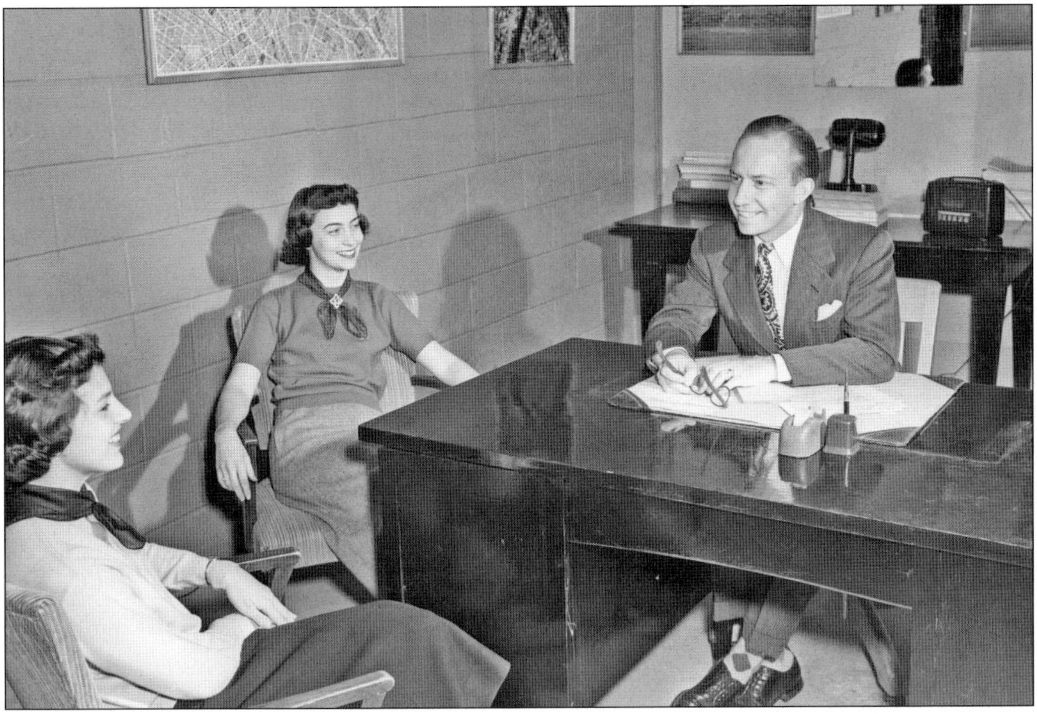

John Courter began his journey at Kansas Wesleyan as a student in the mid-1940s. Upon graduating in 1950, he joined the staff as an admissions counselor. After obtaining his graduate degree from Syracuse University, Courter returned to Kansas Wesleyan to serve as dean of students. In 1979, he received the Alumni Achievement Award. Here, Courter meets with students in his office around 1950.

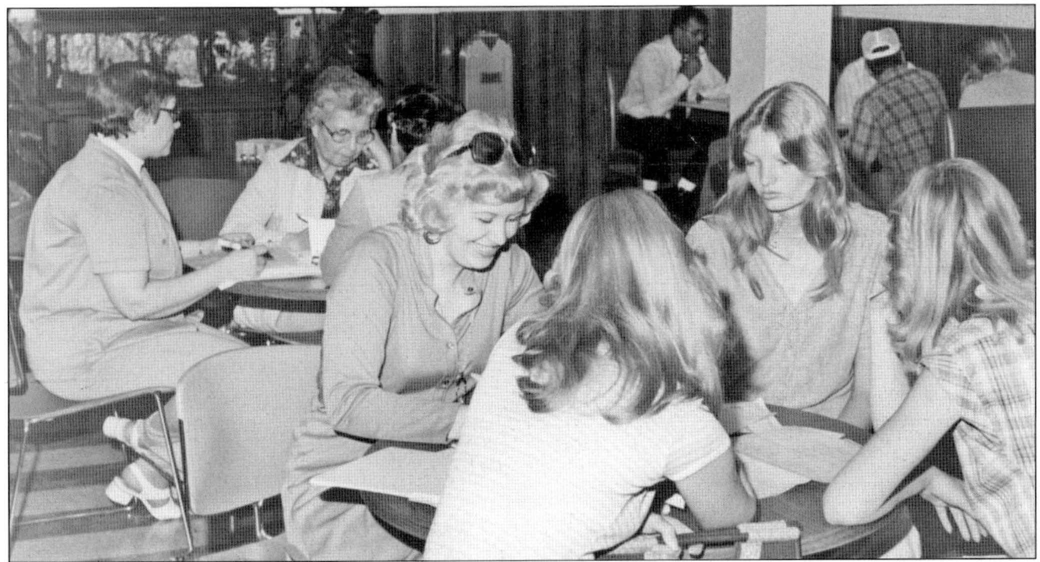

Every fall, students must meet with faculty representatives for registration, as shown here in the fall of 1978. Dr. Sheila Drake, an education professor, assists students in the registration process. In the late 1970s, there were four divisions of studies: humanities; social sciences; natural sciences and mathematics; and applied arts and sciences.

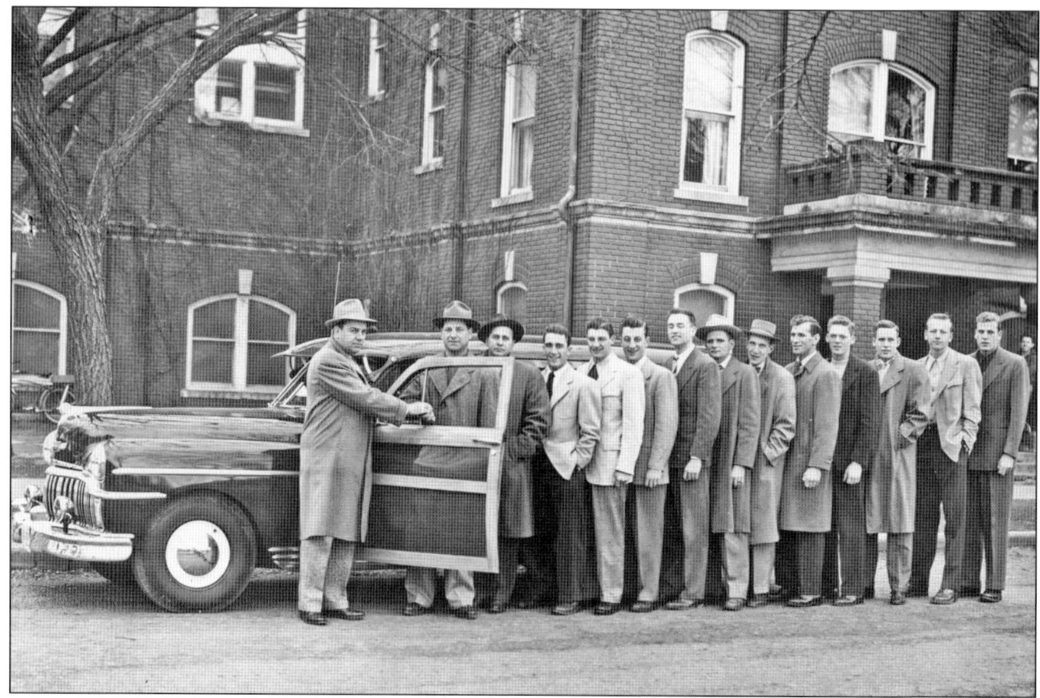

When Wally Forsberg (third from left) replaced Virgil Baer in 1949, he had coaching assistance from Arch Stuck (second from left), Salina's star athlete, nationally known "Gridstar" on the University of Kansas's 1930 Big Six Championship team. The 1949–1950 basketball team played an exciting season, won the conference, and competed at the NAIA National Tournament for the first time. Here, Walter Melton presents the keys to the DeSoto Woody for team travel.

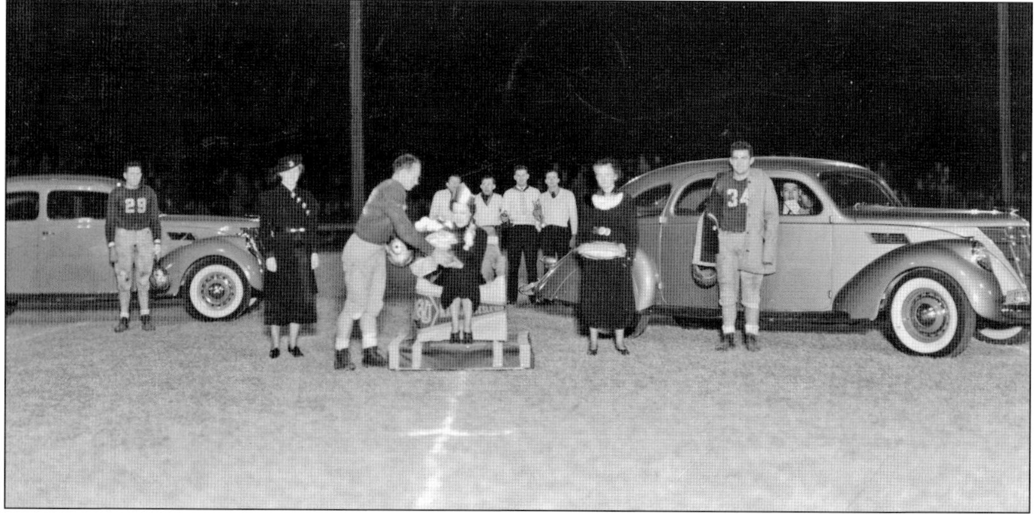

Football queens were selected by the football team. In 1936, Homecoming game sponsor Healey Motors advertised the Lincoln Zephyr automobile (right). During this game against Baker University, captain Amos Morris crowned June Arend Muck, daughter of Rev. Leroy Arend, an alumnus and trustee. Pictured are, from left to right, (front row) Everett Morgan, Doris Lundin Nonkin, Morris, Muck, Eva Lyne, and Lawrence Blair; (back row) varsity quartet Arthur Johnson, Cyrus Pangborn, James Smith, and John VanGundy.

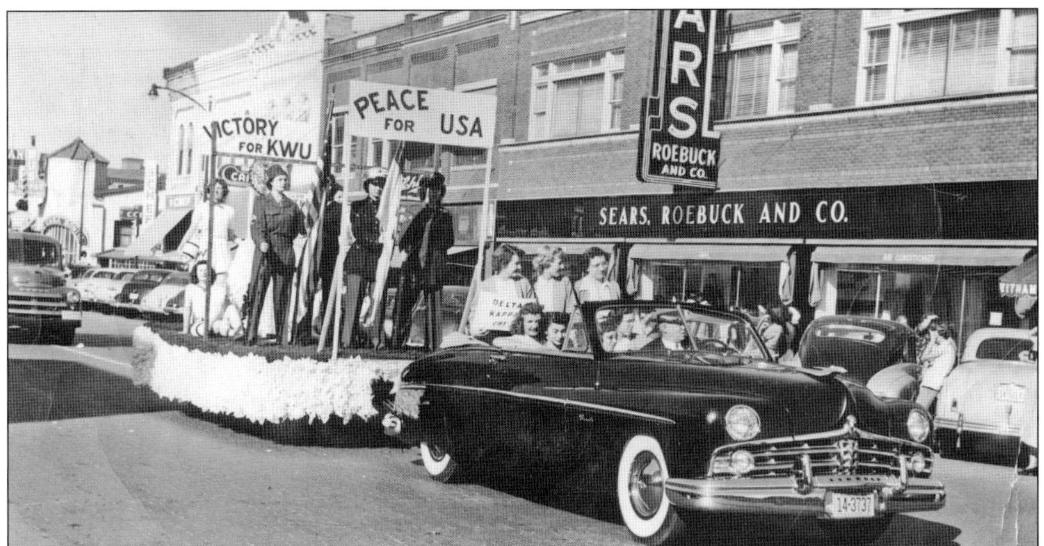

In 1950, all the football queen candidates were members of Delta Kappa Chi. The opening rush event was held at the University Methodist Church with a theme of "South Sea Rush Party." Dinner was at the Brookville Hotel. Delta Kappa Chi's float "Peace for USA and Victory for KWU" took fourth place in the Homecoming parade.

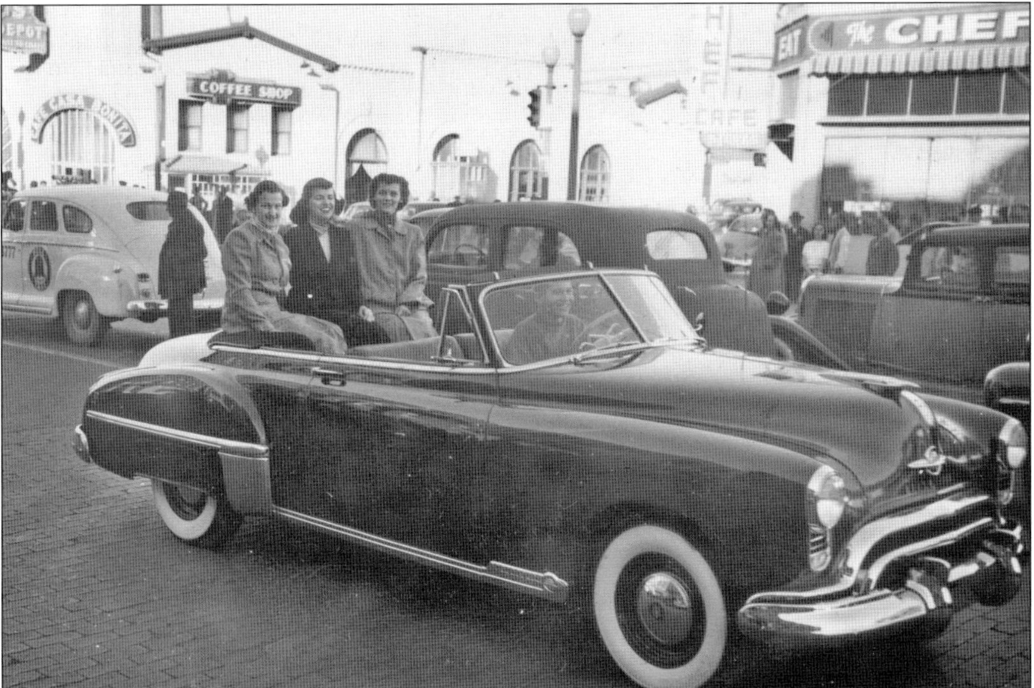

Carl Ramsey operated University Café (1932–1949), at 1416 South Santa Fe Avenue, and Casa Bonita (1951–1963), at 200 North Santa Fe Avenue. University Café was a hangout near campus where student meals were $3.50 in 1937. Ramsey was inducted into the Athletic Hall of Fame in 1987. Seated in the car, from left to right, are Pat Lytal Noyce (Homecoming queen), Beulah Frazell Hulen, and Mildred Gibson Pounds in a parade near Casa Bonita and Chef Café in 1949.

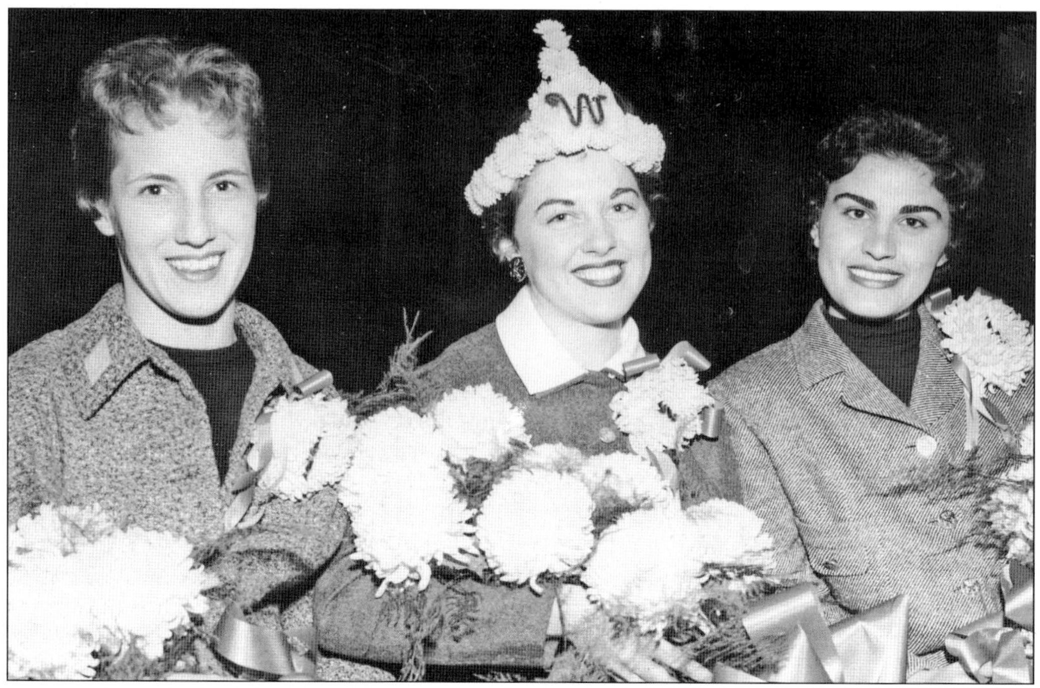

Several crowning ceremonies existed prior to the Homecoming Queen and Miss Wesleyan. In the mid-1920s, representative women were elected as Coyote Queen and Hi-Ki Queen. In 1930, Helen Hall Davis was crowned Queen of the May. Greek life also held annual ceremonies such as Delta Phi Gamma's White Rose Queen. When football stopped during World War II, paper ballots were distributed to all Kansas Wesleyan military. Pauline Sams Roiz, niece of longtime benefactor Earl Corder Sams, was crowned during the Homecoming dance in Miller Hall in 1943. Above, from left to right, are Barbara Cox Culley, Barbara Crampton Walle (1958 Homecoming Queen), and Elaine Maduros Beltsos. Below, from left to right, are Joyce Markle, Anita Gleason Cyrier (1962 Homecoming Queen), and Sylvia Twadell Scott.

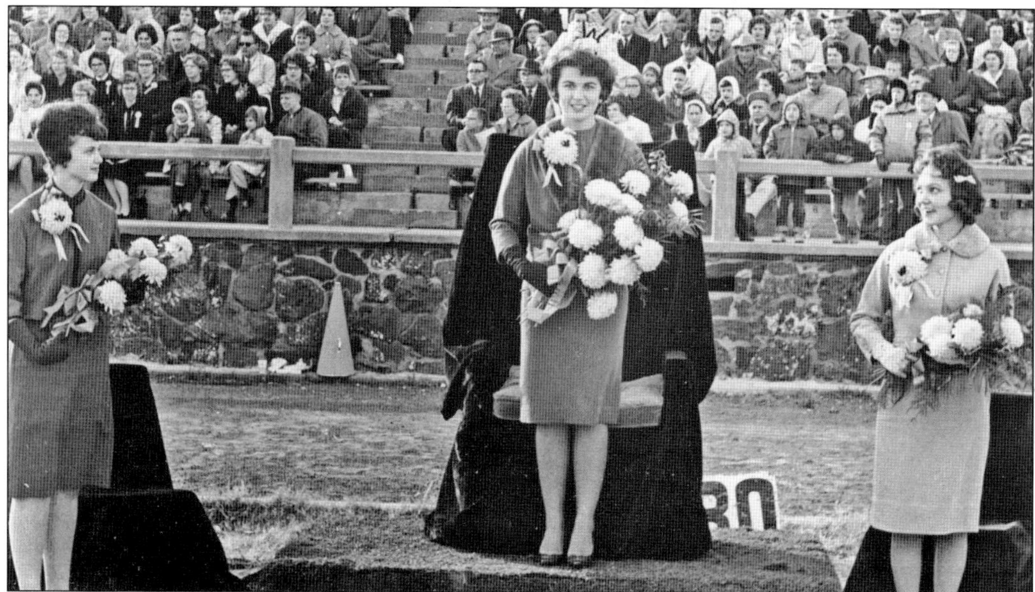

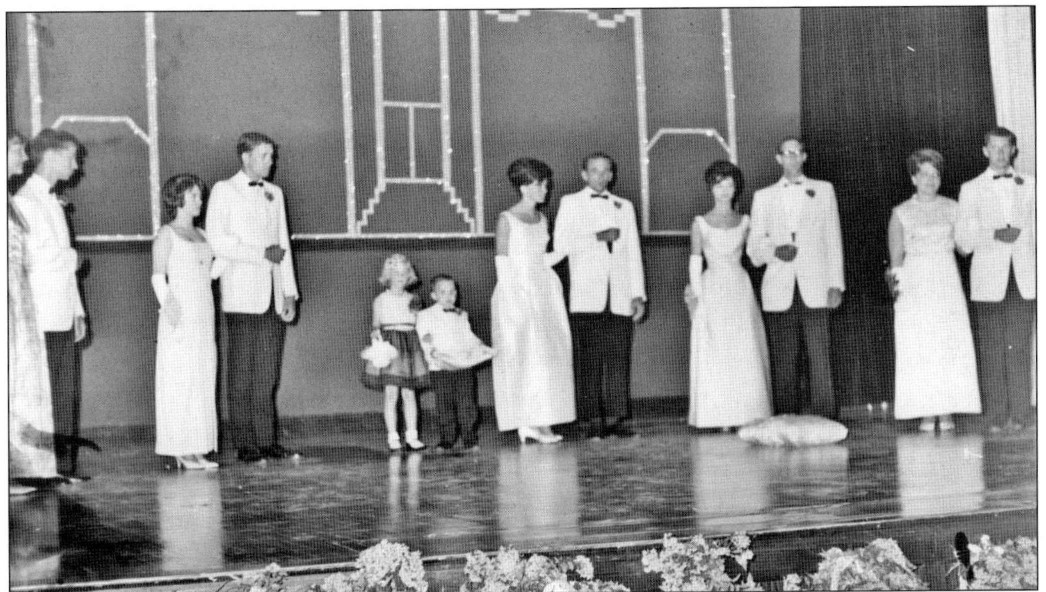

In 1965, the Lilac Fete theme was "Silhouettes in Silver" to commemorate the 25th anniversary of Lilac Fete. After the crowning ceremony, a dance followed in Oakdale Park. A silhouette of Pioneer Hall is seen behind Joyce Markle (center) as she is crowned the 25th Miss Wesleyan with attendants, from left to right, Susan Sullivan Hoisington, Karla Peters Schuster, Jane Blake Beasley, and Jennie Culley Van Gundy.

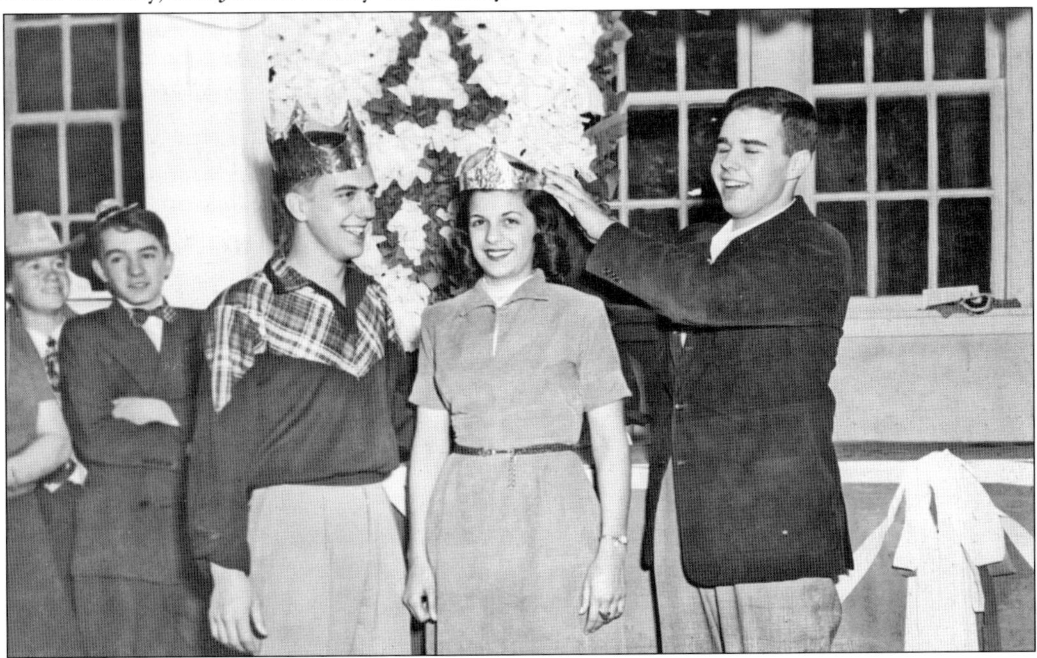

On a Saturday night in April 1951, students turned McAdams Dining Hall into a campus carnival. Carnival-goers enjoyed hot dogs, bingo, and a penny pinch to elect a king and queen. Shown here at the Delta Phi Gamma booth, freshman Nick Agnos and Peggy Bartlett Claypool were crowned by fraternity president Alan Zimmerman. Delta Phi Gamma was formed in 1946. Peggy was a member of Gamma Delta Gamma.

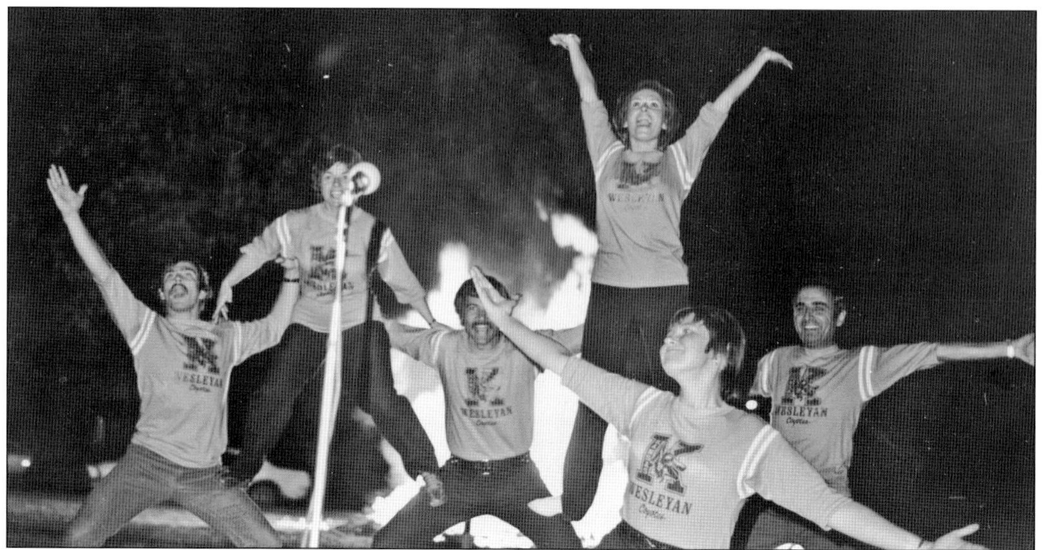

During Homecoming 1978, Michelle Budke was named Homecoming queen. Budke was chosen by the Agree All American Homecoming Queens program to represent Kansas at the Orange Bowl Festival in Miami, Florida. These faculty cheerleaders, led by Dr. Richard Ferrin, cheered on the Coyotes during the Homecoming football game against St. Mary of the Plains.

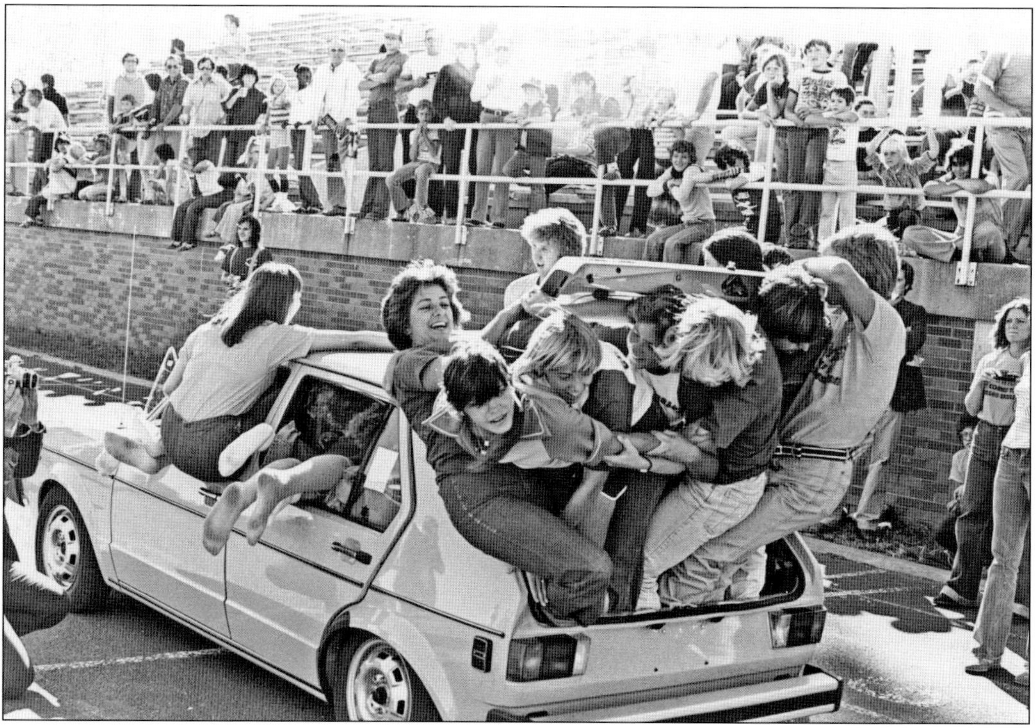

On October 6, 1979, Kansas Wesleyan hosted "Guinness Day Comes to Wesleyan." Several record-breaking attempts were held October 4–6, including the largest tossed salad. Pictured here, students participate in the Volkswagen Rabbit Stuff. They attempted to cram as many people into the car as possible during halftime of a game at Salina Stadium.

Six

Arts and Culture

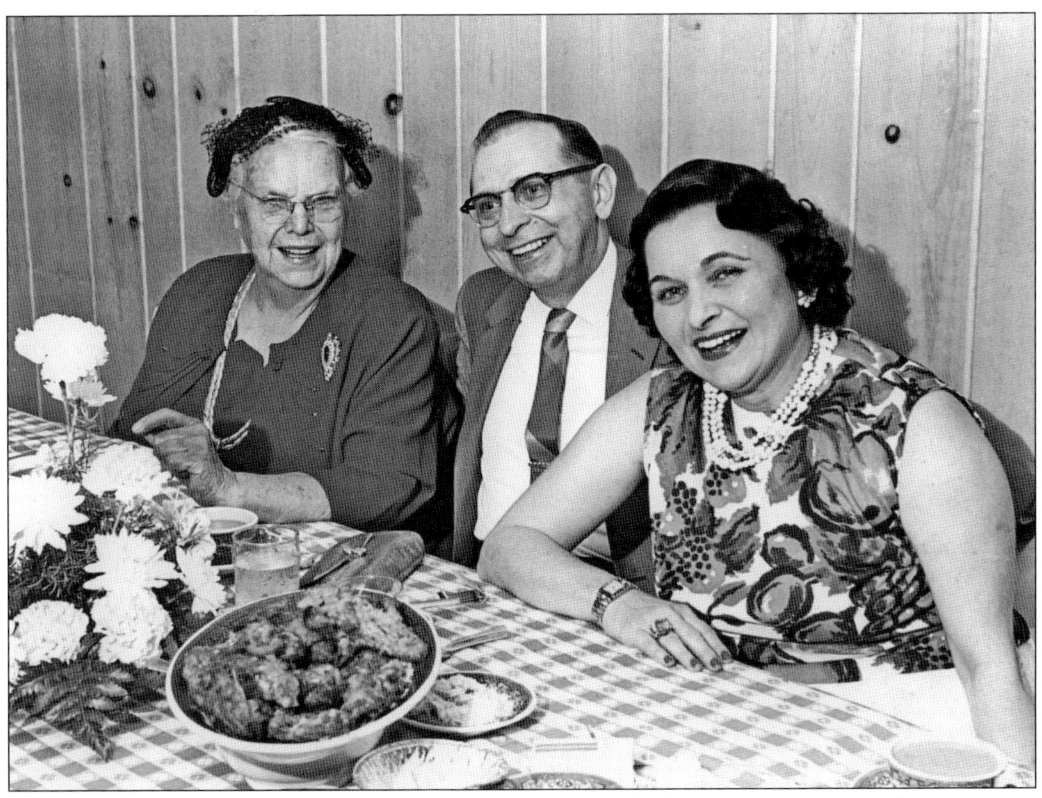

In 1979, music professor Harry Huber (center) retired after 32 years. His wife, Sara, was secretary for the dean and president's office. He continued as organist at University Methodist Church until 2009. In May 1964, Dr. Claire Coci (right) performed a dedicatory recital for the new Shriwise Organ. The Hubers hosted a dinner for Christina Shriwise (left), who sponsored the organ, and Claire Coci at the Brookville Hotel.

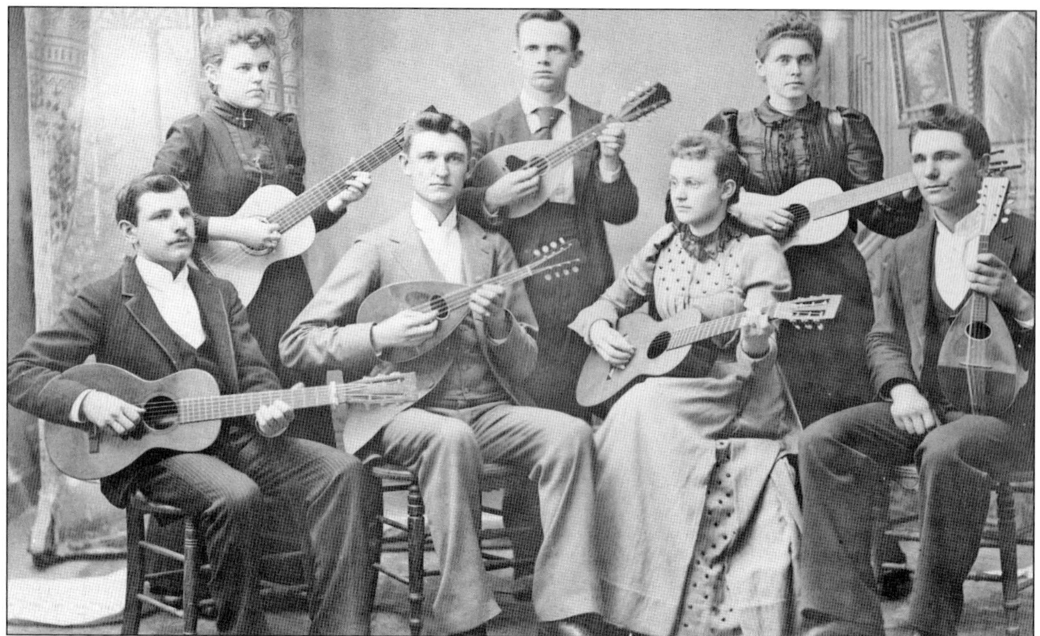

On June 16, 1892, Edith Collins Hagerty Bishop became the first female to graduate from the university. In the evening, entertainment was provided by the Mandolin Club at Salina's Methodist Episcopal Church. From left to right are (first row) Clarence Matson, Fred Bull, Ruth George and Charles C. Eberhardt; (second row) Mattie Shanks Poe, Robert Postlethwaite, and Harriett Thompson Collins.

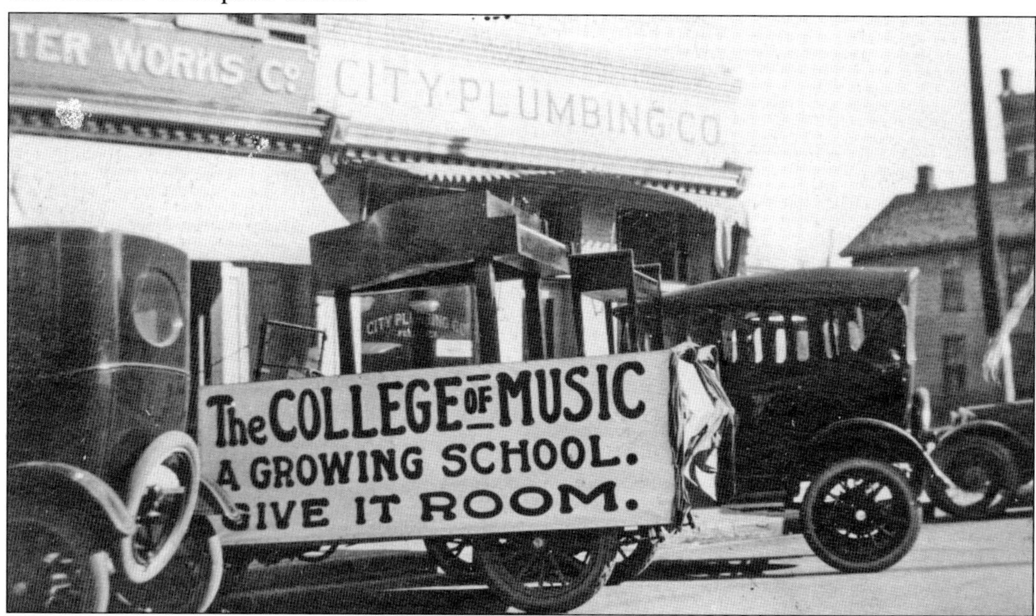

In 1888, the university hired Andrew Jackson Guile Jr. as the first director of the school of music. Music studios moved to various locations, including the business college. The College of Music was once located in downtown Salina over the Palace Theatre at 145 South Santa Fe Avenue. In 1920, the theater did not make improvements to the studio space and plans were begun to create studio space on the main campus.

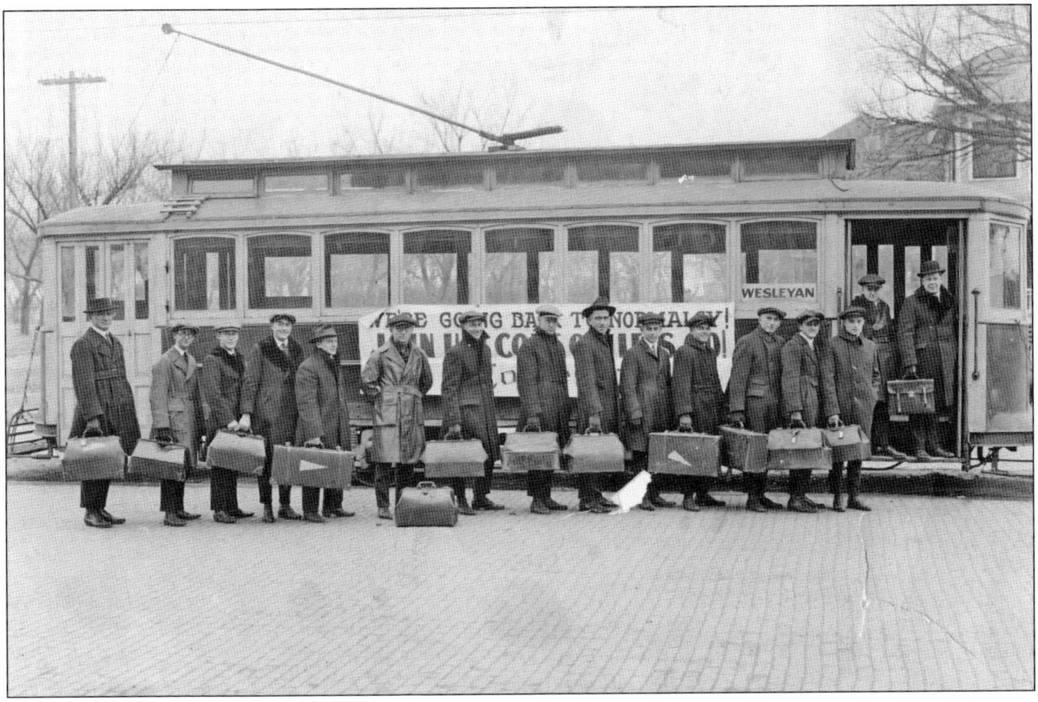

In 1917, Baker University graduates Ernest Lincoln Cox and Everett Foster arrived in Salina to teach at the Kansas Wesleyan College of Music. Both professors received training in Berlin, Germany. Cox valued community involvement from the city, and he reinforced traditional music instruction and introduced new opportunities. Students participated in glee club, voice recitals, and Chautauqua events. Here, Cox boards a streetcar with the glee club in March 1922.

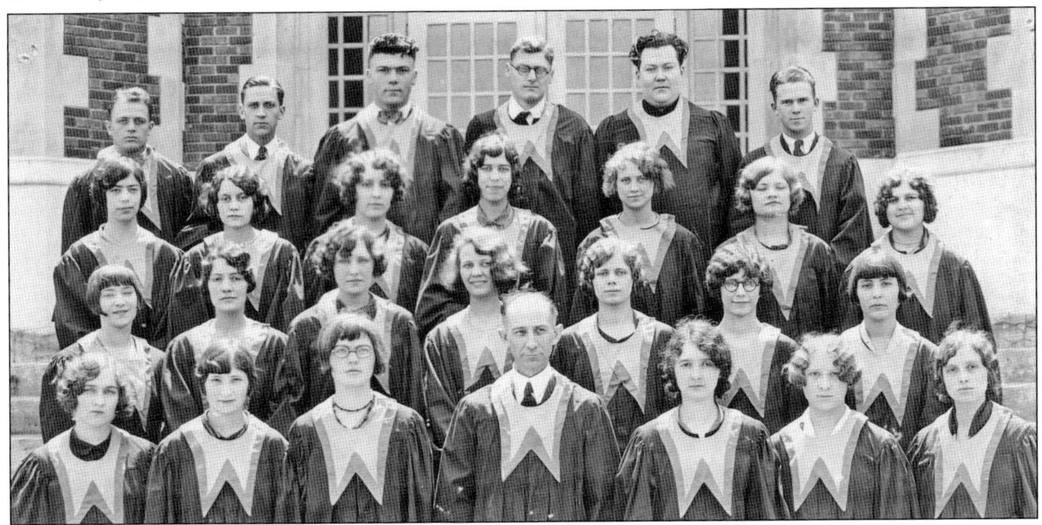

Prof. Ezra Weis, dean of the College of Music, led the department with the assistance of Prof. Carl Jessen and his wife, Pearl Fannie Adair Jessen. Students gave performances throughout the year. After the holiday season, the Chromatic Club, a group of students dedicated to musical studies, performed operas and musicals, such as *H.M.S. Pinafore* by Gilbert and Sullivan. Weis is pictured with the philharmonic choir around 1930.

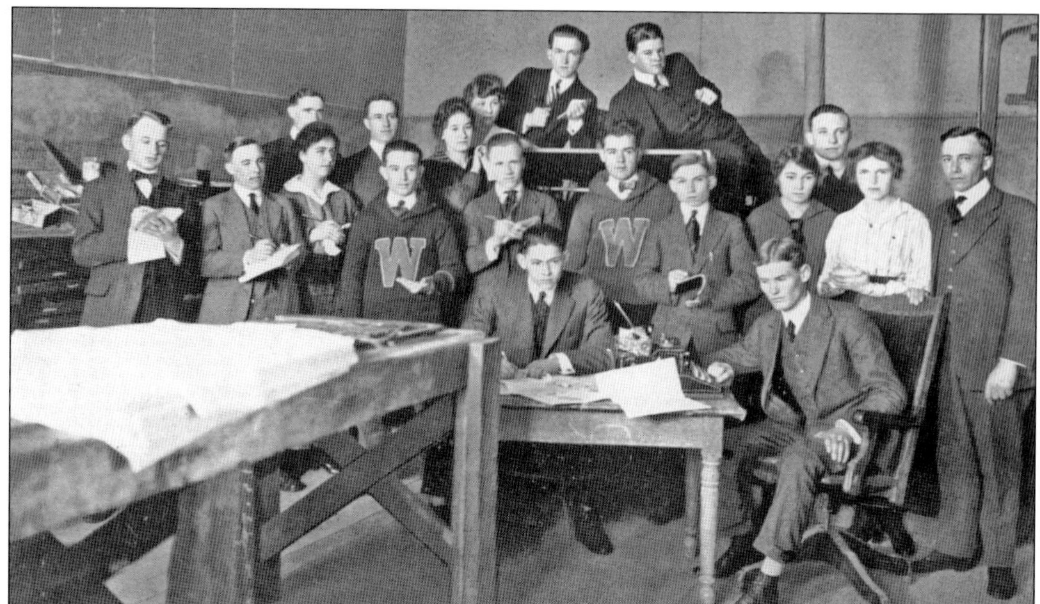

The school newspaper was once named the *Wesleyan Lance* and *Wesleyan Advocate*. By the 1890s, it was known as the *Advance*. Around 1917, the newspaper staff (above) had a vision to create the University Printing Company and garnered support from local printshops for the project. At the time, the *Advance* and the *University Kansan* were the only university newspapers to print on campus. The journalism department hosted the Kansas State Intercollegiate Press Association meeting, with newspaper and yearbook editors, business managers, and journalism students from 14 universities in Kansas. Art professor Lauretta Bennett Peters provided students guidance with the layout of graphics and photographs. Below, editorial skills continue under editor Rosalie Dillinger Menhusen (center left, pointing at paper) and assistant editor Marlene Loyd Falk (left) with staffers around 1960.

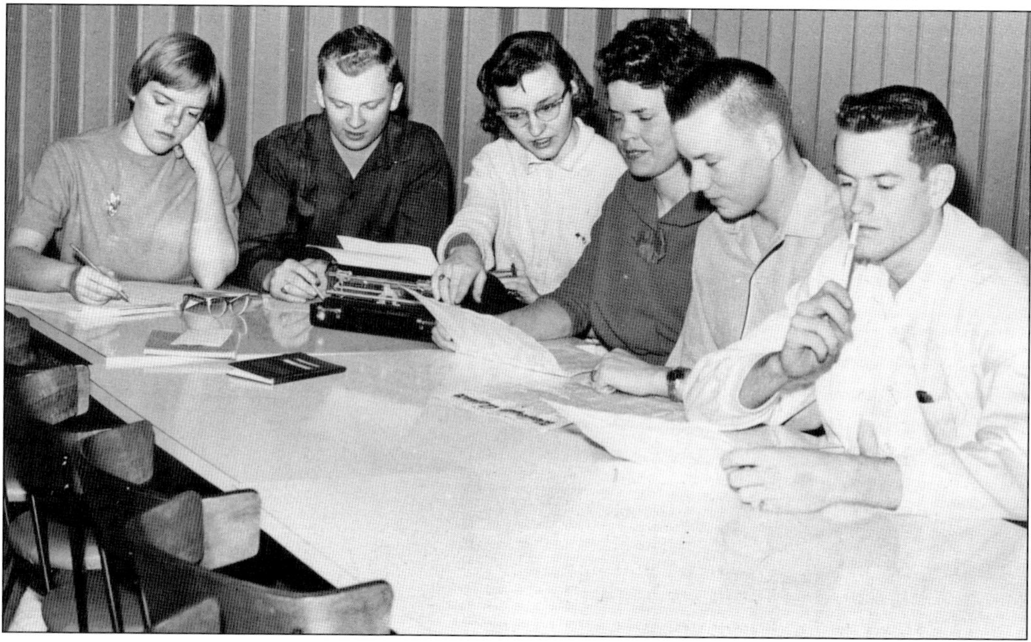

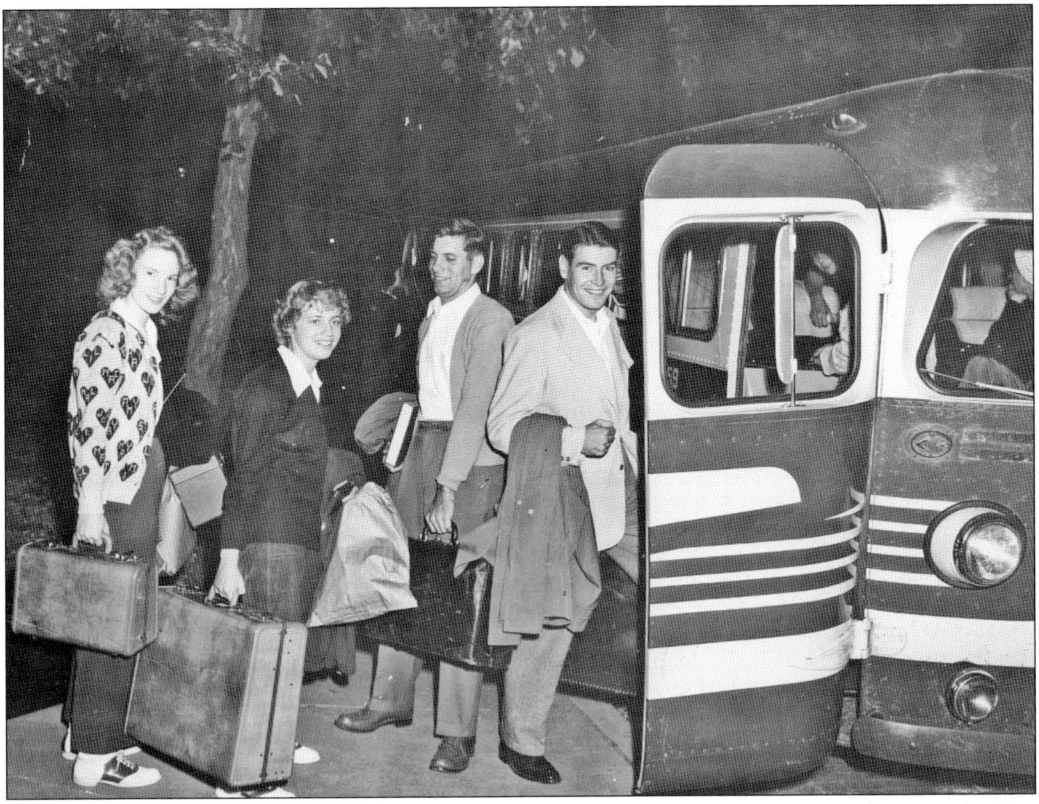

In October 1947, four representatives of the student publications attended the Associated Collegiate Press convention at the University of Minnesota's School of Journalism. From left to right are Betty Feldman Curtis, Jean Clark Joyce, Ed Miner, and Chris Burns. The school newspaper, the *Advance*, received a first-class award the year prior. Those editors credited were Virginia Harz Muninger and Don Gallion.

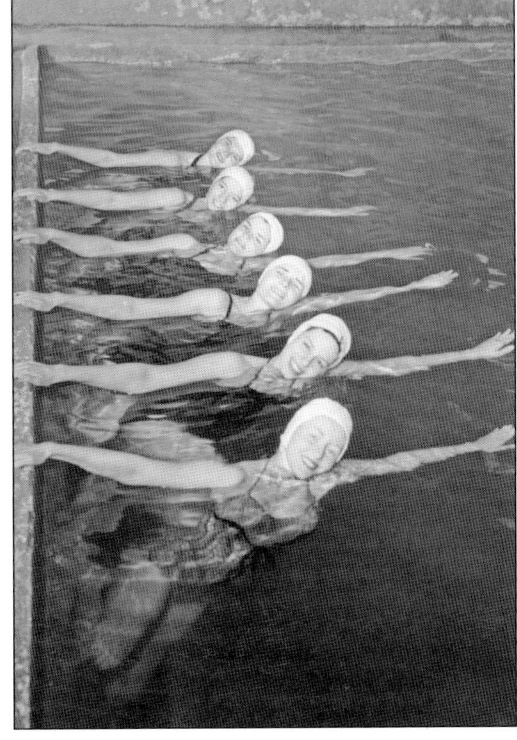

During the 1950s, the university hosted High School Days, which typically included a full preview day of activities offered to potential students. The Wesli-Annes demonstrated their dance and athletic skills during a water show in King Gymnasium's pool. A group of modern dance students had the opportunity to attend Emporia State University's master dance class, taught by José Limón, a well-known dancer and choreographer.

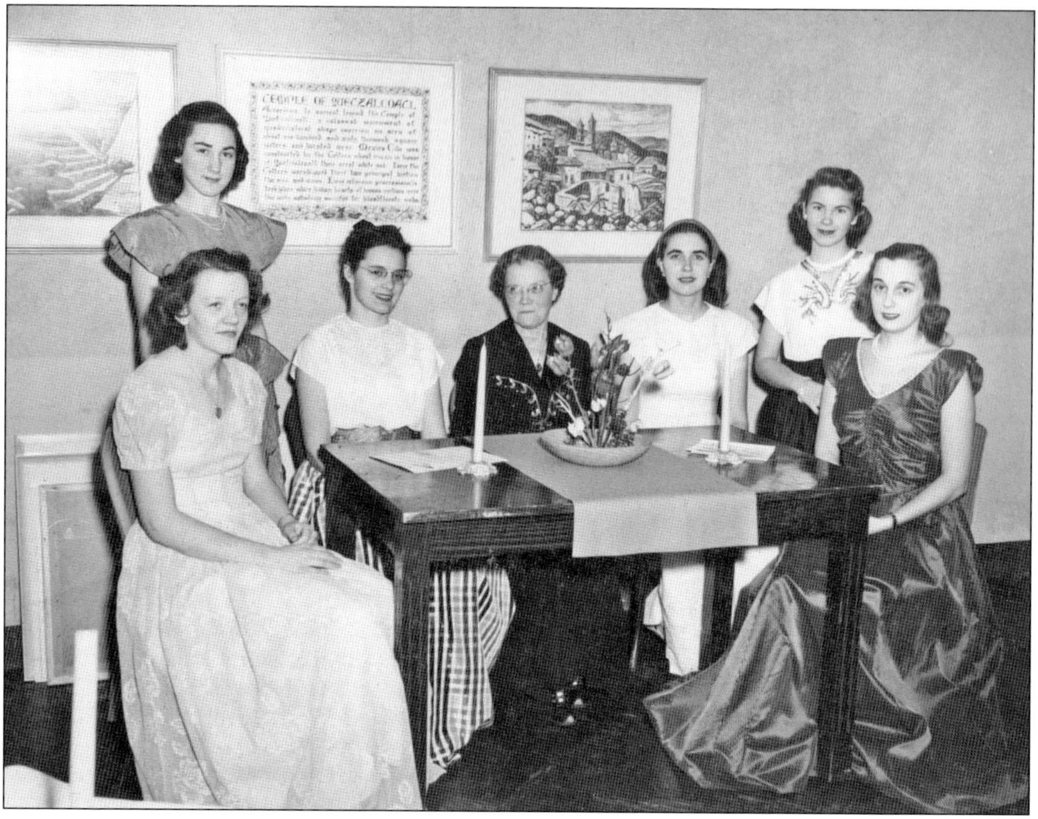

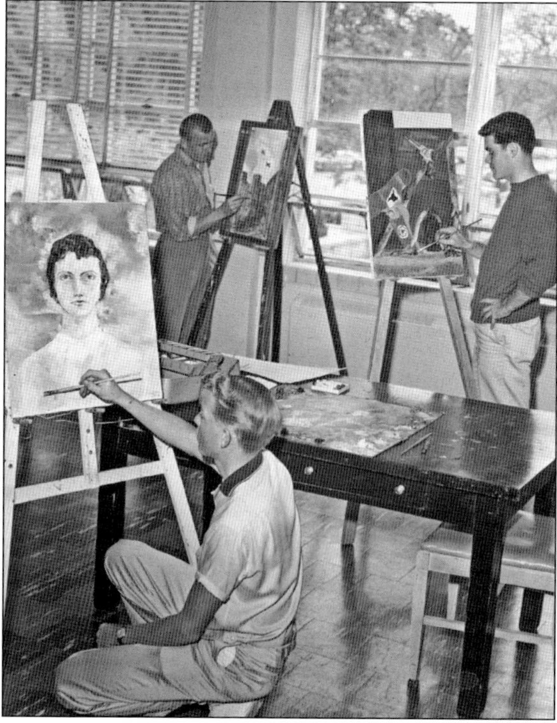

From 1886 to 1888, art was taught by Mary Delahay and Mary Barton. Hallie Hubbard taught for one year in 1897, and President Hagerty's wife taught art in 1901. Around 1910, the university officially formed an art department and hosted its first exhibit. A small gallery was in Schuyler Hall, and an art studio was in Lockwood Hall. Lauretta Bennett Peters grew the presence of the art department from 1912 to 1934. For the next two decades, Prof. Edna Tuttle led the art department. She brought artist Birger Sandzén to campus for special exhibits and lectures. Kappa Pi National Art sorority (above) includes, from left to right, (first row) Helen Stephenson, Ruth Briney Ross, Professor Tuttle, Margaret Nickels Goodenow (president), and Evelyn Knapp Cole; (second row) Virgie Rawlings and Joan Buehre Patterson. At left, students work on paintings in class.

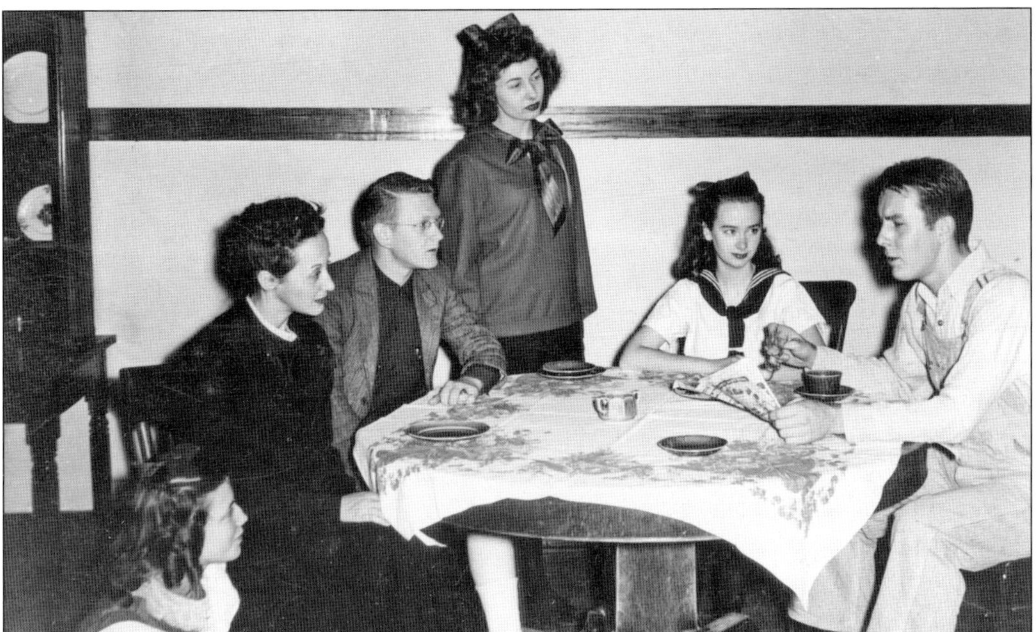

In December 1946, students presented a popular production of John Van Druten's play *I Remember Mama*, under the direction of Prof. Lilybelle Carlisle. The play had a successful run on Broadway in the preceding years. According to the *Salina Journal*, the audience was enthusiastic over the performances and costumes. Among those pictured here are Jeanette Clark Joyce, James Joyce, Dorothy Beck, Virginia Harz Mininger, and Richard Spalding.

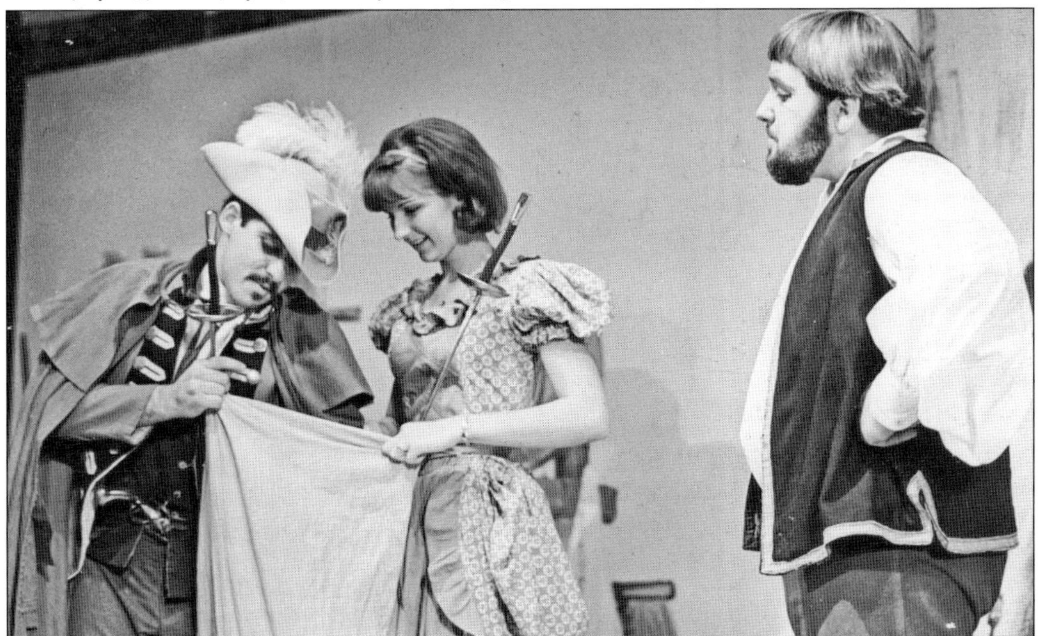

In March 1967, Prof. Lloyd Frerer directed Bronson Howard's play *One of Our Girls*. Frerer chose the play based upon his coinciding doctoral research on the playwright at the University of Iowa. In this photograph, the character the Count, portrayed by Frank Darytichen, looks on at his fellow cast members.

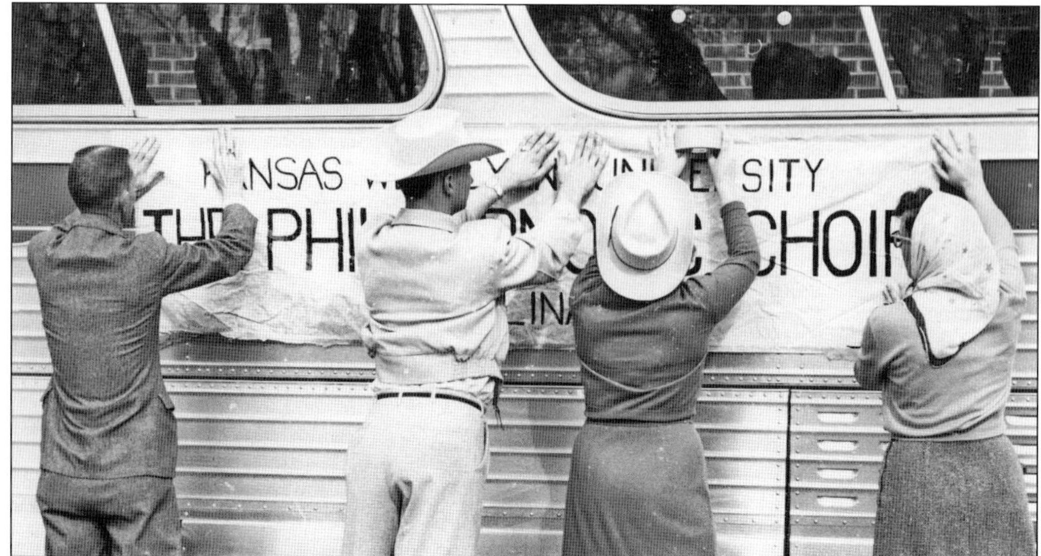

The Kansas Wesleyan Philharmonic Choir completed its 13th annual concert tour in 1951. A total of 62 students traveled to the Grand Canyon, singing for an Easter Eve vesper service to tourists gathered for sunrise service. They also made stops in New Mexico and Colorado. Director Leon Wilgus led the choir in performances of masterpieces by Bach and Brahms. Wilgus brought the choir national recognition.

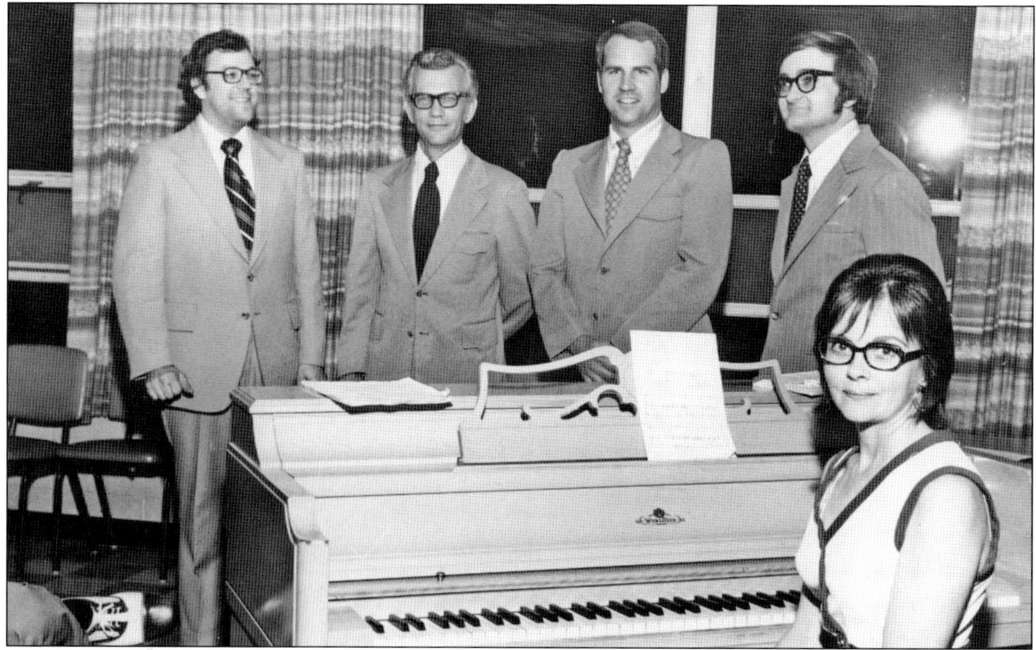

In 1976, Chaplain Steve Fink left to pursue his doctorate. He coordinated host families, chaperoned students abroad, and was instrumental in the campus ministry program, Counterpoint. Many attended his speech at the peaceful antiwar rally outside Pioneer Hall in 1972. Fink's work at the United Nations prompted an Alumni Distinguished Service Award in 1980. Faculty pictured here are, from left to right, Fink, Orville Voth, Bill Anderson, Bill Worley, and Pat Taylor (seated).

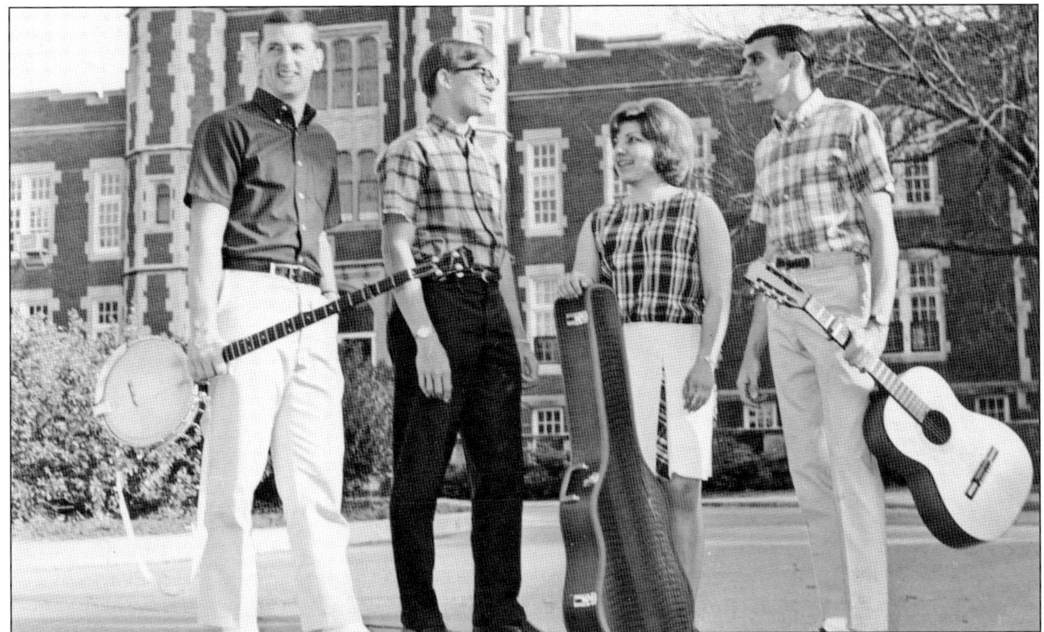

The popular Cat Canyon Singers sang folk songs. In January 1966, the group performed with others including the Madrigal Singers to welcome Schilling Manor families to Salina. Photographs taken during the event were mailed to First Infantry Division troops in Vietnam. From left to right are Randy St. Clair, Bill Forbes, Jennie Culley Van Gundy, and Penn White.

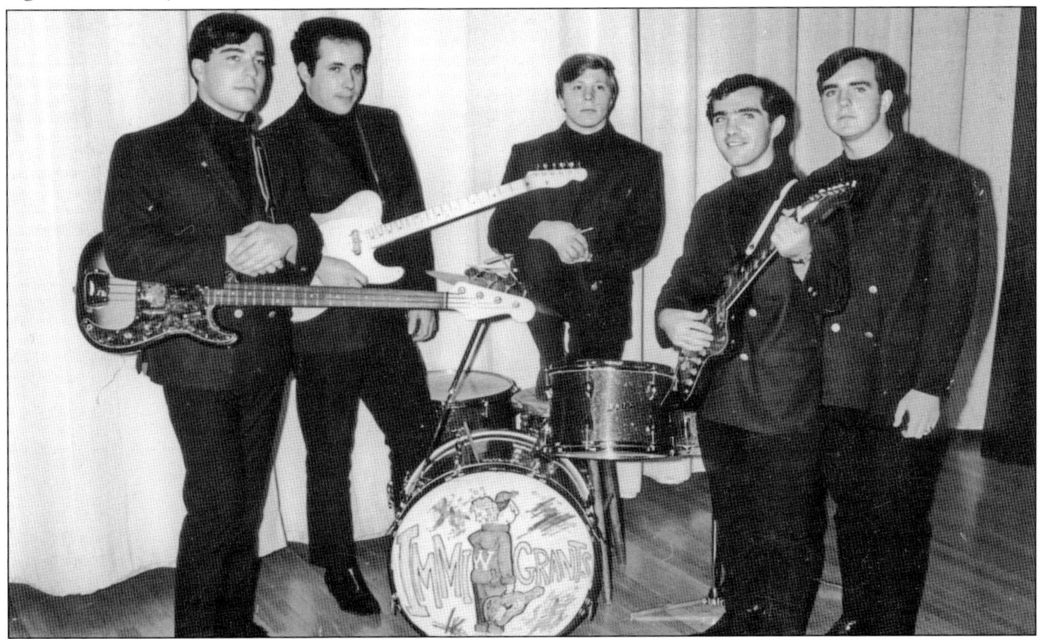

In 1966, New York and New Jersey students formed the rhythm and blues band the Immigrants. The band's album *Immigrants on the Move* was recorded in Sams Chapel and features "Time to Say Goodbye Now." In 2015, drummer Nicholas Petron (center) received the Division of Fine Arts Outstanding Alumnus award. From left to right are band members Dave McKay, Ray Leavitt, Petron, Dick Reilly, and Ed Reilly.

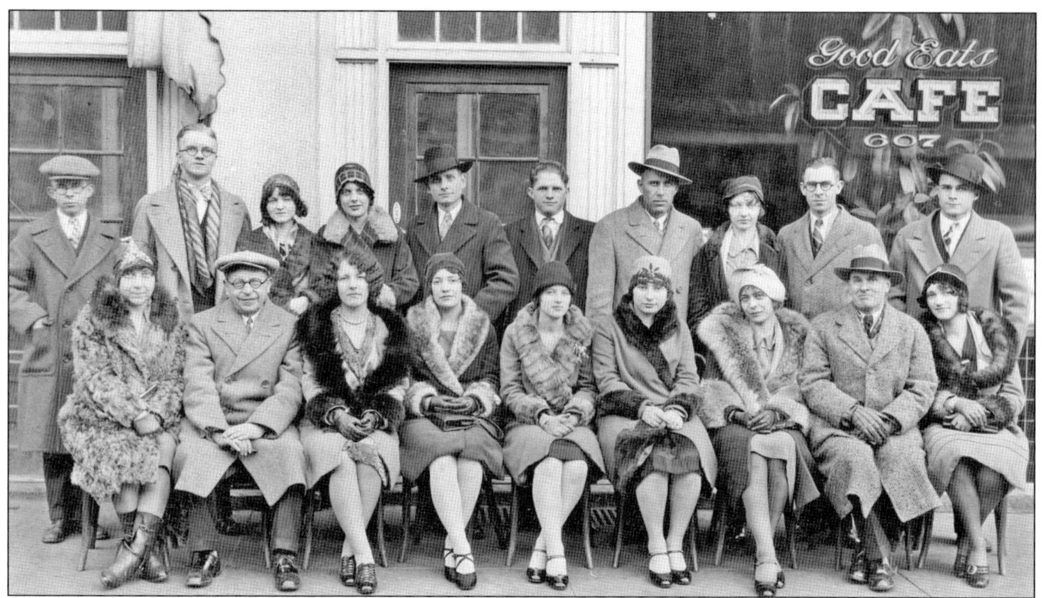

On February 12, 1929, the Kansas Wesleyan Business College Broadcasting Club traveled to Milford, Kansas, for a second year to be a featured entertainment act on KFKB Radio. The station was owned and operated by John R. Brinkley, a radio entertainment pioneer. Music professor Karl E. Hurst led the group, which performed many different readings, solos, and duets. The program received excellent reviews nationwide. Above is the Broadcasting Club on the trip outside the Good Eats Café in Junction City. Prior to and after teaching at Kansas Wesleyan, Professor Hurst also taught at the Goldsboro School of Music in Goldsboro, North Carolina. Below, Hurst stands on the steps of the unfinished Pioneer Hall with the Kansas Wesleyan University band around 1928.

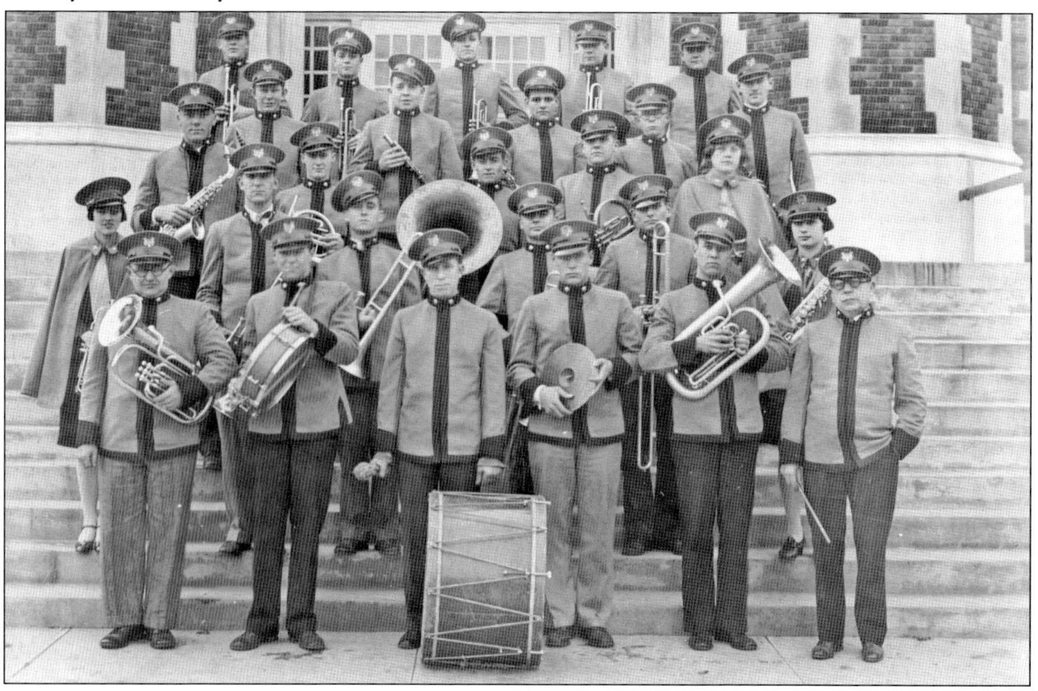

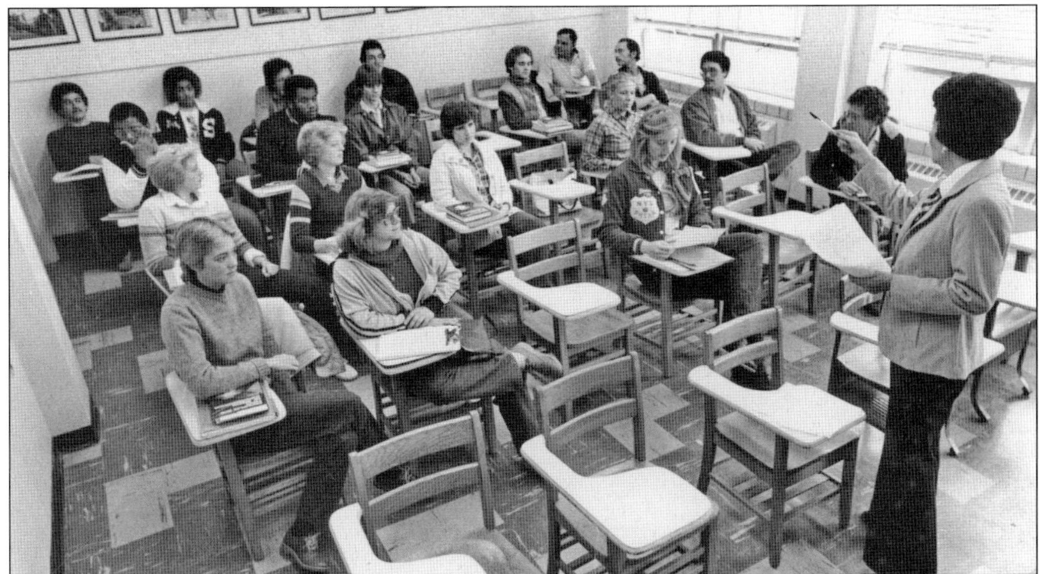

When Prof. Kay Dudley arrived on campus, there were only two speech classes offered, and her diligence established a speech degree. Alumni recall numerous news clippings and photographs lining the walls of Dudley's office. She beamed with optimism, living by a motto that was in a speech by President Bratton: "We expect you to expect the best in us." In 1981, she received the Student Congress Distinguished Service Award.

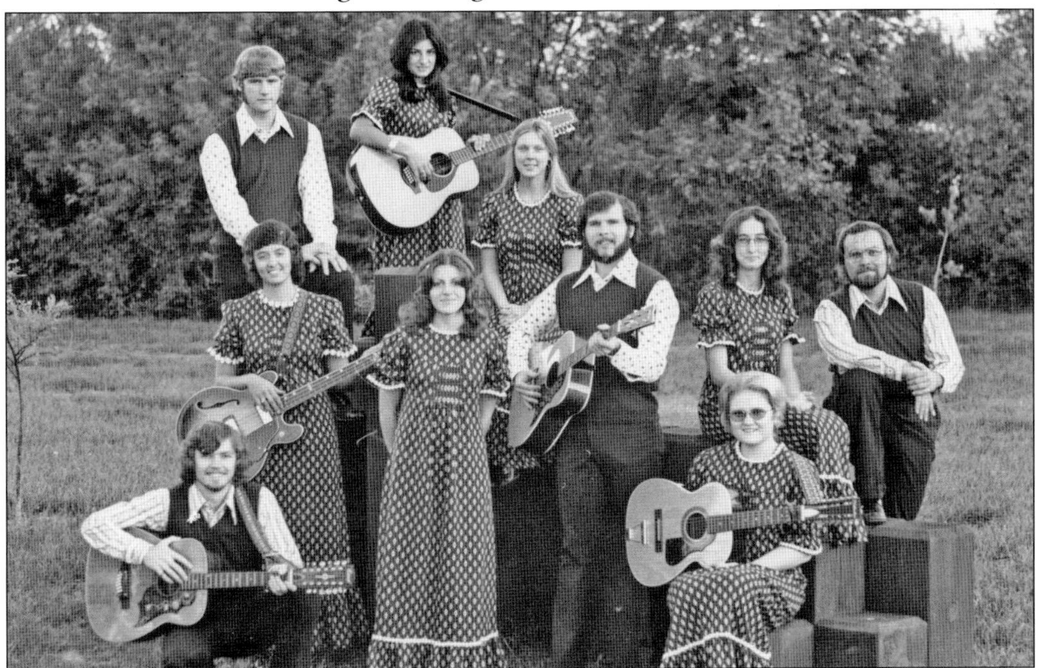

The 1970s student musical ensemble the Wesleyan Singers performed and recorded contemporary folk songs with lyrics conveying messages of moral significance. As the group grew in popularity, its audience expanded nationwide, including a special performance at the Capitol Hill United Methodist Church in Washington, DC, during the US bicentennial celebration. This group was under the direction of Prof. William Anderson.

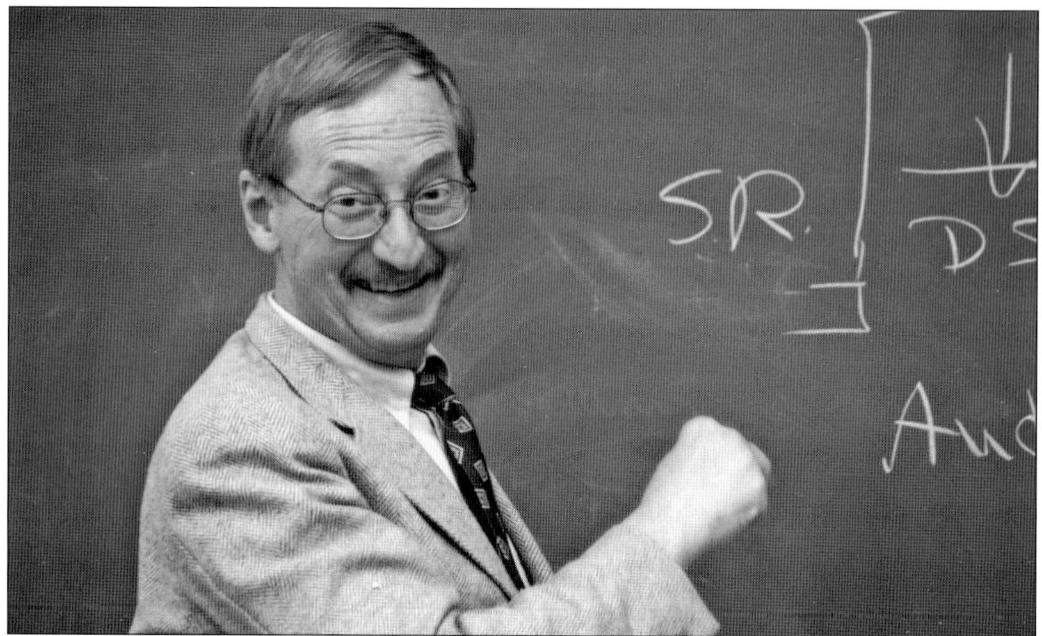

In 1987, Dr. Eric Marshall (above) and Barbara Marshall joined the faculty in the speech, theater, and communication department. In the decades to follow, these professors brought an invigorating spirit to the department. The Marshalls' first play on campus was Oliver Goldsmith's 18th-century comedy *She Stoops to Conquer*. In 1988, the theater department reintroduced summer productions with the Kansas Arts Excellence Grant, funded by Southwestern Bell. The first summer students performed *Picnic*, which resonated with the community because portions of the movie version were filmed in Salina. The following summer, students performed N. Richard Nash's 1950s play *The Rainmaker*. The main character, portrayed by Jernard Burks (below), exudes optimism for rain when a Western town faces drought conditions. Burks's final undergraduate acting performance, *Fences*, was in the spring of 1990, and he has achieved a successful acting career.

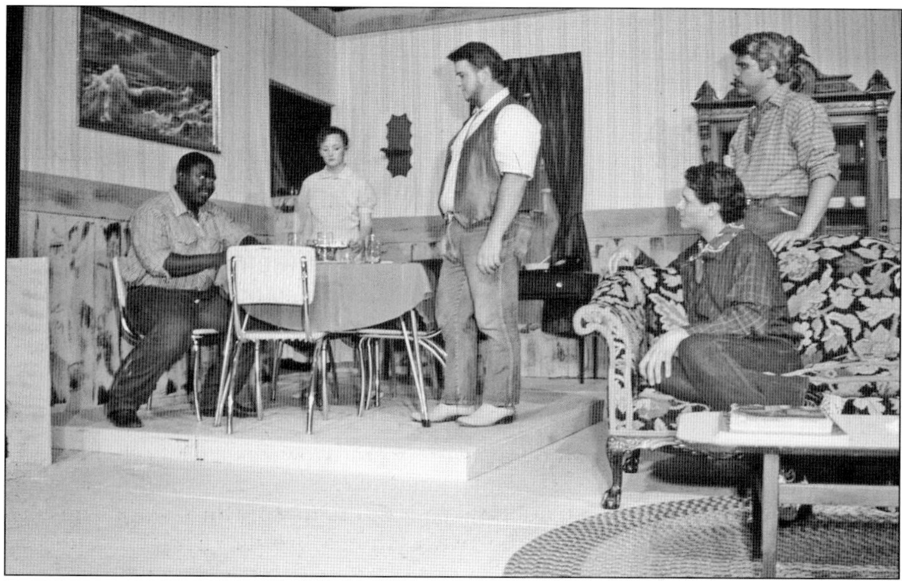

Seven

Go Coyotes!

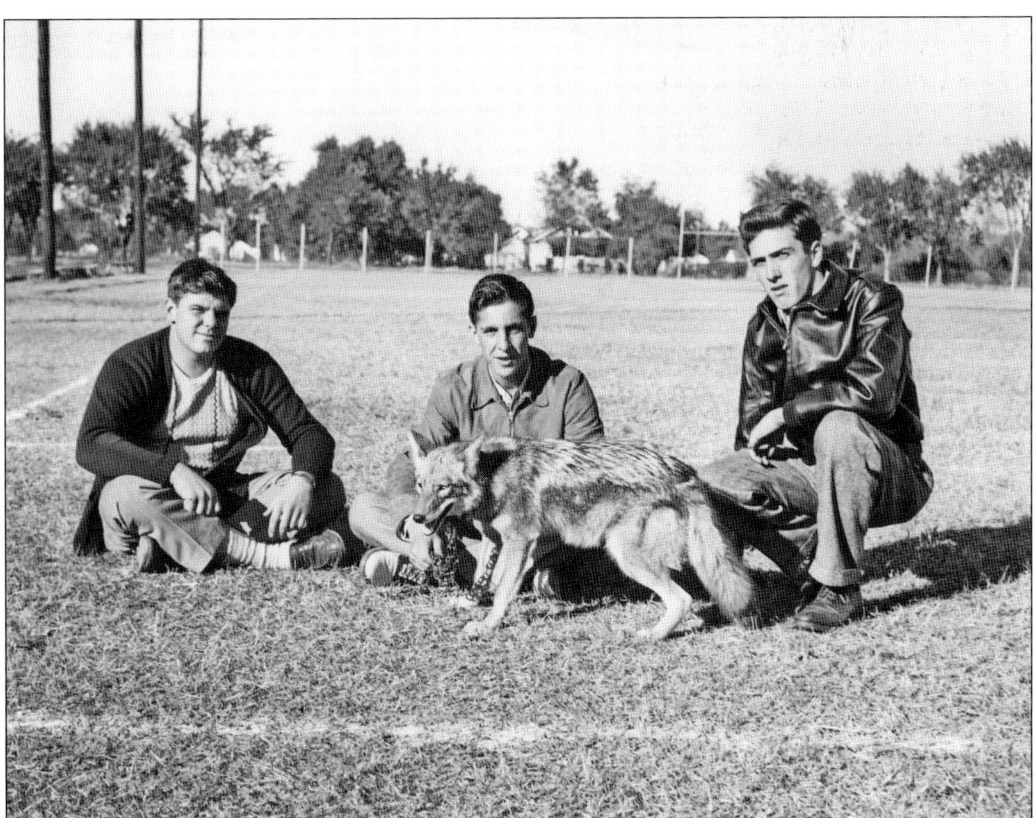

Before the coyote mascot was adopted, the teams were known as the Preachers, Methodists, and Wesleyans. In December 1915, students voted to call the yearbook *Coyote*, and it was suggested to take a vote of the student body to make the mascot the coyote. The coyote is a plains native and is considered one of the swiftest animals in the world. Pictured here are the keepers of the coyote around 1948.

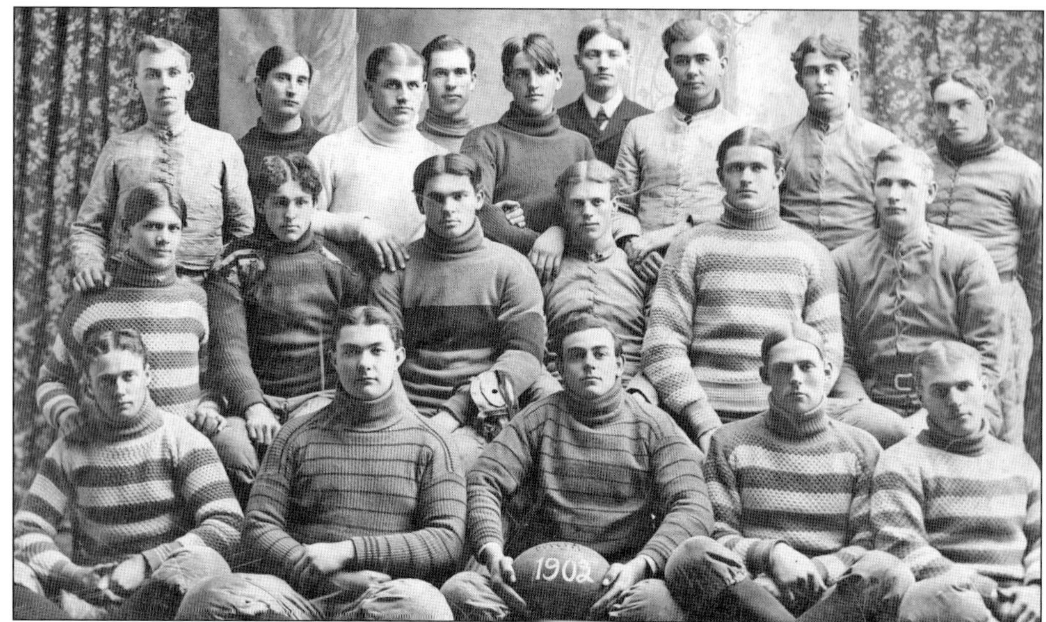

The 1902 football team was victorious over Salina Normal University 16-0. Pictured here, the team includes Clyde Orlando Marietta (second row, far right) and Clarence Edmund Rarick (second row, third from left). Marietta later joined the Kansas Wesleyan faculty. Rarick, a former West Point cadet, participated in Wesleyan's military department. Rarick also served on Kansas Wesleyan's board of trustees and became president of Fort Hays State University during the Great Depression.

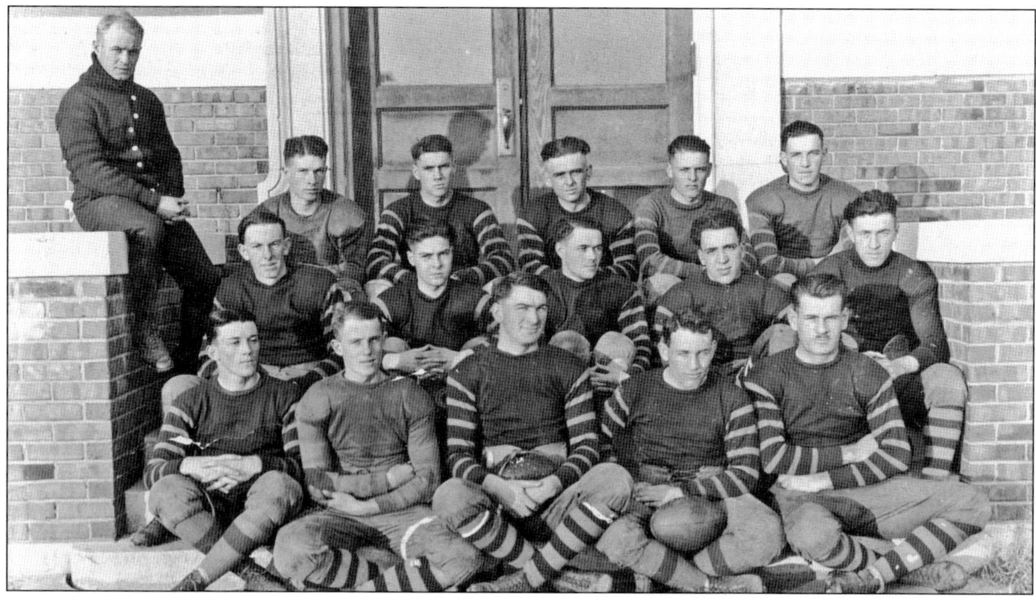

In 1920, athletic director Albert King hired J. Elwood Davis (seated, left) to coach football, basketball, and track. Davis was football captain at the University of Iowa. A year later, the Mackies arrived in Salina to successfully lead the athletic programs for two decades. Alexander Brown Mackie, an alumnus of Ohio Wesleyan, and wife Ruth Law Mackie, who trained at Ohio State University, previously led high school athletics in Athens, Ohio.

Before the advent of today's modern electronic scoreboards, someone had to update the scores manually. It was also important to have the scores of other games of interest from the area to keep people updated. Louise Medcraft is shown at the scoreboard in 1924 during the football game with the Bethany Swedes.

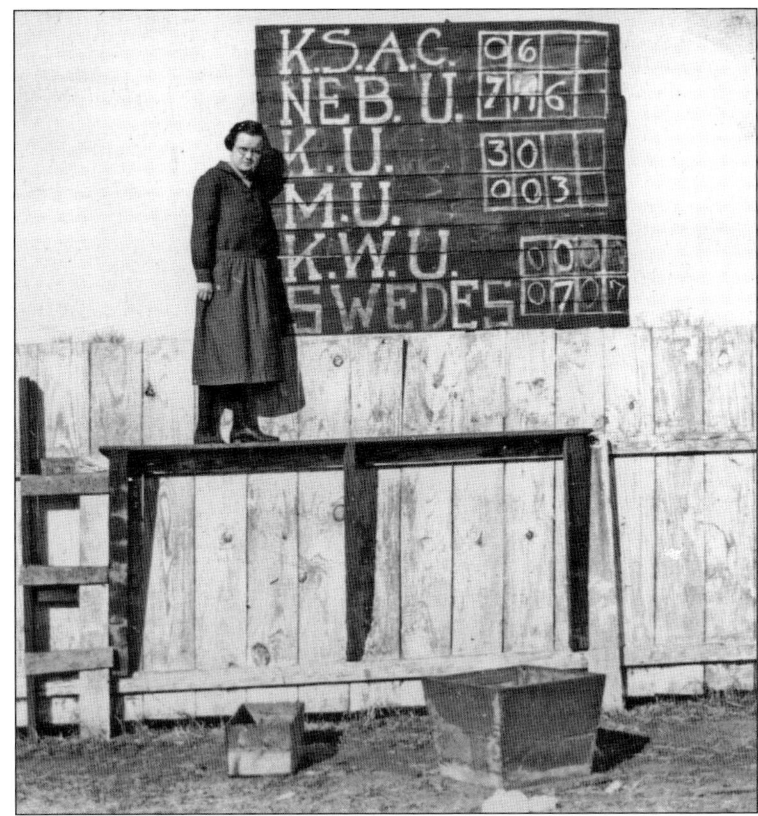

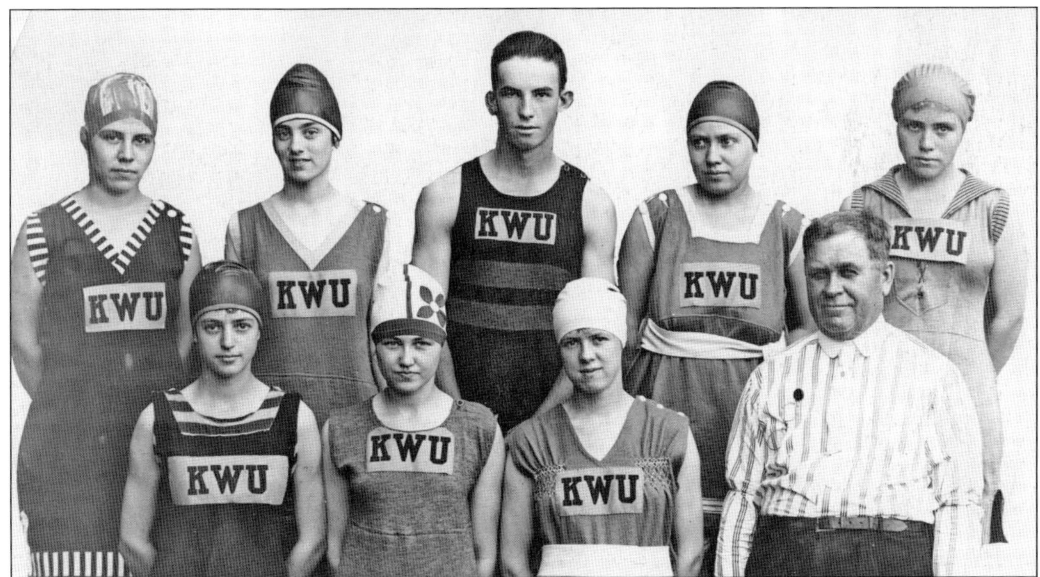

In 1916, headlines drew excitement when teenager Mary Campbell Palmer (first row, second from left) swam 66 laps in record time in Kansas Wesleyan's pool without pause. This prompted regular swimming instruction and competitions in conjunction with the Salina Swimming Club. Campbell Palmer was an alumna and professor and became the dean of women in 1930. (Courtesy of the Smoky Hill Museum.)

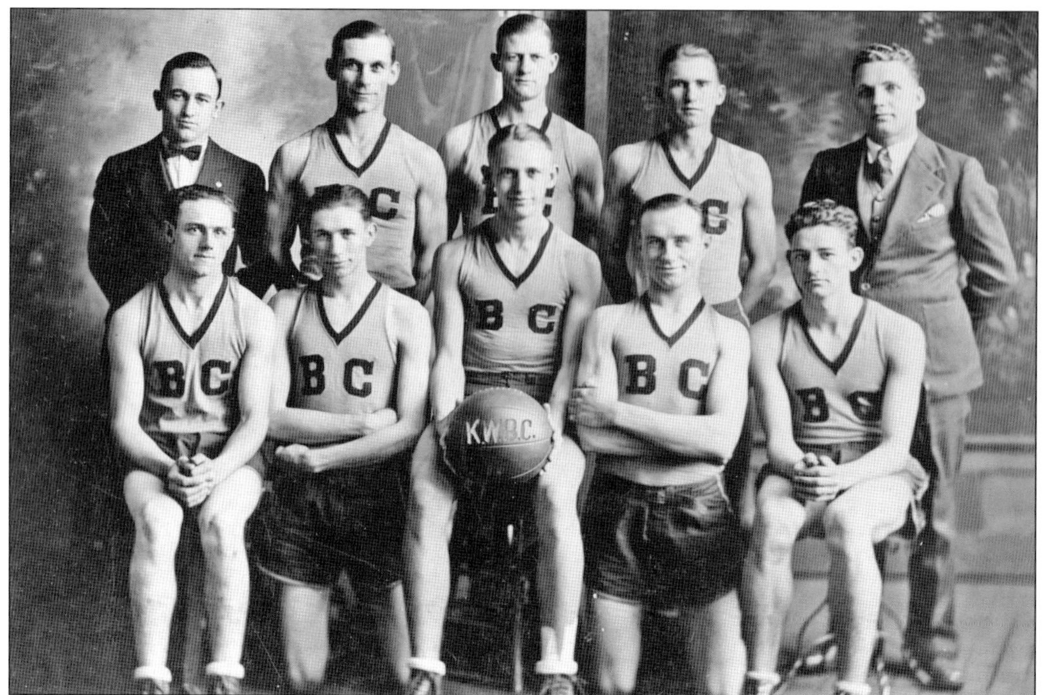

In the mid-1920s, Sam Green led athletics at the Kansas Wesleyan Business College under the supervision of Alexander Brown Mackie on the main campus. Green was known for his scientific method of coaching. He was engaged in the Salina community, volunteering his time to many groups. Shown here is Green (back row, far right) with the 1926–1927 basketball team along with star and team captain Leroy Sandberg (with ball).

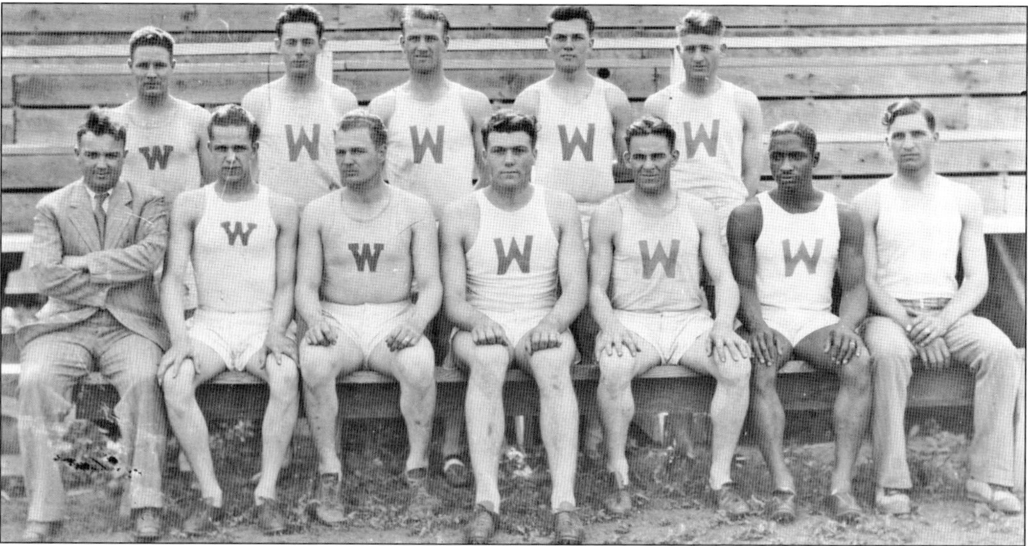

The 1928 track team was captained by Martin Isaacson and Stanley Hermann. Both were standouts in the state in all events. Isaacson was the high-point man nearly every time he stepped on the track for the Coyotes. Hermann continued his track career, winning a myriad of medals in the Senior Olympics. Both are members of the Kansas Wesleyan Coyote Athletic Hall of Fame.

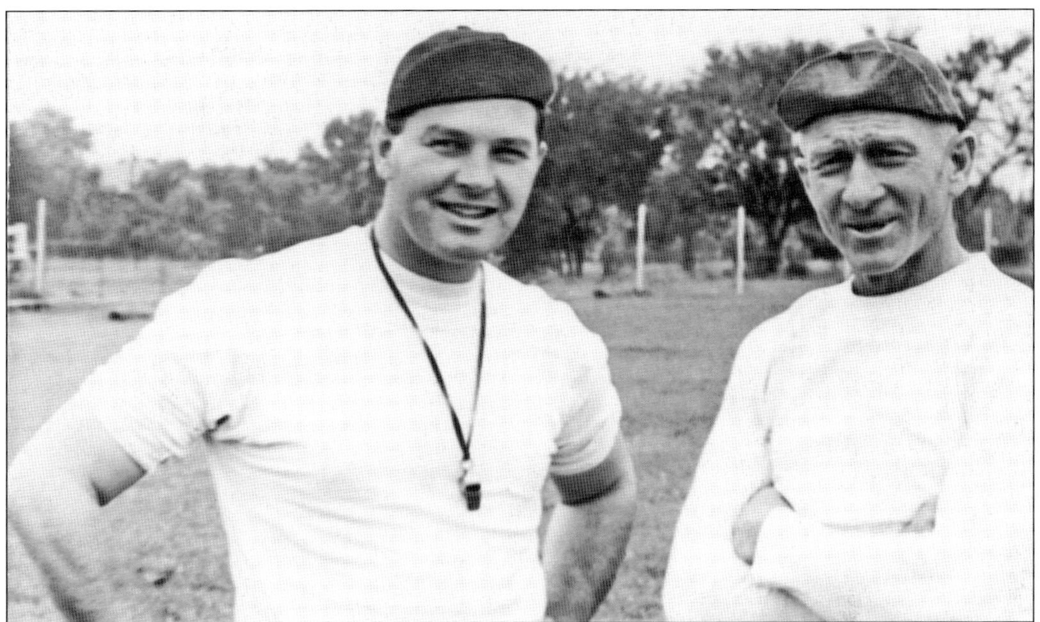

Coach Virgil Baer (left) and assistant Charlie Purma survey new prospects. Baer, a 1936 alumnus, was the university's first ever All-American and a three-time All-Kansas Collegiate Athletic Conference (KCAC) pick. He and teammate Sidney Smith led the football team to three KCAC titles from 1934 to 1936. Baer revived athletic programs after they had been suspended during World War II. Purma taught industrial arts and later coached football at Pittsburg State and basketball at Junction City High School.

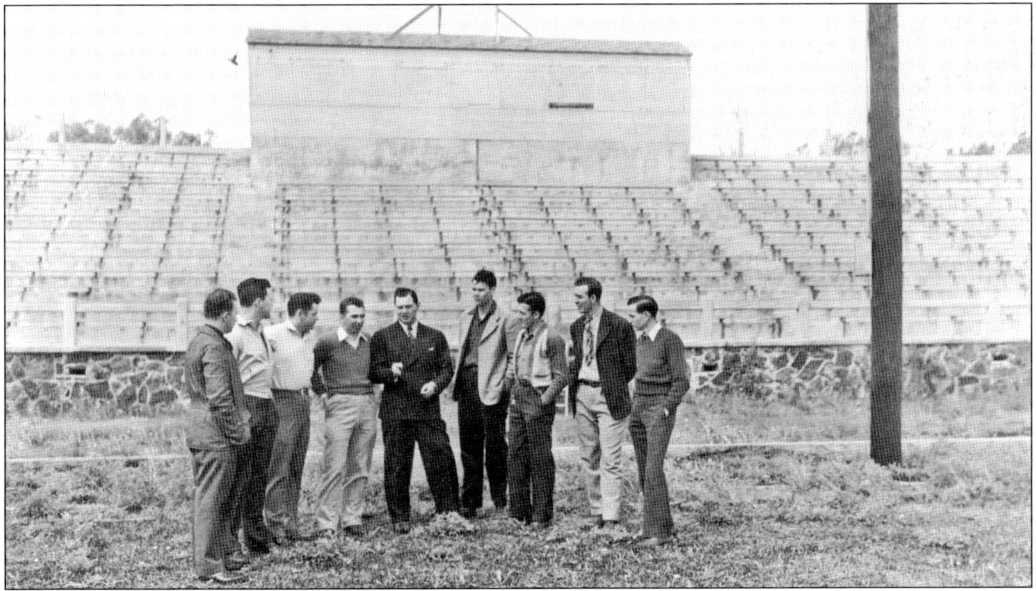

In the spring of 1946, coach Virgil Baer talks with alumni athletes and returning players about fall athletics at Martin Stadium. From left to right are Francis Starr, Donald Eugene Newell, Charles Pugh, John Ritter Jr., Baer, Delmer Furrow, Ed Doherty, Don Bennett, and Harold VanPelt. Baer rebuilt and reinvigorated the athletic program after a period during World War II without competition.

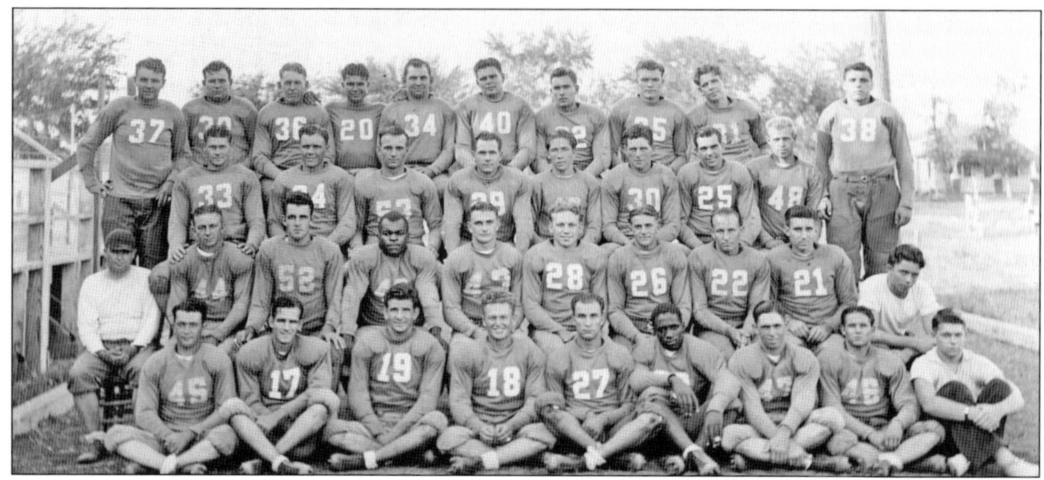

The 1936 KCAC Champion football team won the program's third straight title under coach Alexander Brown Mackie. Mackie was 78-52-13 in 17 seasons leading the Coyotes, including the school's only undefeated and unscored-upon season in 1927. Everett Morgan was named Honorable Mention AP Little All-American that season. Morgan, Everett Watson, Earl VanCleef, Amos Morris, and Lawrence Blair were All-KCAC selections. The Everett Morgan Strength Training Center is named in his honor.

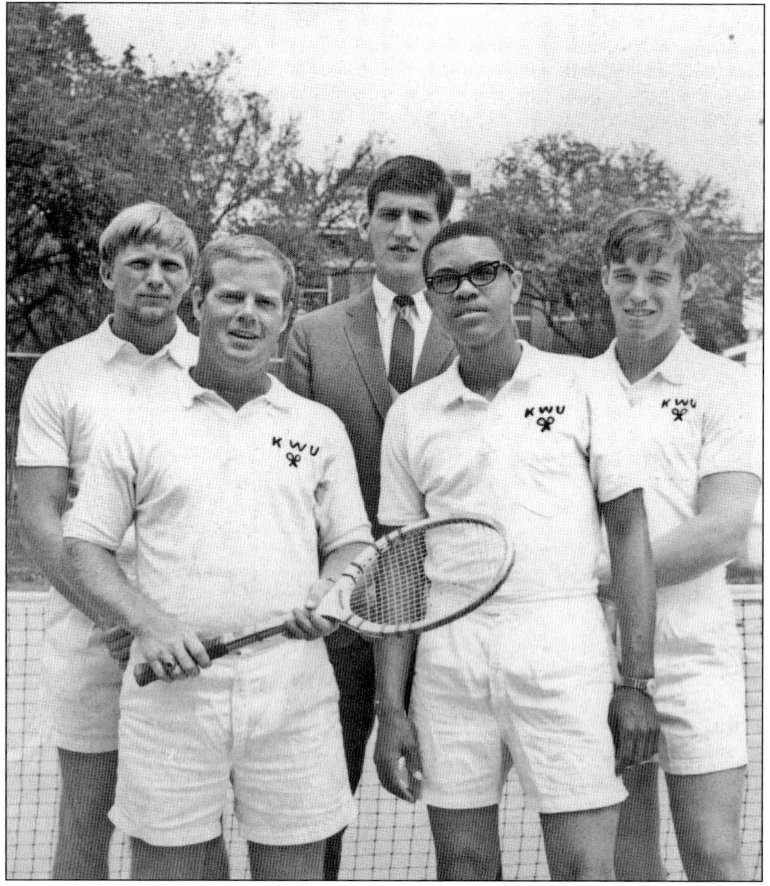

Tennis was played on campus as early as the 1890s. The 1907 men's team included exceptional players and noted champions, and a women's team formed by the end of the academic year. Tennis was discontinued in 1981. It was reinstated in 2000 and has continued since with full men's and women's teams. Pictured here is the 1967 squad, led by coach Sam Paul (center, in suit).

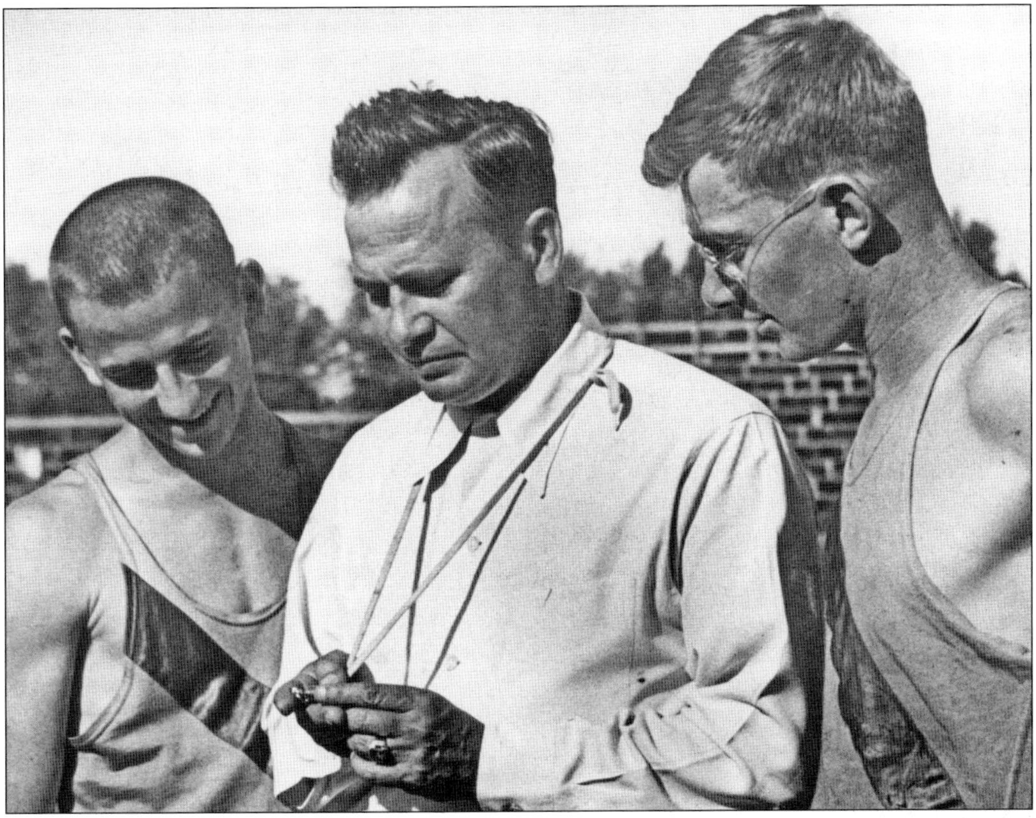

Wally Forsberg (center) coached basketball, football, and track in the late 1940s and early 1950s. Forsberg led the Coyotes to a National Association for Intercollegiate Basketball Championship appearance in 1950, a feat not achieved again until 2007, when the team won the KCAC and appeared in the NAIA Division II National Tournament. Here, Forsberg discusses strategy with athletes Keith "Peanuts" Mueller (left) and Phil Nemeth during a track meet.

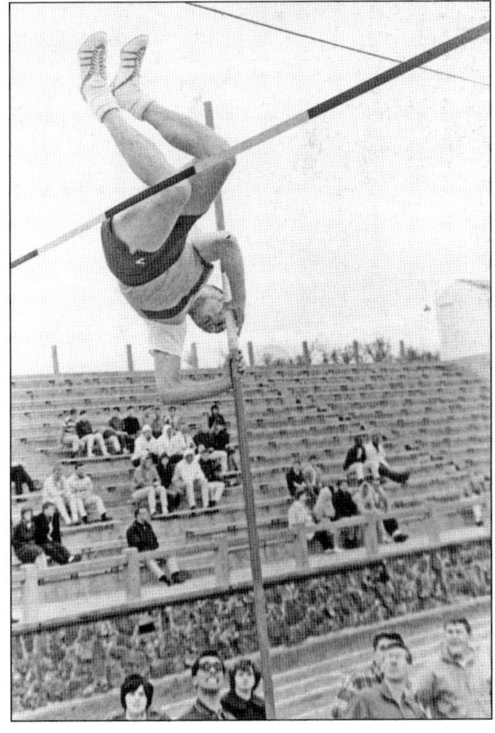

Track and field got its start in the late 1890s. Kansas Wesleyan has sponsored both indoor and outdoor track teams. After several years of not having a usable facility on campus, track returned to campus in 2015 with the opening of the Olson Family Track at the Graves Family Sports Complex. Here, John Cox vaults his way to a school record in the pole vault in 1965.

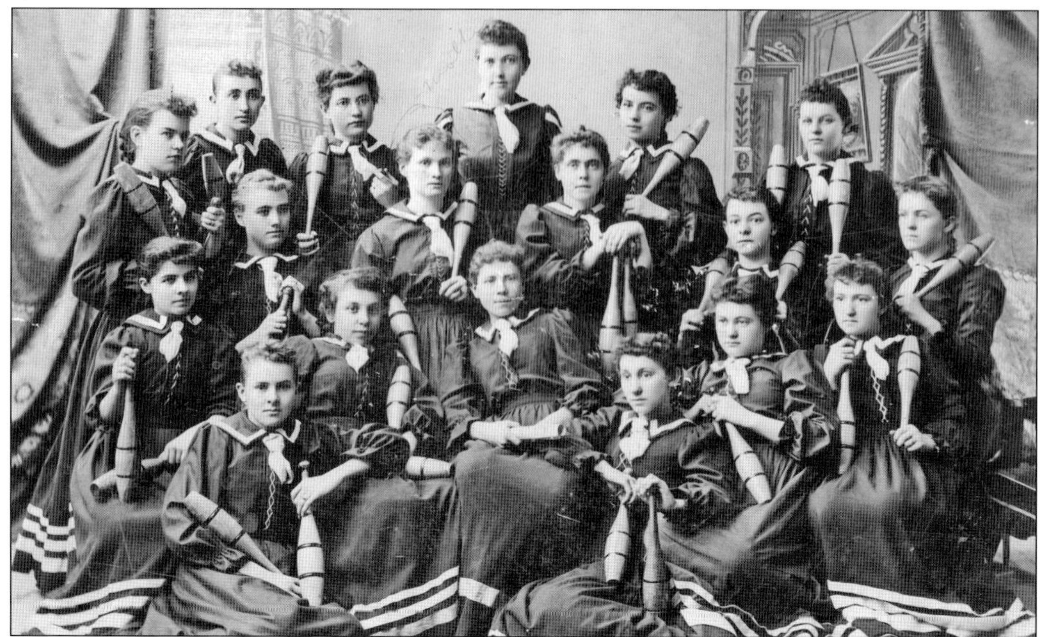

On December 4, 1893, the Ladies Athletic Club performed under the direction of Prof. (and later president) George Hagerty and led by Rose Koepsil. The performance included club drills and a labyrinth march. At the conclusion of the performance, the audience was entertained by several musical acts. The following day, the club had this photograph taken at Atherton's Studio. (Courtesy of the Smoky Hill Museum.)

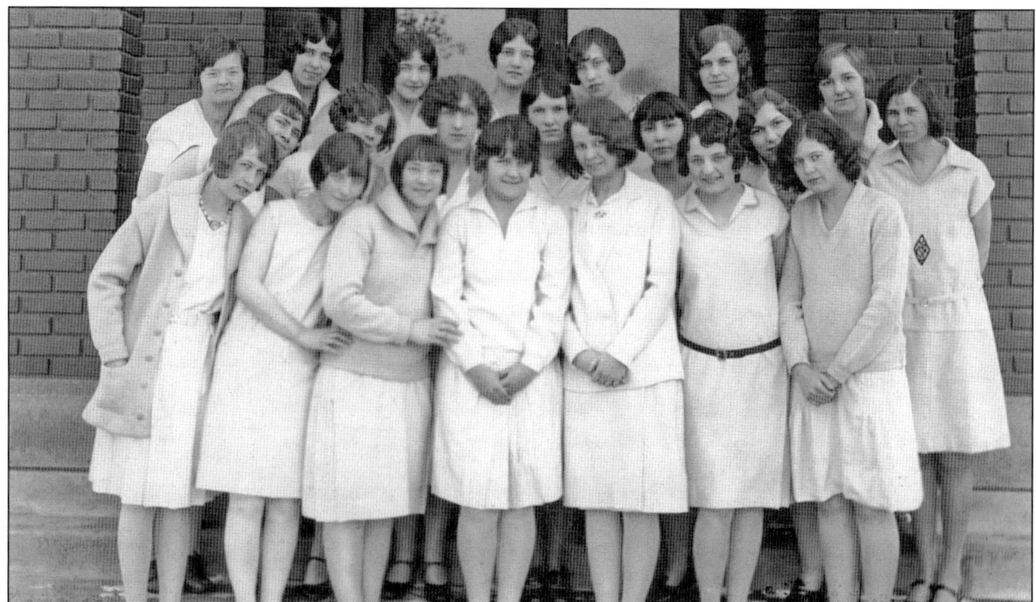

By the 1890s, the Women's Athletic Association was established. As the group evolved, it competed in various sports against associations from other institutions. By the 1920s, colleges across the nation decided on a point system for membership. By the late 1920s, Kansas Wesleyan required 100 points for membership and 1,000 points to receive a purple sweater with a gold *W*. Pictured is the 1929 Women's Athletic Association.

The Women's Athletic Association, once informally known as the Wesleyan Anns, promoted and fostered women's athletic activities. In the 1930s, Ruth Law Mackie was at the helm of women's physical education. She phased out basic gym work and ushered in calisthenics and a wide variety of athletic sports. In 1935, Bess Mellard was the only member to achieve the point requirements to earn the *W* sweater.

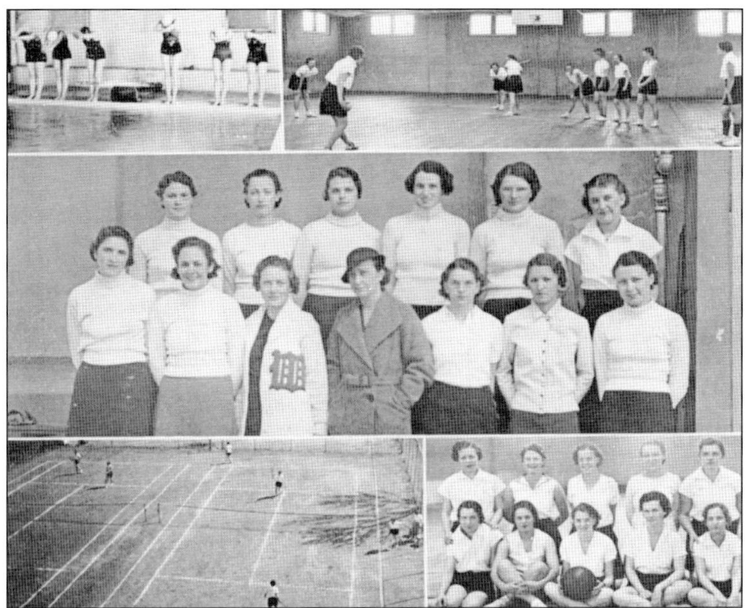

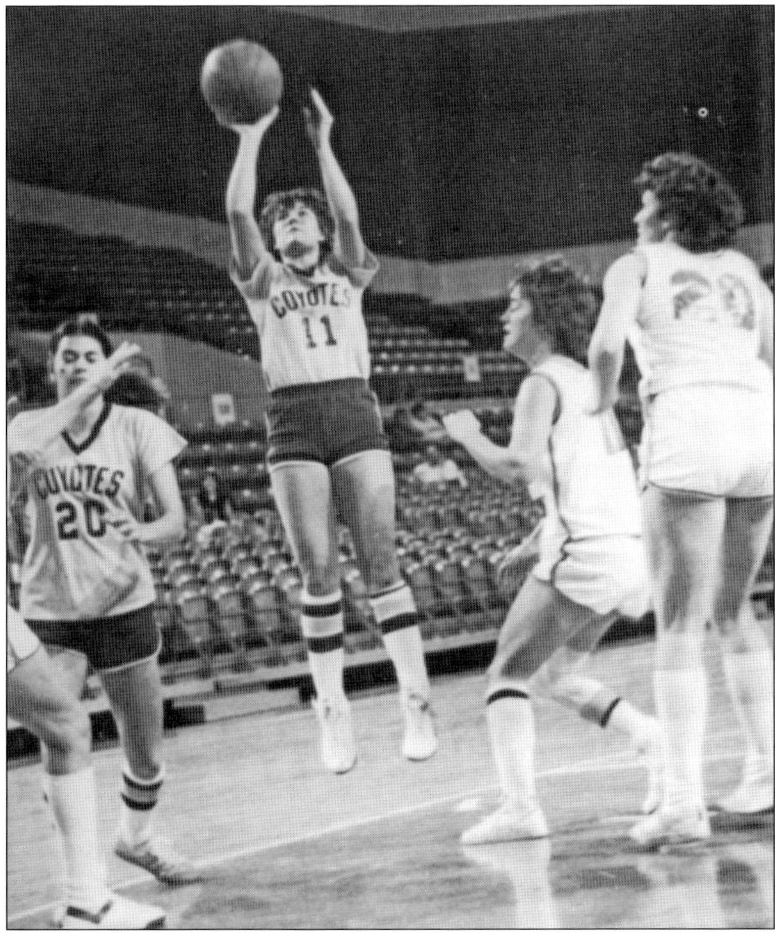

After forming in the late 1960s, the women's athletic teams were formally recognized by the university in 1971–1972. The 1982–1983 season was the first for alumnus coach Tracy Rietzke leading the volleyball, women's basketball, and softball teams. Rietzke later led the 1987–1988 basketball team to the program's first KCAC title. Here, Karla Campbell shoots while Kim Reitz gets ready to rebound in a game against Marymount at the Bicentennial Center.

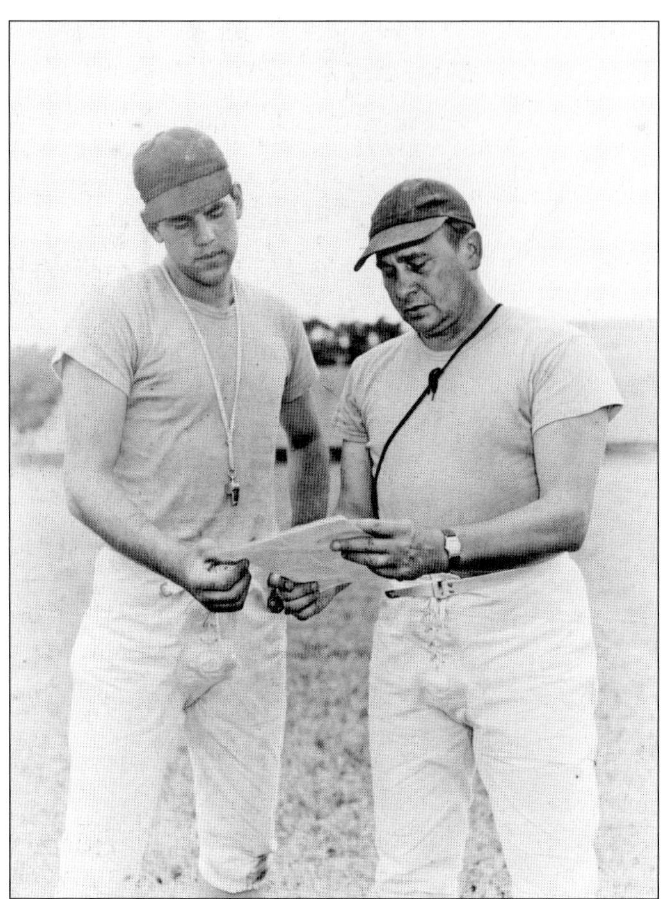

Coach Gene Bissell came to Salina in 1950 with the intent of coaching here for a couple of years before heading west. He never left, becoming the all-time wins leader in football history with 116, but was more than a coach for thousands of student-athletes. Bissell instilled high character values in his players, and it carried over into his everyday life. Pictured are Coach Bissell (left) and coach Wally Forsberg.

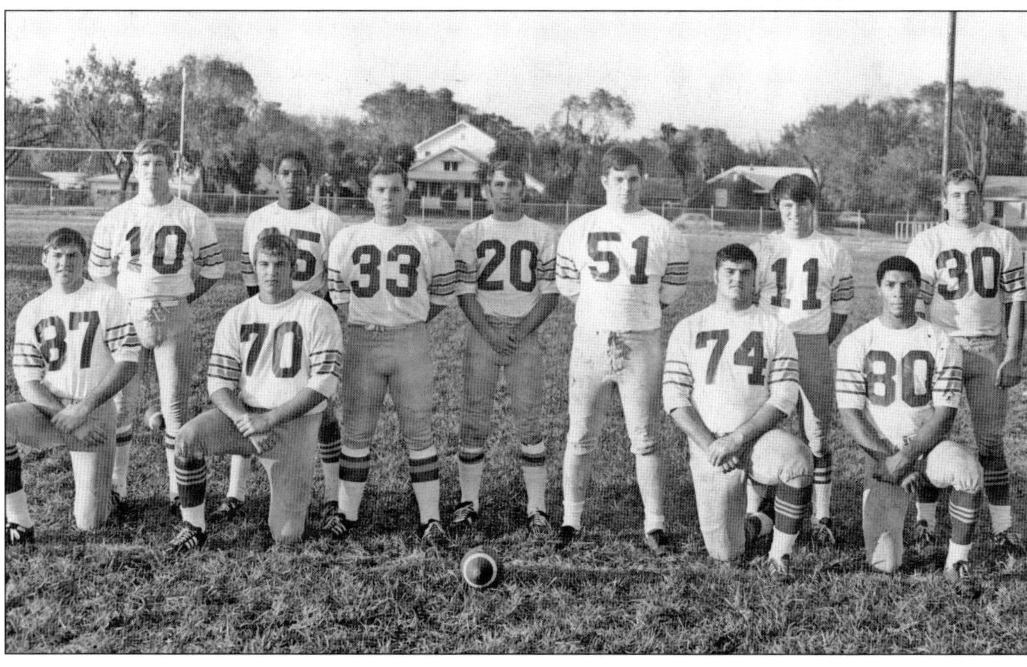

The 1969 KCAC champions were 8-2 and won the KCAC North Division. The Coyotes easily won all their division games with the exception of a hard-fought 7-6 win over Ottawa University. The Coyotes faced Sterling College for the KCAC Championship, beating the Warriors for a second time that season and giving the team its first football championship in over a decade.

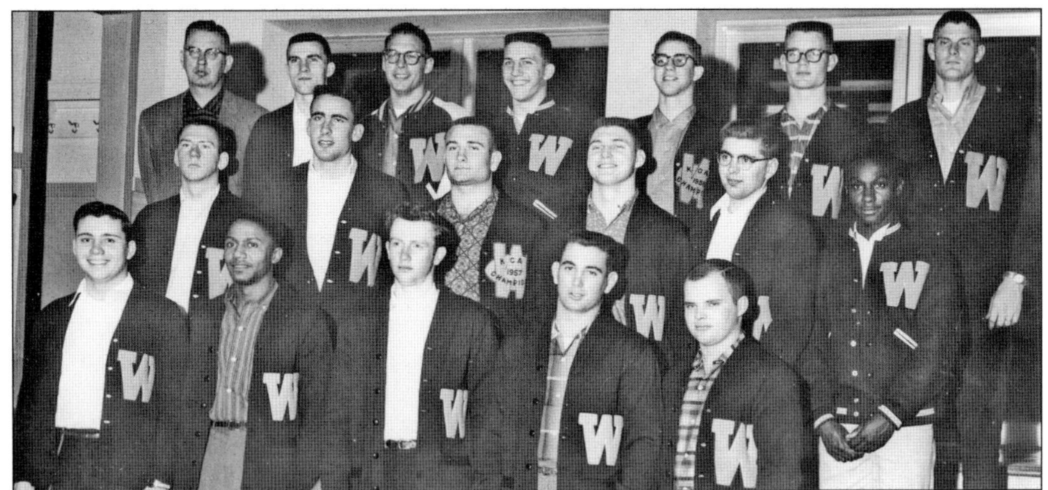

The Varsity Club provided a scholarship for a freshman athlete. Each year, the members would speak with prospective students on what was known as High School Day. In 1960, coaches Gene Bissell and Swede Backstrom were cosponsors of the club. Backstrom coached and served as athletic director for several years at Kansas Wesleyan. The 1960 Varsity Club is pictured with coach Swede Backstrom (top row, far left).

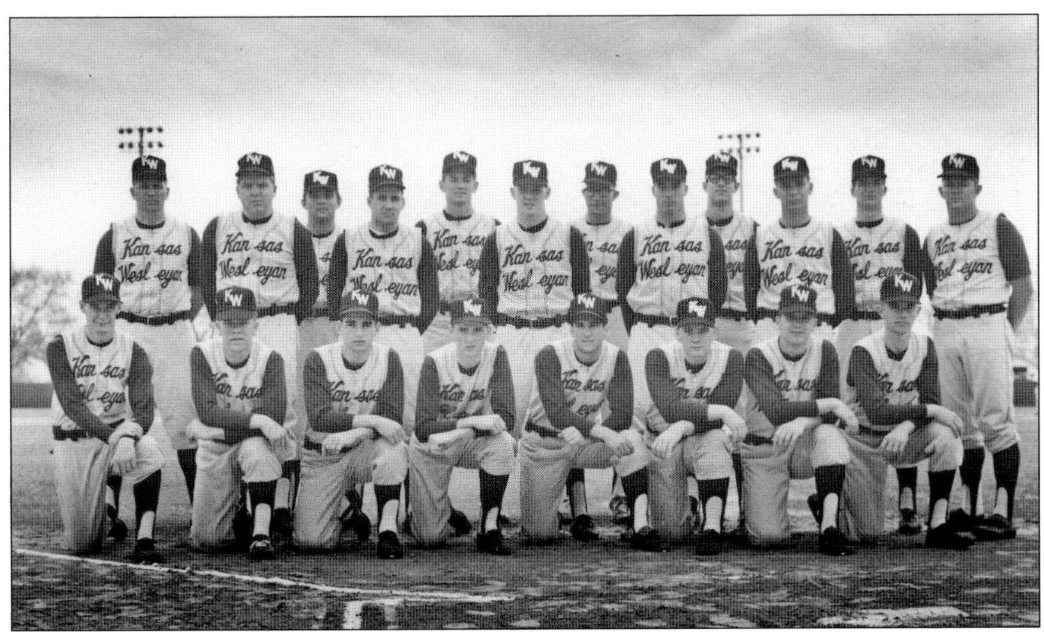

Baseball was played for a second season in 1967 after being revived following a 19-year hiatus. That year, the team was 15-6 overall but did not win the KCAC Championship, which went to the Presbies of the College of Emporia. The Coyotes placed four on the All-KCAC team that season: Phil Coleman, Steve Eich, Kelly Rudolph, and Don Swartz.

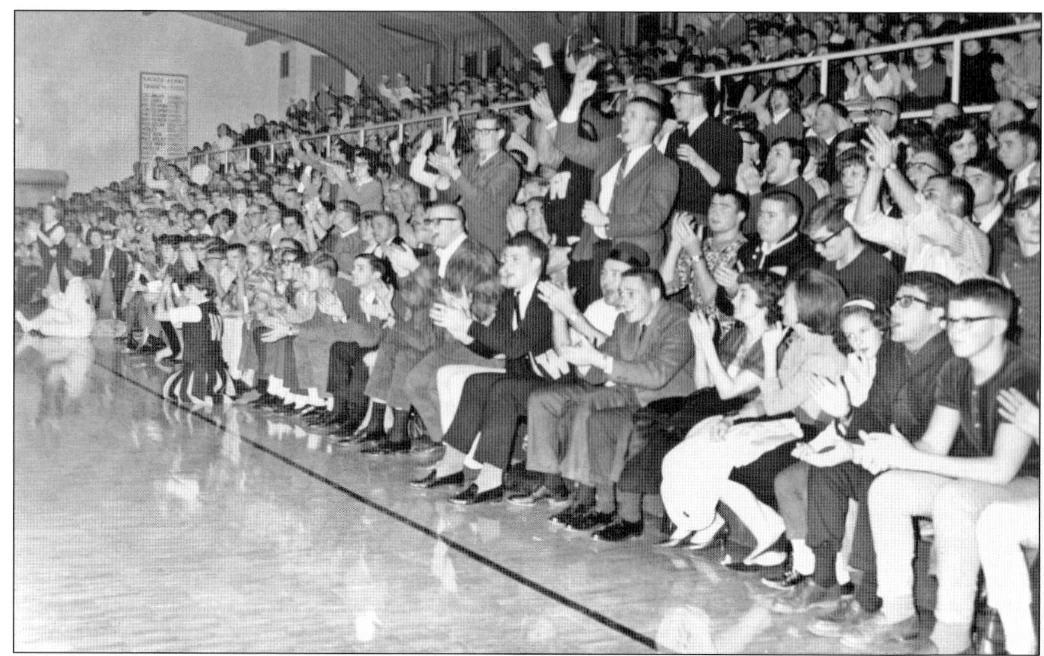

There was a hum on campus about having a walkout if the basketball team broke its 20-game losing streak against the Bethany College Swedes prior to the January 8, 1966, meeting between the rivals. That night, it was standing room only inside Sacred Heart's gymnasium as the Coyotes pulled off the 69-61 victory over their archrivals. Pictured above, over 2,000 spectators filled the gym, and some were not allowed in the doors. Some climbed on the roof of the gym and looked in the windows. As the game ended, Dean Paul Renich and other faculty declared the following Monday a holiday. Below, the crowd was ecstatic over the win and helped the team lift coach Ken Cochran on its shoulders. Assistant coach Ken Straight (left) joins in excitement.

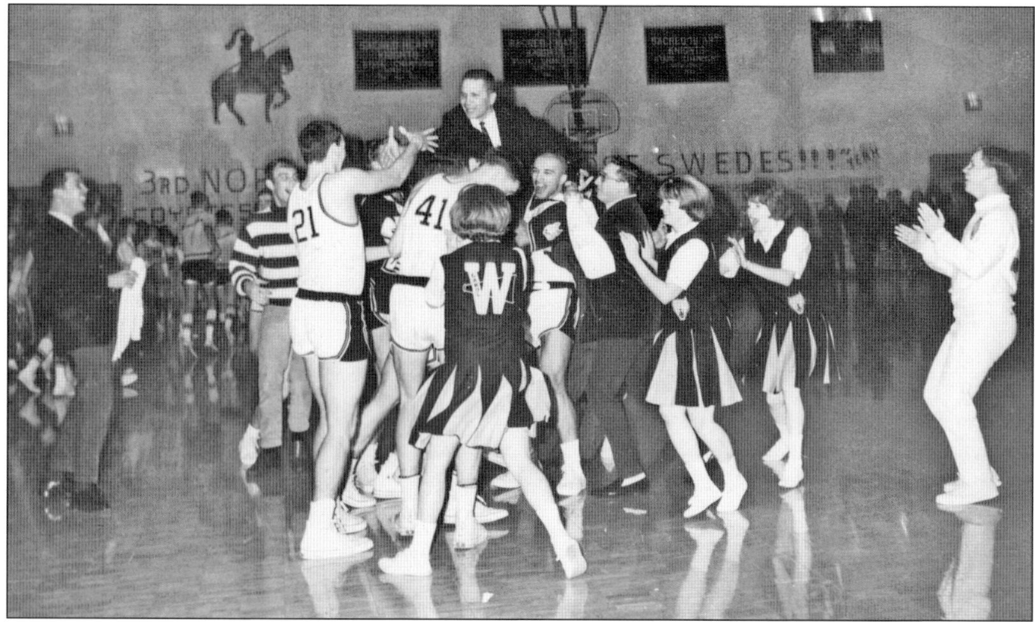

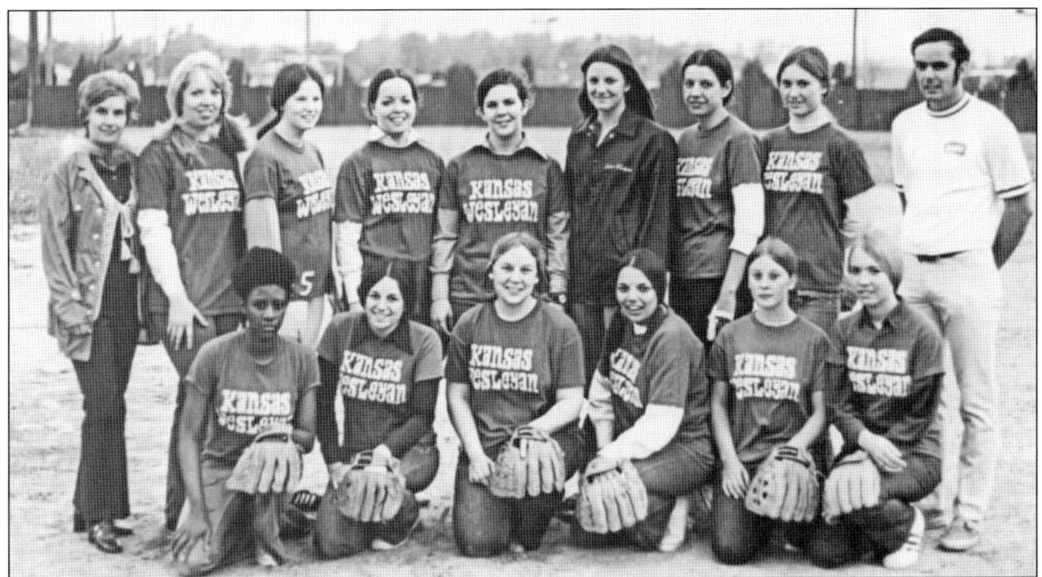

Women's athletics have been important for most the university's history. However, until Title IX, women's athletic teams at Kansas Wesleyan played intramurals. Alumna Ginny Zook Bevan was a pioneer under Title IX and worked tirelessly to promote women's sports. She coached volleyball and softball in 1972. In 1999, she received the Distinguished Service Award on Founder's Day. Bevan is pictured with the softball team.

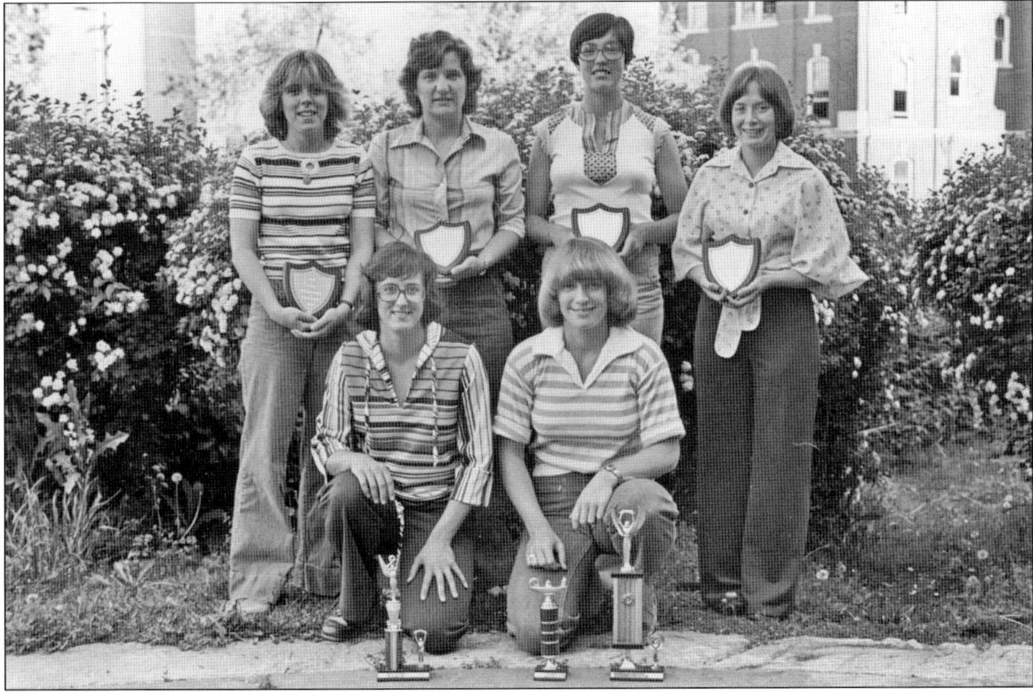

On May 7, 1978, the booster club sponsored its first Women's Athletics Banquet at the Cavalier Club. From left to right are (first row) Carolyn Sias Wiggins (Most Outstanding Athlete) and Jill Rietzke Ptacek (Most Valuable Player); (second row) Carol Hall White (basketball), Jackie Douglass (softball), Jessi Burnham Stang (volleyball), and Lynette Wallace (track).

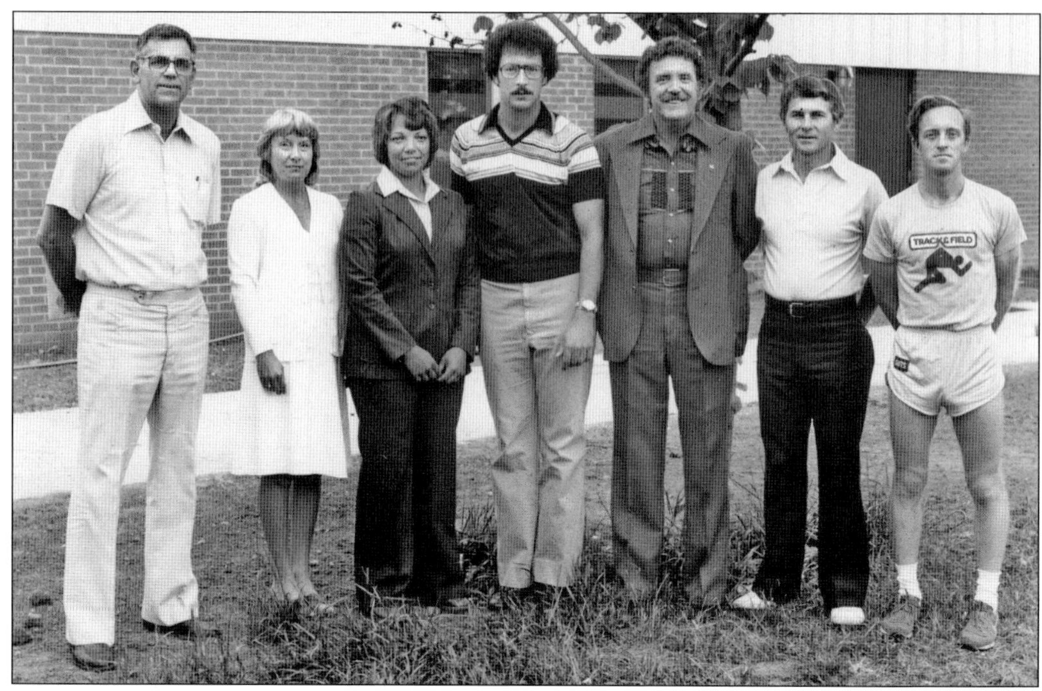

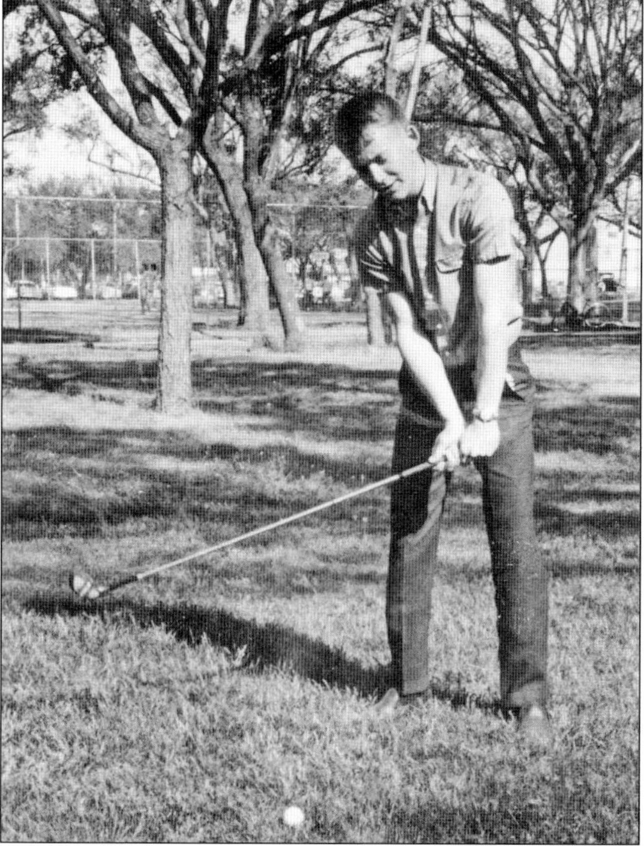

The 1981 athletic staff includes, from left to right, Gene Bissell (athletic director), Ginny Bevan (Health, Physical Education, and Recreation professor), Marcia Troutfetter (volleyball and softball), Sheldon Woolery (women's basketball), Bill Stevens (men's basketball), Jon Bingesser (football), and John Kernan (cross-country and track). Several coaches brought championship experience to the Kansas Wesleyan athletic programs at that time, including Bissell, Bingesser, and Kernan.

Golf at Kansas Wesleyan has had a long-standing tradition. The Coyotes won the KCAC title in 1970 and won several National Small College Athletic Association National Championships in the late 1990s under coach Jim Crawford. Here David Zook, a member of the 1961 golf team, gets in some practice shots.

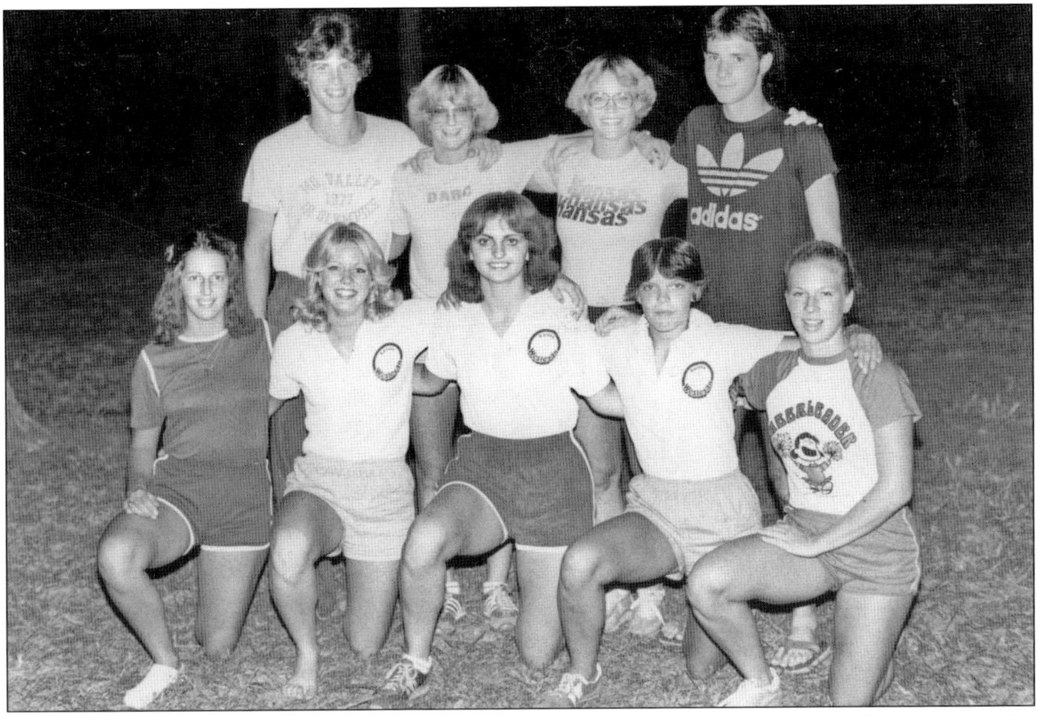

Go Coyotes! Cheerleaders have a long history building spirit on campus. Cheering on the teams has always been a key part of the game-day experience. In the late 1990s, under the direction of coach Georgia Rupp, Wesleyan began a competitive cheer team that qualified for national competitions in Florida. The competitive cheer teams won three straight KCAC championships in 2013, 2014, and 2015, and the competitive dance team won its first conference title in 2015. The 2016 competitive cheer team qualified for the NAIA Invitational for the first time when the NAIA became the first collegiate governing body to sponsor a competitive cheer and dance national championship. Pictured here are cheerleading squads from 1980 (above) and 1979 (below).

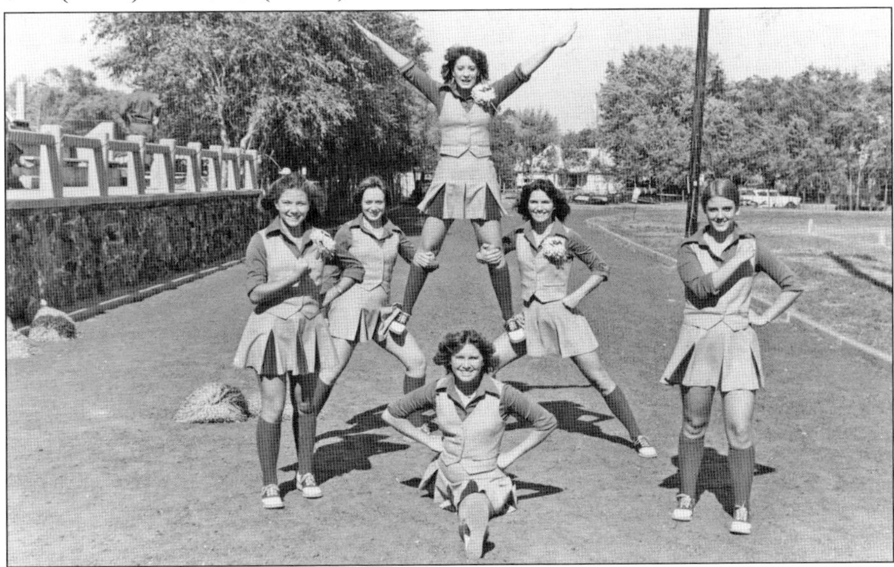

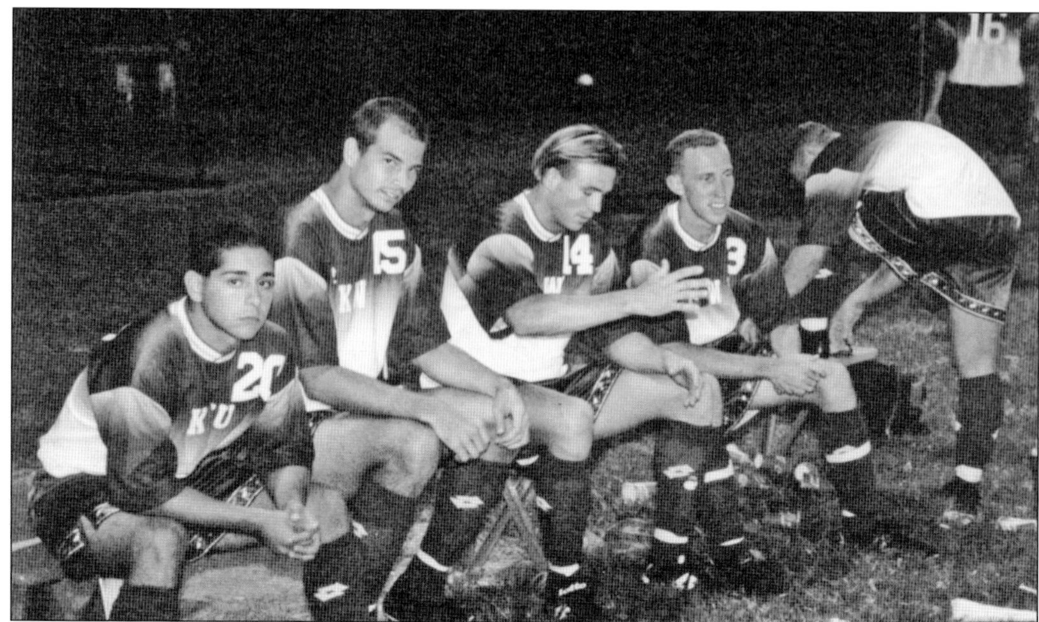

In the mid-1960s, Kansas Wesleyan international students often played soccer on campus, and the university fielded a club-level team in 1982. In 1996, soccer made its official debut, and the men's team won the KCAC in its first season that year. Soccer has been one of the most successful sports on campus since the program's start. Since 1996, the program has won over 63 percent of its matches, captured 19 KCAC Championships, and made six appearances in the NAIA playoffs. While the women's team did not enjoy immediate success like the men, when Mike Dibbini became coach in 2005, the Coyotes quickly ascended to national prominence, winning several conference championships and being consistently nationally ranked, posting a 183-46-17 record overall and a 102-5-1 mark in the KCAC through the 2015 season. Pictured below is the inaugural women's soccer team in 1996.

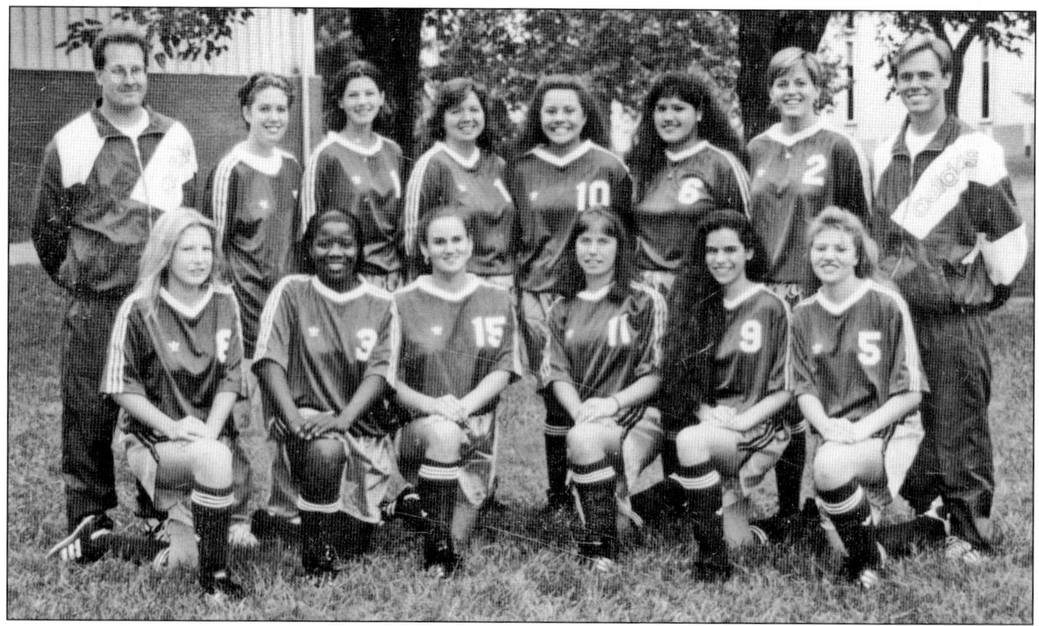

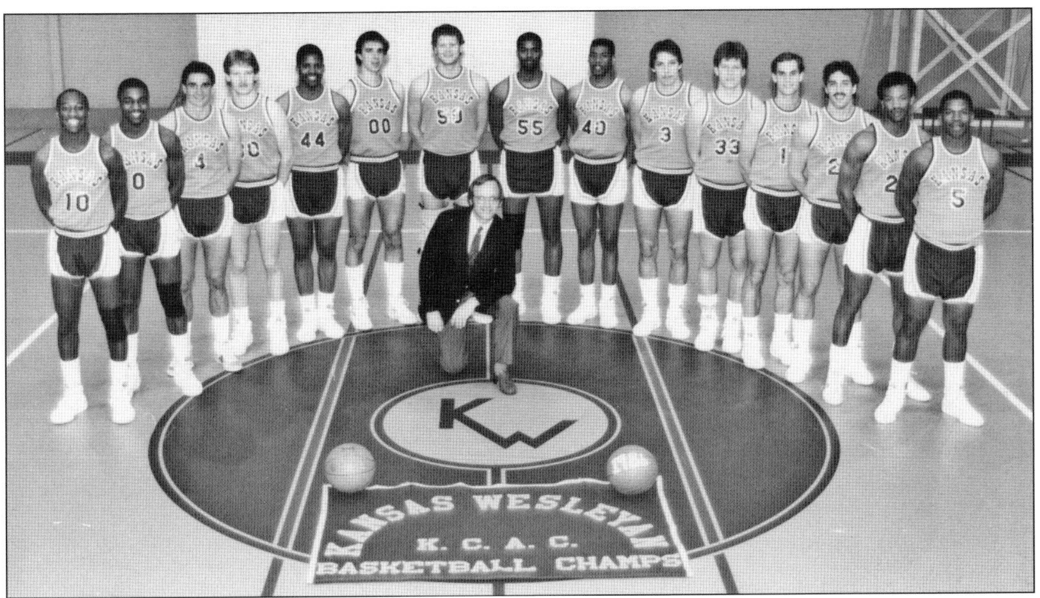

In his fourth year, Jerry Jones led the men's basketball team to its first KCAC title in 10 years. Jones left after the 1988 season and returned in 1995 at the request of the university's administration. Jones led the Coyotes to the 2000 KCAC Championship, coached until the 2006 season, and is the all-time wins leader at the school. He also served as athletic director for several years through 2005.

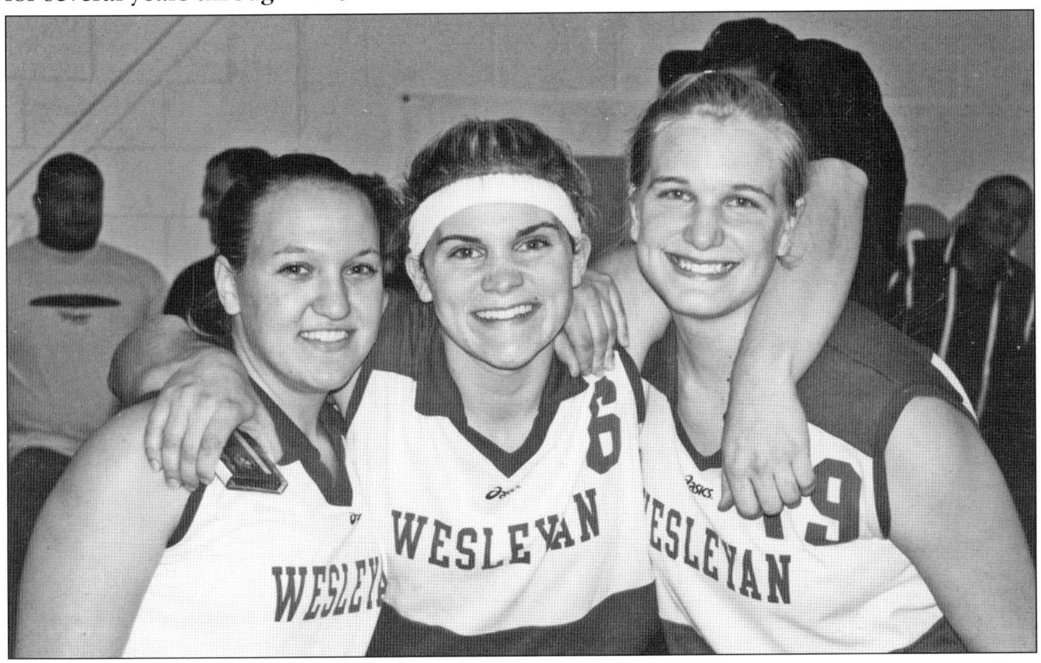

With very early roots on campus, volleyball has been played off and on during the university's history. The sport regained traction in the 1960s and was formally recognized at Kansas Wesleyan in 1971. The program has enjoyed many recent successes in winning conference championships. Pictured are, from left to right, Kelly Gingrich, Natalie Williams, and Rachael Dobelmann around 2000.

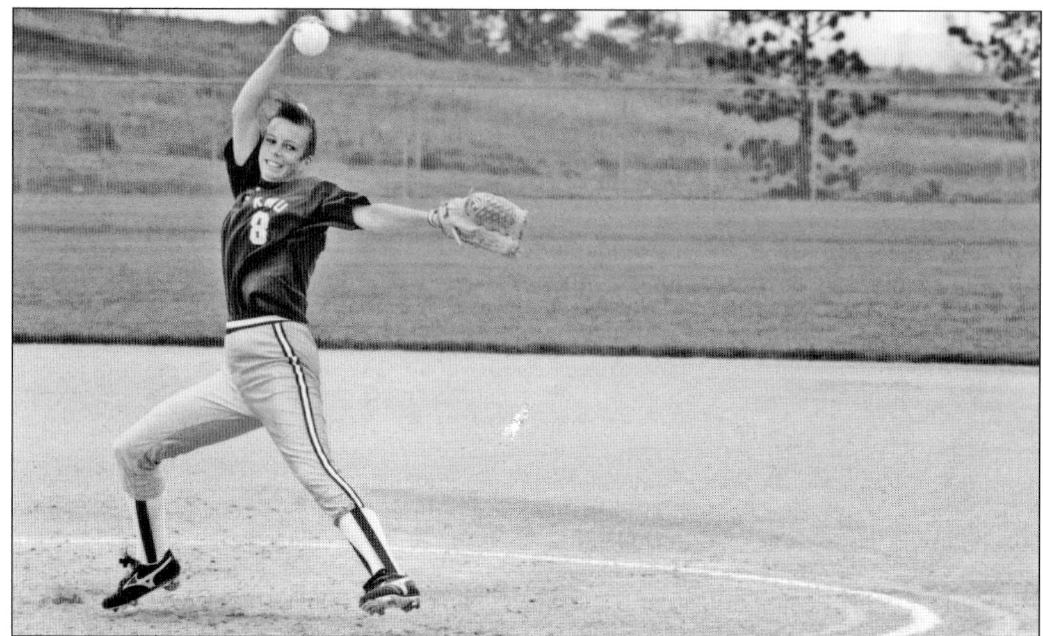

Softball has been one of the most successful women's sports on campus. During an incredible run between 1983 and 1999, the team finished no worse than third in the KCAC regular season or tournament. The team won the NAIA District 10 title in 1994. Leslie Zielinski Lazzarini, pictured around 1994, was part of four straight conference championship teams under coaches Russ Martin and Kevin Blaskowski.

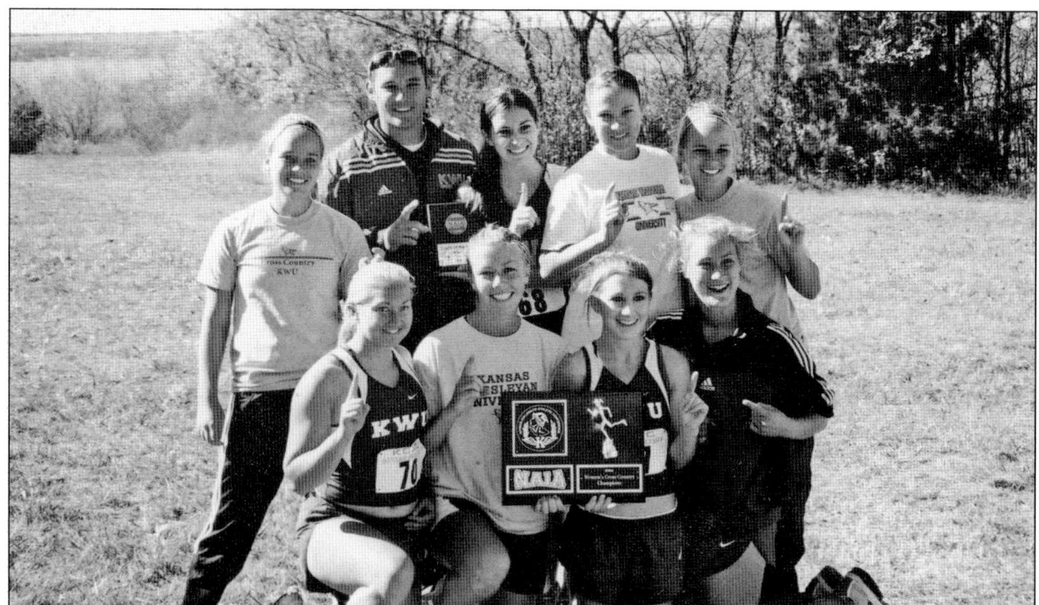

Kansas Wesleyan's women's cross-country team won its first ever KCAC championship in 2004. Led by first-year coach Zach Kindler, the team featured several athletes who also competed in other sports at the university. Sophomore Nicole Heptig captured the KCAC individual title. The 2004 team featured two All-KCAC runners and two Honorable Mention All-KCAC runners, and Kindler was the KCAC Coach of the Year.

Eight

The Second Century

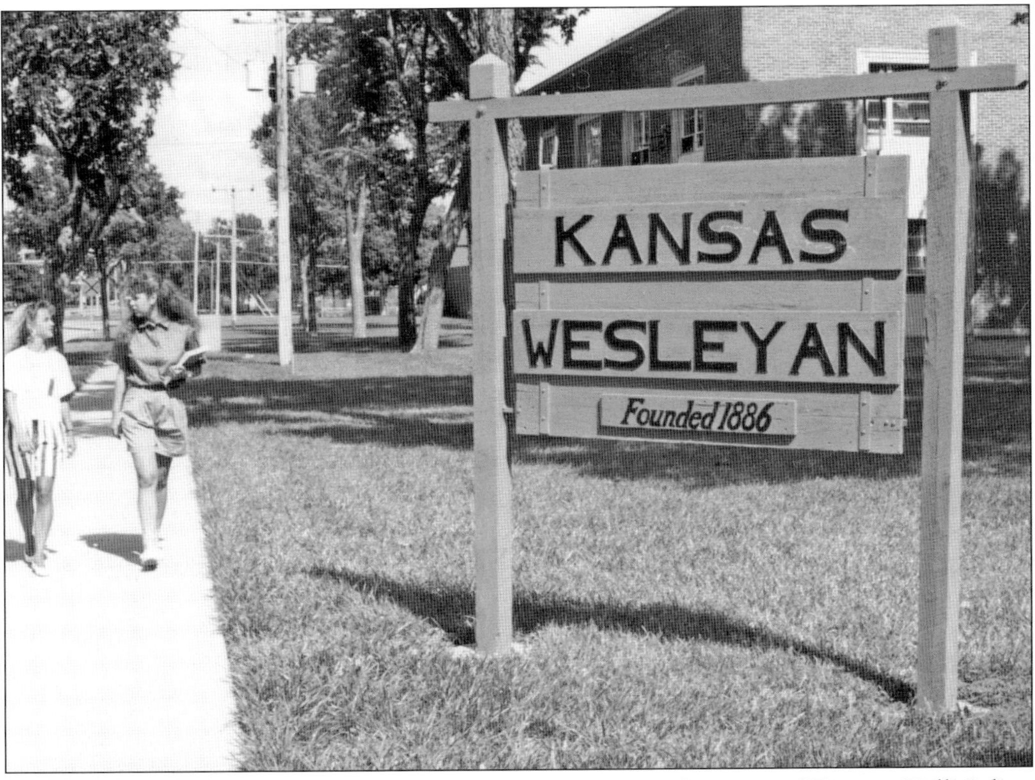

In 1986, the university held its centennial celebration. On the steps of Pioneer Hall, Salina mayor Merle Hodges read a proclamation during the Founder's Day celebration proclaiming February 19, 1986, as "Kansas Wesleyan Founder's Day." Shortly after the reading, purple and gold balloons were released as a symbol of new dreams for the next century. The ushering in of the next century brought forth many successful fundraising campaigns to strengthen the campus.

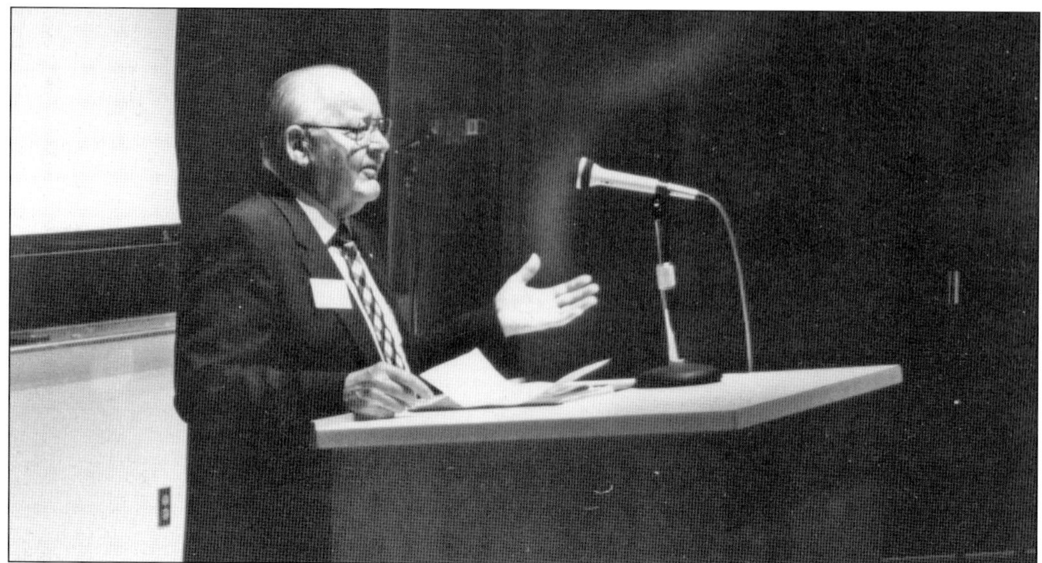

In anticipation of a new century of higher education, the university kicked off a new fundraising campaign in November 1985. The launch of the Second Century Campaign was held in Heritage Hall at the Bicentennial Center. Politician Bob Dole was unexpectedly unable to attend the launch due to extended Senate activity. His speech was broadcast via satellite. Dole emphasized developments in education funding, especially in regards to private colleges. Pres. Marshall Stanton spoke stressing the importance of planning for the future. Past Trustee and longtime supporter William H. Graves Sr. (above) called to the audience to start making plans to support the university's fundraising efforts. Below, President Stanton (fourth from left) discusses the campaign with William H. and Helen Graves (seated left) and Frank and Emma McBride (seated right). The man between the Graveses and Stanton is unidentified.

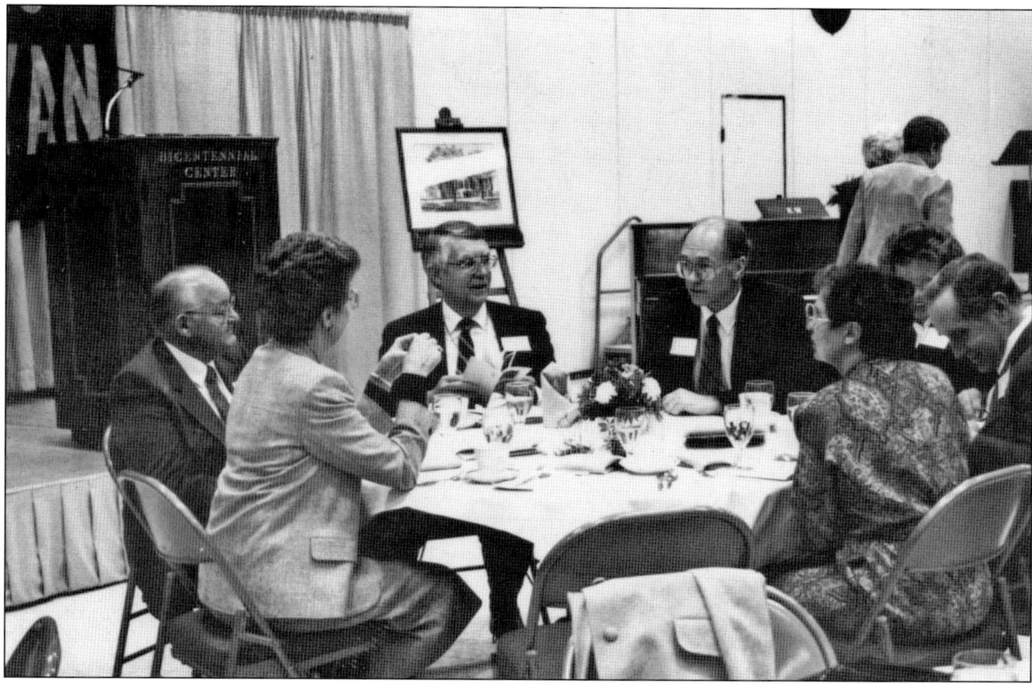

In October 1984, Rev. Marshall Stanton was inducted as president in Sams Chapel. Prior to the presidency, Stanton served five years on the board of trustees and as chairman of the Student Life Committee. He served as district superintendent for Hutchinson District's United Methodist Church. Cindy Wunder inferred in the *Advance* that Stanton had started a revival on campus to help it prosper and grow. When he took the job, he knew it would be a challenge, stating, "The ability to encourage the rest of the administration and staff through good human relations. All of these things must be incorporated to assure that the 'nuts and bolts' of the college work as well as continue the perseverance of the vision of the school's mission." Over the next two decades, Stanton had a restorative influence and effectively guided the university.

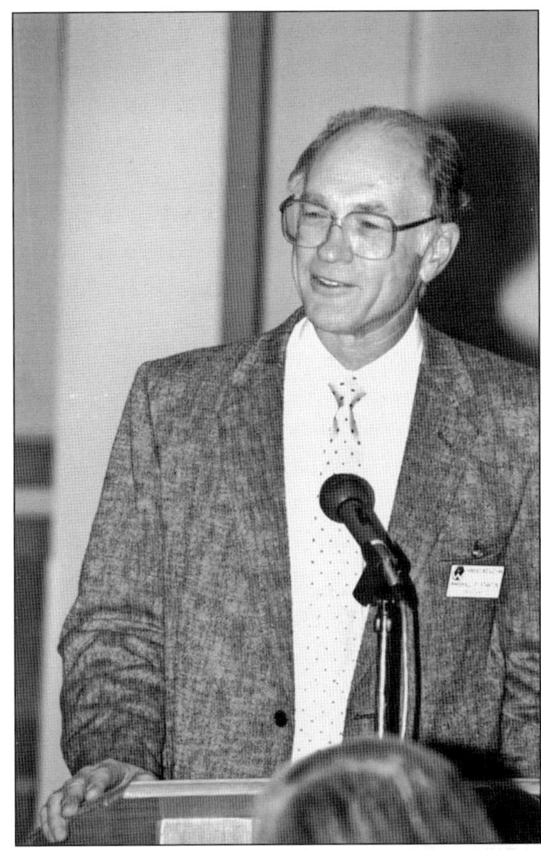

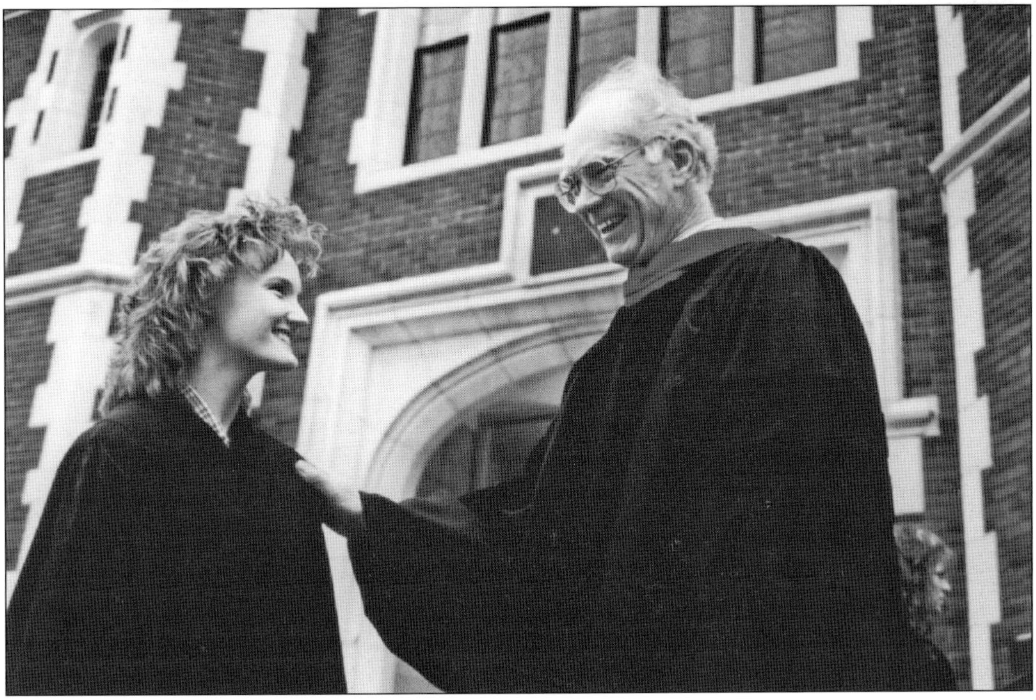

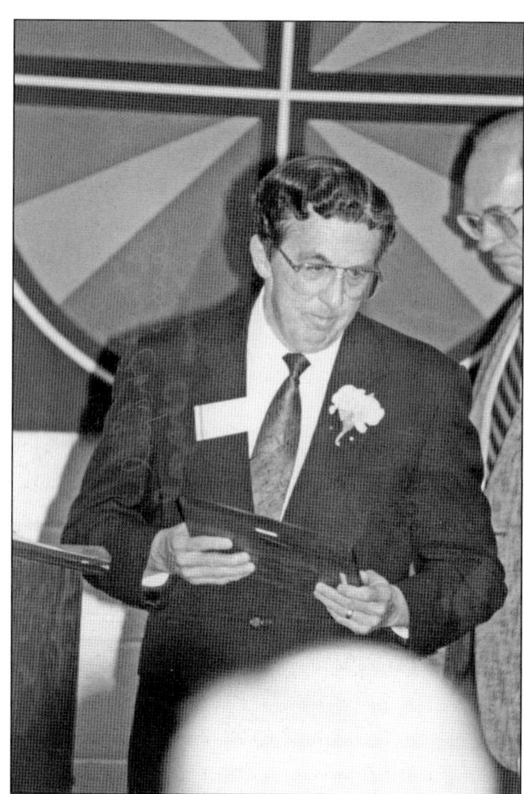

Shown here, Richard Blackburn received the Alumni Achievement Award in 1988. He managed several college student unions and became director of Association of College Unions–International. His parents, Edgar and Anona Shaw Blackburn, were both alumni. In the 1920s, Edgar attended the business college, while Anona pursued studies at Kansas Wesleyan's conservatory of music. Richard's grandmother Hattie Park Shaw attended Kansas Wesleyan's preparatory academy. Richard's wife, Fay, is also an alumna.

The Coyotes enter Muir Gymnasium through a crowd of fans prior to the January 20, 1988, meeting with the Bethany College Swedes. Tim Parker leads the Coyotes out of the tunnel. Wesleyan was victorious over the Swedes that night 69-59 behind a season-high 20-point effort by Billy Smith.

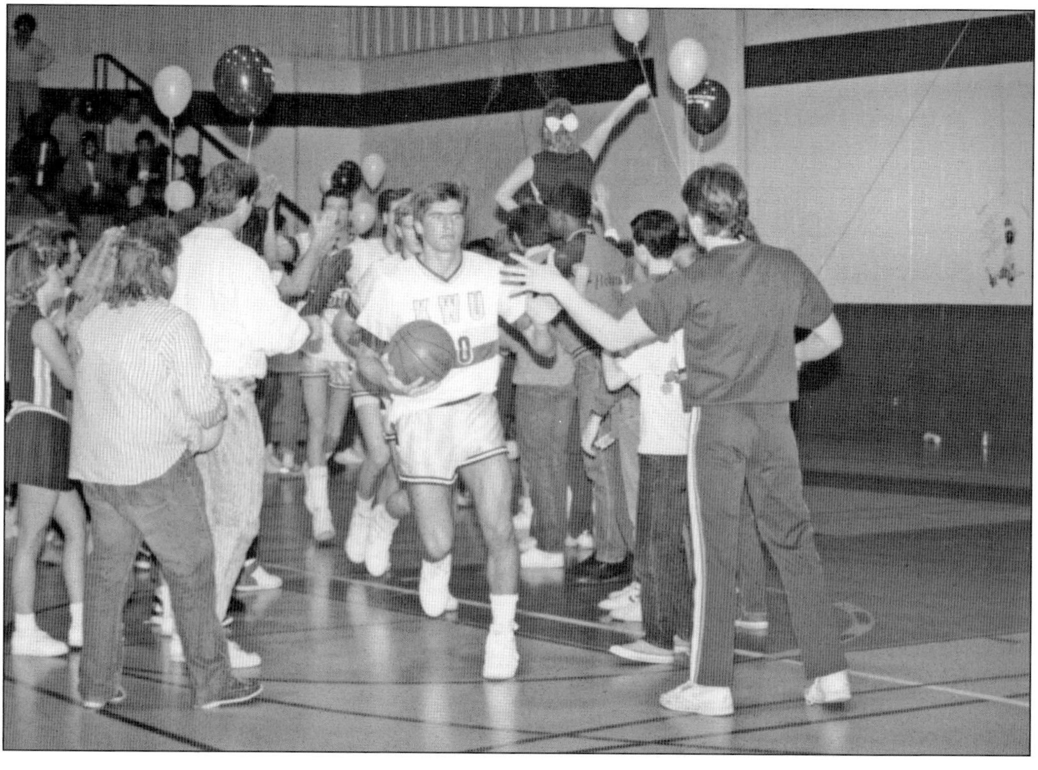

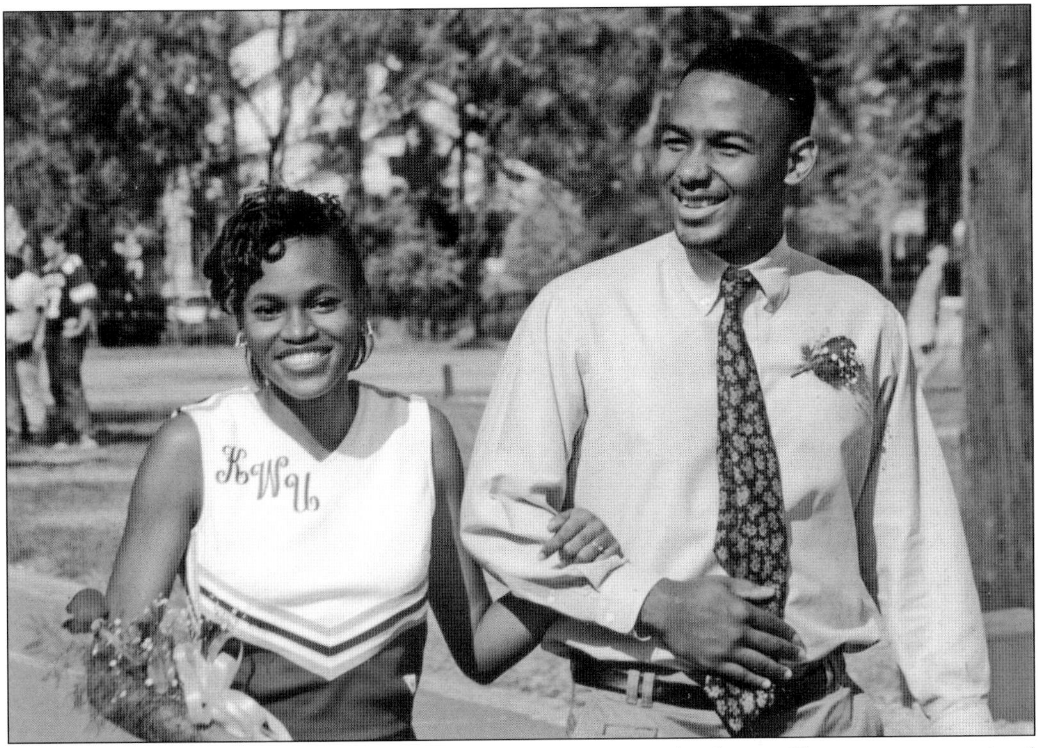

In 1990, the Homecoming theme was "As Time Goes By," and Rebecca Chopp was recognized with the Alumni Achievement Award. Chopp is currently the chancellor of the University of Denver, where Kansas Wesleyan's first graduate, Henry Milton Mayo, and his children worked. Here, Kevin Chevis is escorting Ronda Harrison, Homecoming queen. She was a cheerleader, student ambassador, and president of the multicultural organization in association with the Student Development Office.

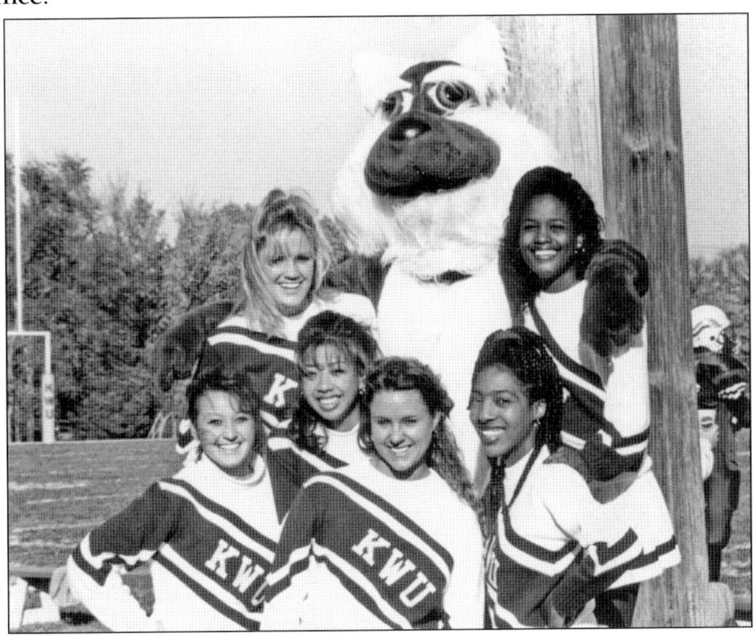

In 1994, Kansas Wesleyan received a new Coyote mascot costume. While the mascot costume has not changed in many years, several new costumes have been purchased since. In late 2004, there was a competition to name the mascot. In January 2005, the name Casey was introduced along with a new costume. Cheerleaders are pictured with the new Coyote mascot costume around 1994.

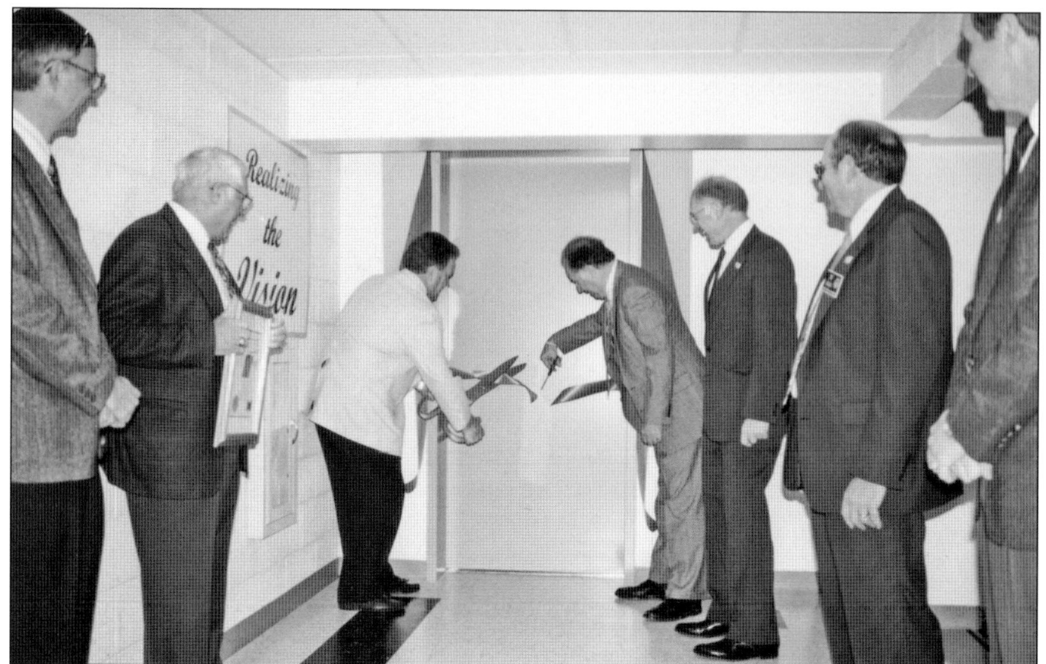

On September 23, 1994, a ribbon-cutting was held to celebrate the addition of the elevator in Pioneer Hall. The elevator was made possible through the $8 million Realizing the Vision Campaign. School Specialty Supply in Salina donated $100,000 towards the elevator's installation, making Pioneer Hall handicap accessible.

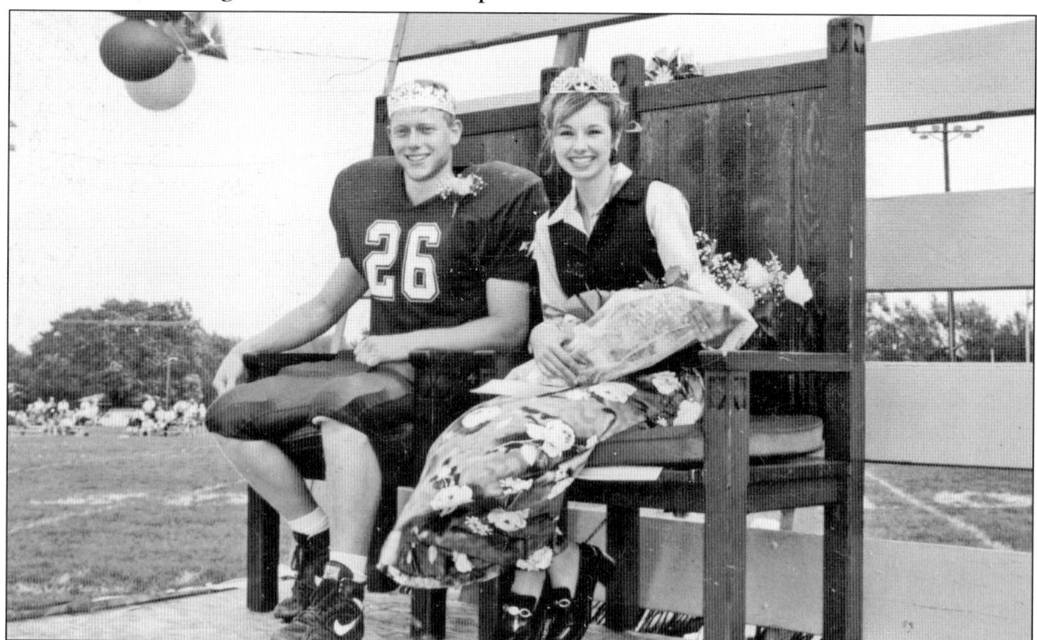

Angela Pope Rhodes and Justin Rhodes were crowned Homecoming royalty on October 11, 1997. Justin was the first to be crowned Homecoming king, starting a new tradition on campus. The Coyotes faced Sterling College in the game, winning 36-20 in coach Dave Dallas's first season with the team. This was the second straight victory that season.

From the late 1990s through early 2000s, the speech, theater, and communication department provided strong academic, extracurricular, and hands-on experience. Theater students participated in two productions per year, and communications students produced film segments at Salina's community access television studio inside Memorial Hall. This provided students access to state-of-the-art editing equipment. Kassie Courange Gilmore (left) and Prof. Barbara Marshall are pictured around 2000.

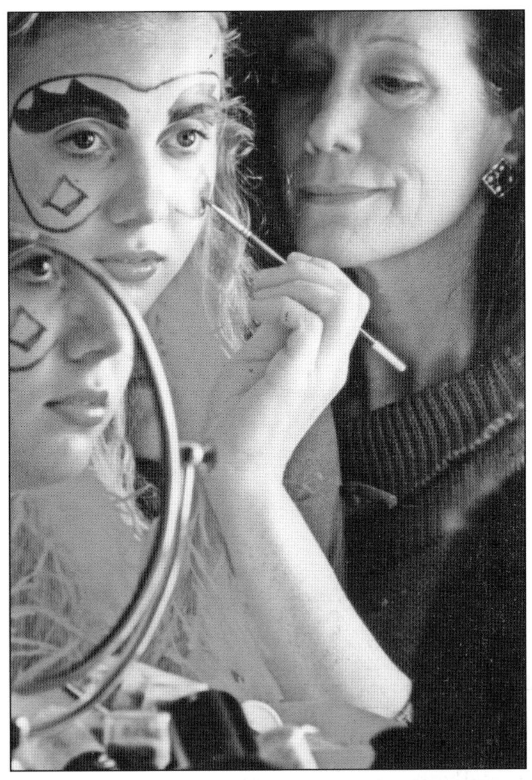

On orientation weekend in 1994, the Coyote mascot was tied to a cottonwood tree at the south end of Pioneer Hall. This event, the Ceremony of the Cottonwood, aligned with the 1990s university theme, "Catch the Spirit." As the university valued school spirit, it hired a campus spirit director responsible for the cheerleading and dance team and oversaw the Ginny Bevan Wellness Center. Pictured here is an excited student crowd around 1998.

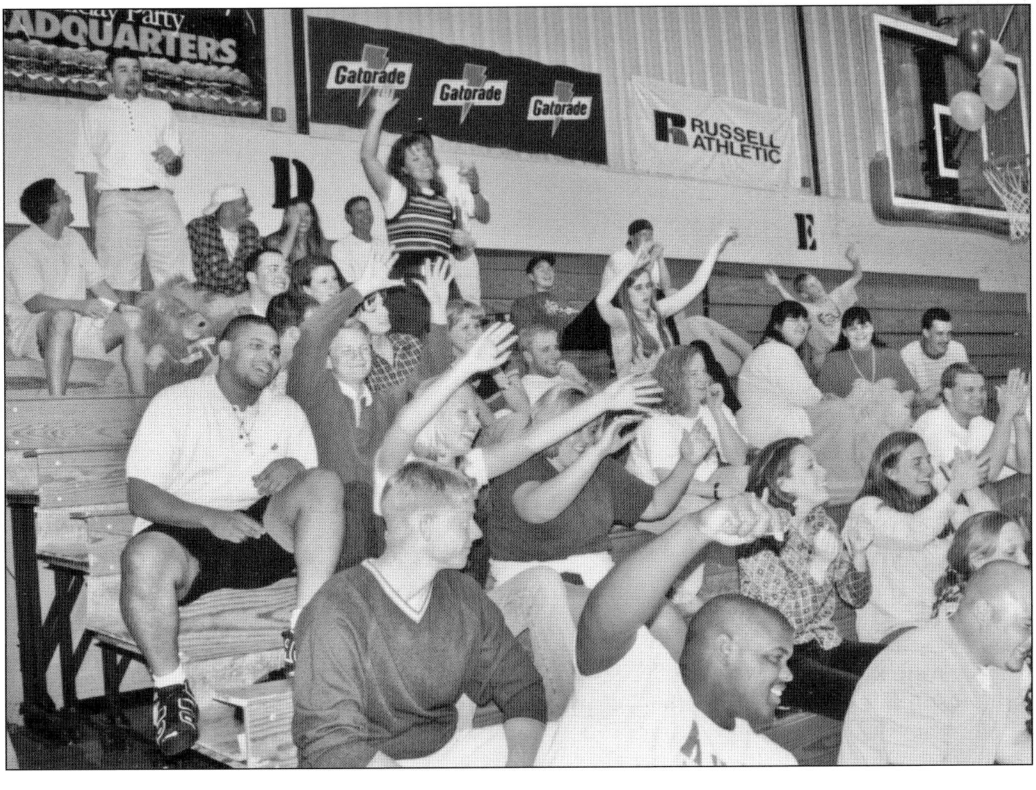

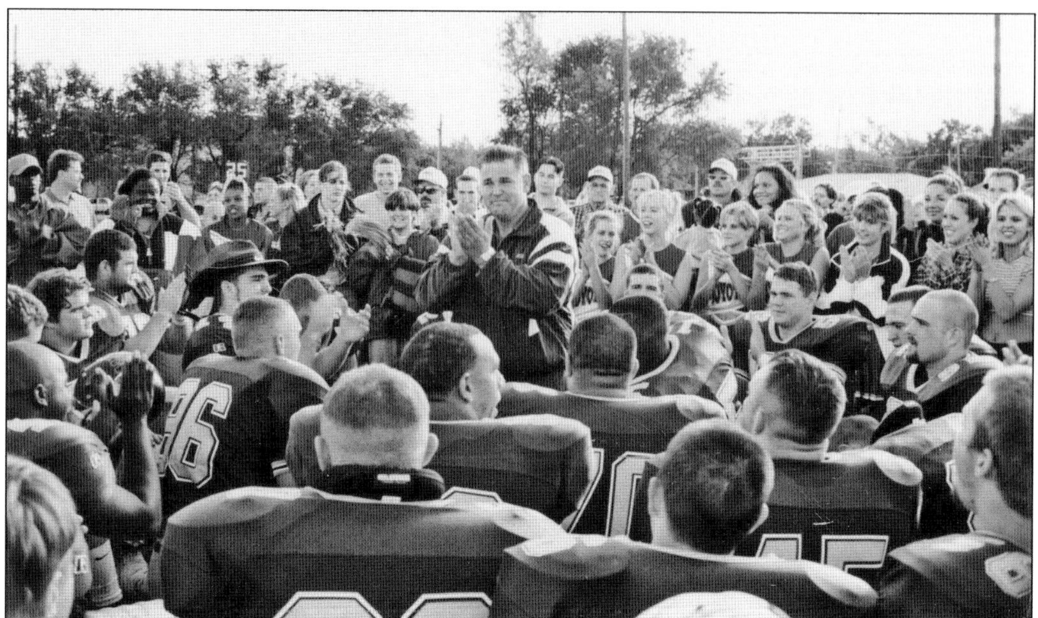

Football coach Dave Dallas talks with the team after defeating Ottawa 21-14 during the "Purple Craze" Homecoming in 1998. It was Coach Dallas's first win over Ottawa, where he coached for eight years before coming to Kansas Wesleyan. Coach Dallas's teams won the KCAC Championship in 2001 and 2002 and coached the Coyotes for 17 seasons. After the game, Dallas let the players cut his hair to celebrate the victory.

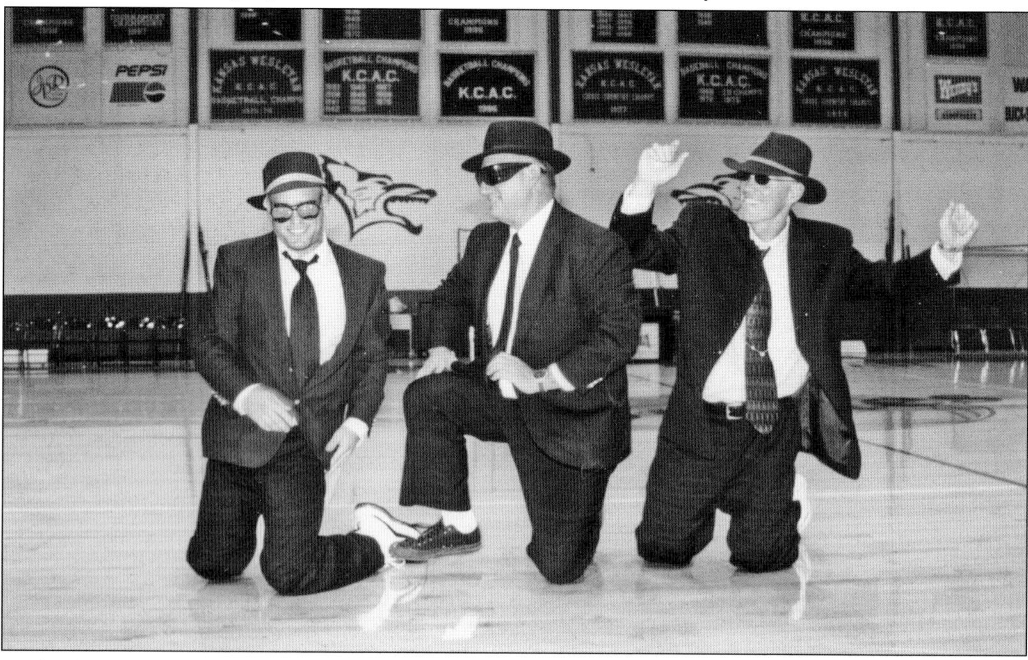

Basketball coaches, from left to right, Brandon Lesovsky, Jerry Jones, and Jon Bishop dressed up like the Blues Brothers for a skit during Midnight Madness prior to the start of the 2000–2001 basketball season. The team won the KCAC conference title and NSCAA National Championship the previous season, which brought renewed excitement to Muir Gymnasium.

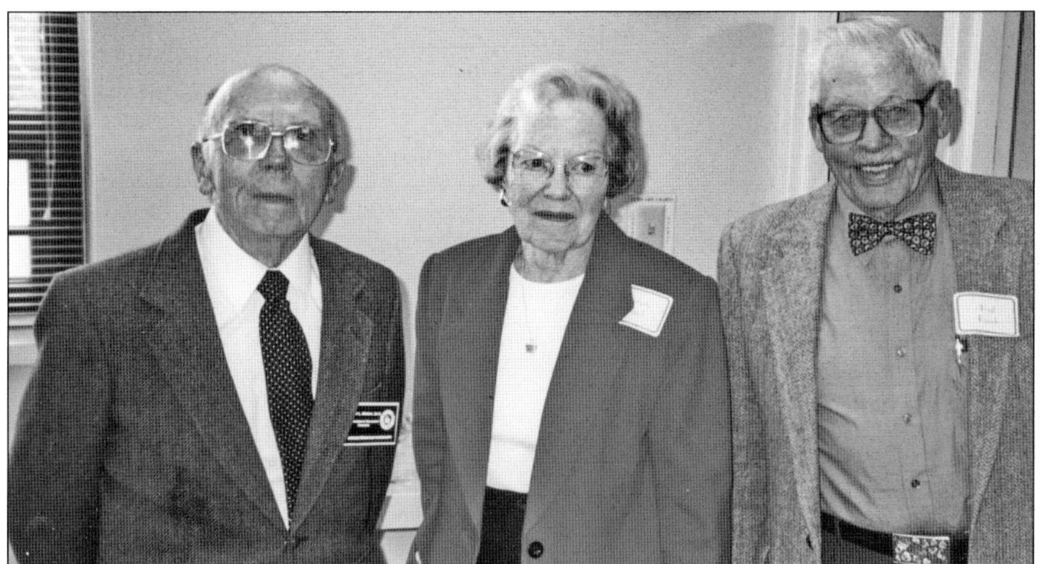

In the mid-1990s, the Launching the Next Century campaign proved successful, assisting with building the endowment, providing operational support, and funding several capital improvement projects. When people were approached to contribute, many discussed their fond memories, attributing them to the best years of their lives. Influential and inspirational retired faculty member Dr. Albert Nelson (left) is pictured above with former university president Paul Renich and his wife, Roberta, around 2000. Although the campaign was ambitious, the $7.5 million raised exceeded its goal. Below, from left to right, student Jaime Blackwell, honorary cochair Gov. Bill Graves, and Sen. Pat Roberts celebrate a successful end of the Launching the Next Century Campaign with students.

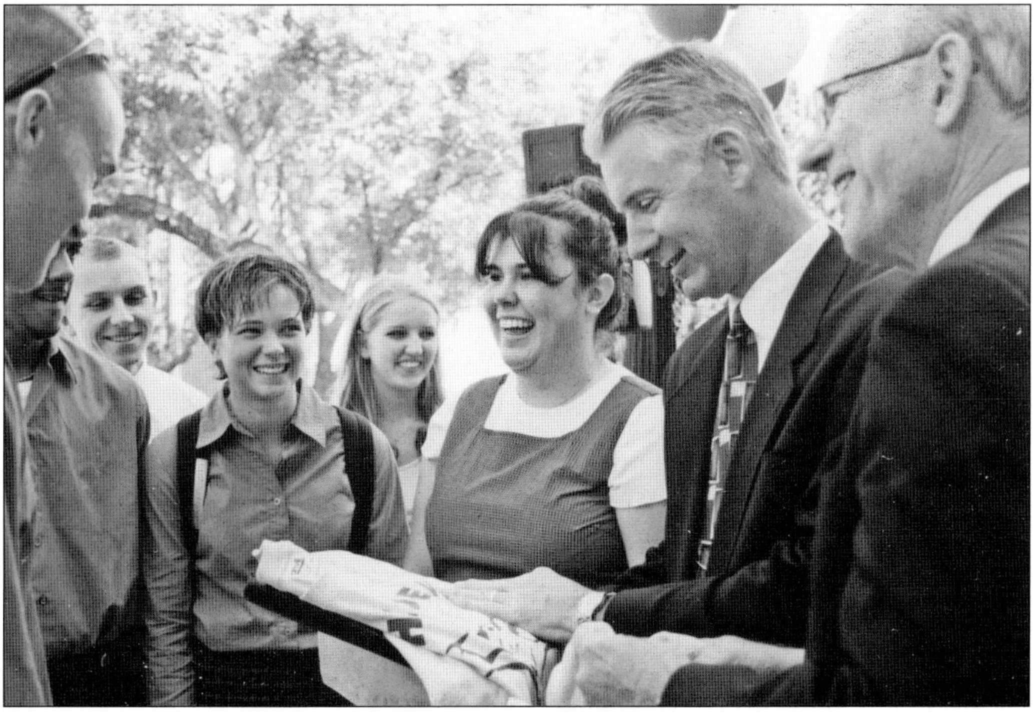

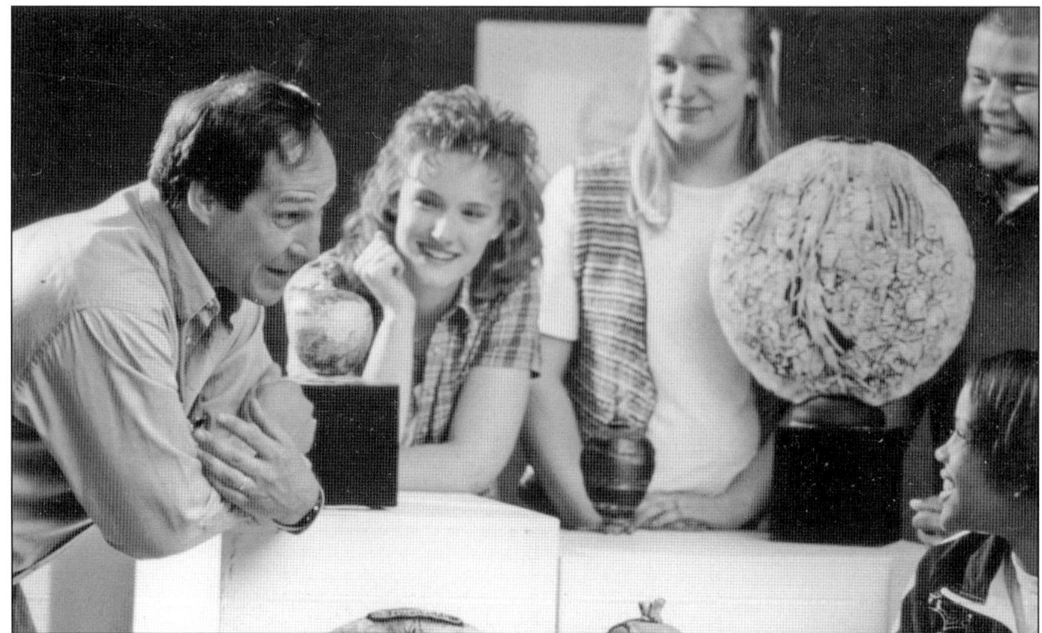

In 2008, art professor Brad Anderson (left) guided students through a ROPE (research, objectives, programming, and education) project, coming up with the university slogan "Connections of a Lifetime," focused on lasting connections made on campus. In 2010, Anderson received the Exemplary Teacher of the Year Award. He continues to maintain connections to Kansas Wesleyan as executive director of Salina Arts and Humanities. Anderson is pictured with students around 2000.

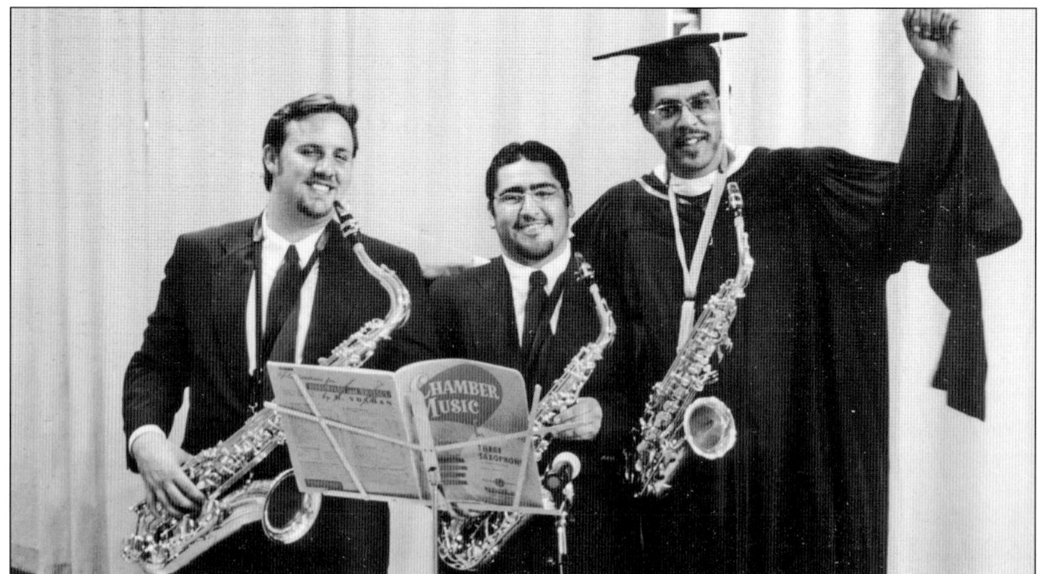

Bill McMosely, director of bands from 1998 to 2013, was an inspirational professor and mentor. In 1999, he created a pep band to energize the crowds. After retirement, he remains involved in the Salina music community with the Salina Jazz Academy and is the conductor for the Salina Municipal Band. From left to right are Nate Daniels, Jake Montoya, and McMosely around 2001.

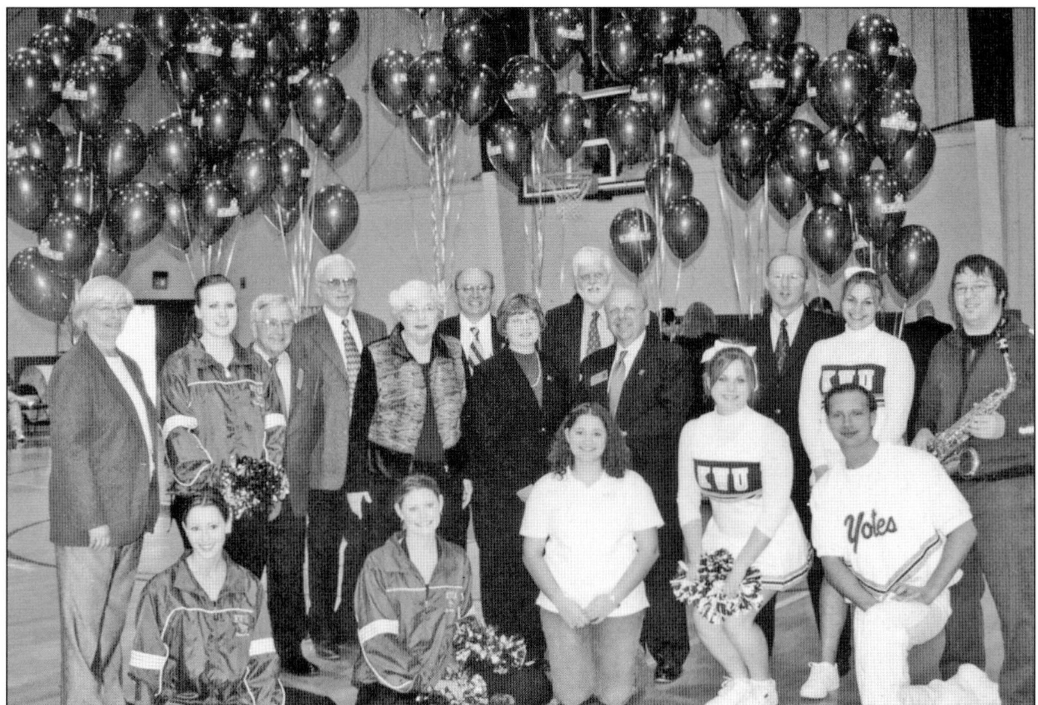

Above, members of the fundraising committee for the Student Activities Center, including Pres. Philip Kerstetter, Barbara Hauptli, Brad Botz, and Phil Coleman, gather in Muir Gymnasium for a celebration marking the completion of the fundraising for the project. The new center provided students with a gathering place on campus, new coaches' offices, a fitness center, and a new basketball arena, Mabee Arena, which remains the best basketball facility in the KCAC. This new space has also provided a place for the university to welcome community involvement through the Hauptli Student Center and the Brown Mezzanine. Below, members of the women's basketball team cheer on the Coyotes at the Homecoming football game in 2011. (Below, courtesy of Montric Santee.)

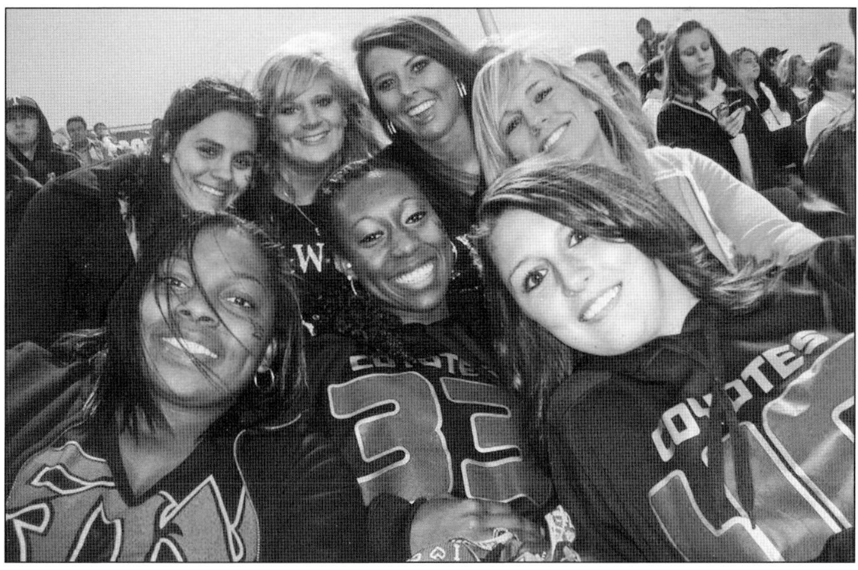

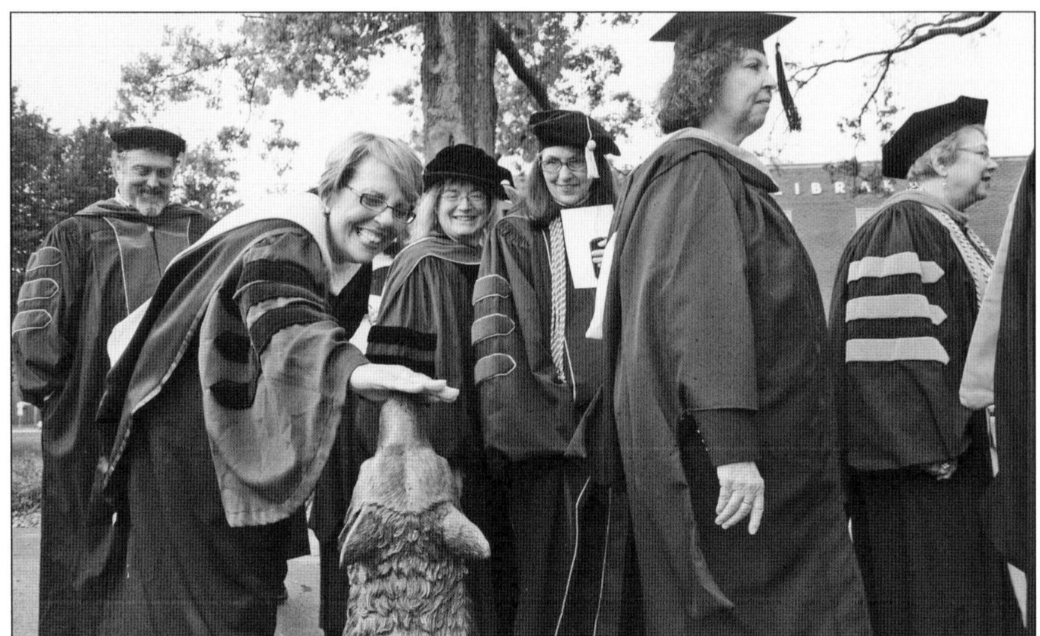

New traditions have emerged on campus. While Fletcher Lamkin served as university president, the Bolen Coyote statue was dedicated in October 2010. This gift from Pat and Linda Bolen was in honor of Pat's father, Dan. Above, Kathleen Barrett-Jones rubs the Coyote's nose. In 2011, another tradition began with the Night with the 'Yotes athletics fundraiser. This event features an award named after Gerald Lilly (below, right), a dedicated supporter of campus events for over 50 years. In 2012, soccer coach Mike Dibbini (below, left) presented Barrett-Jones (below, center) the award. Dibbini was a part of the first soccer program as a student-athlete in 1996. As Kansas Wesleyan's soccer coach, Dibbini established the program as a national power, and he currently leads Kansas State University's first soccer program. Dibbini received the Young Alumnus Award in 1999. (Above, photograph by Tanner Colvin.)

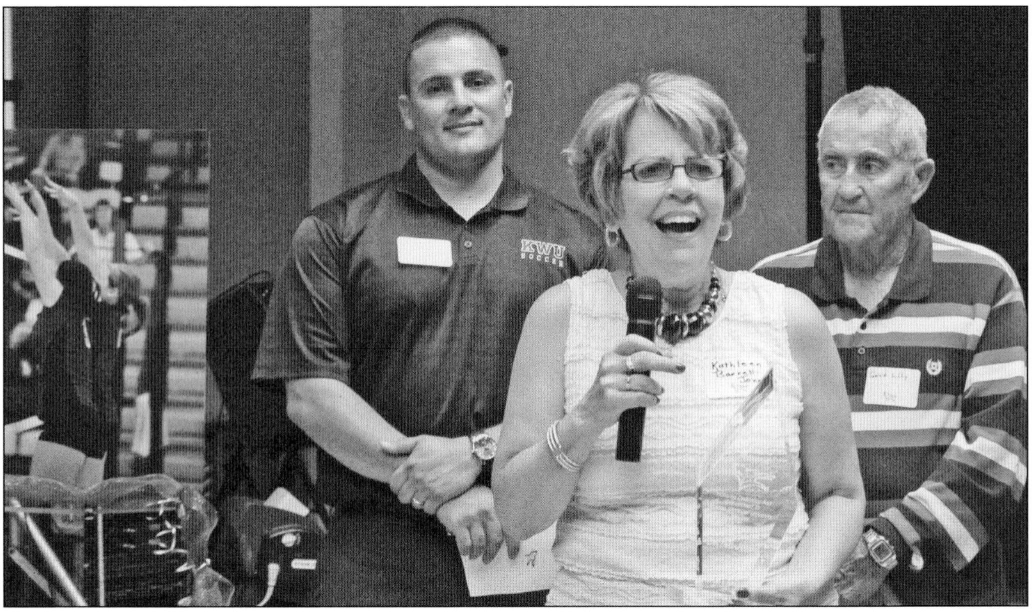

Nine

The Expanding Community

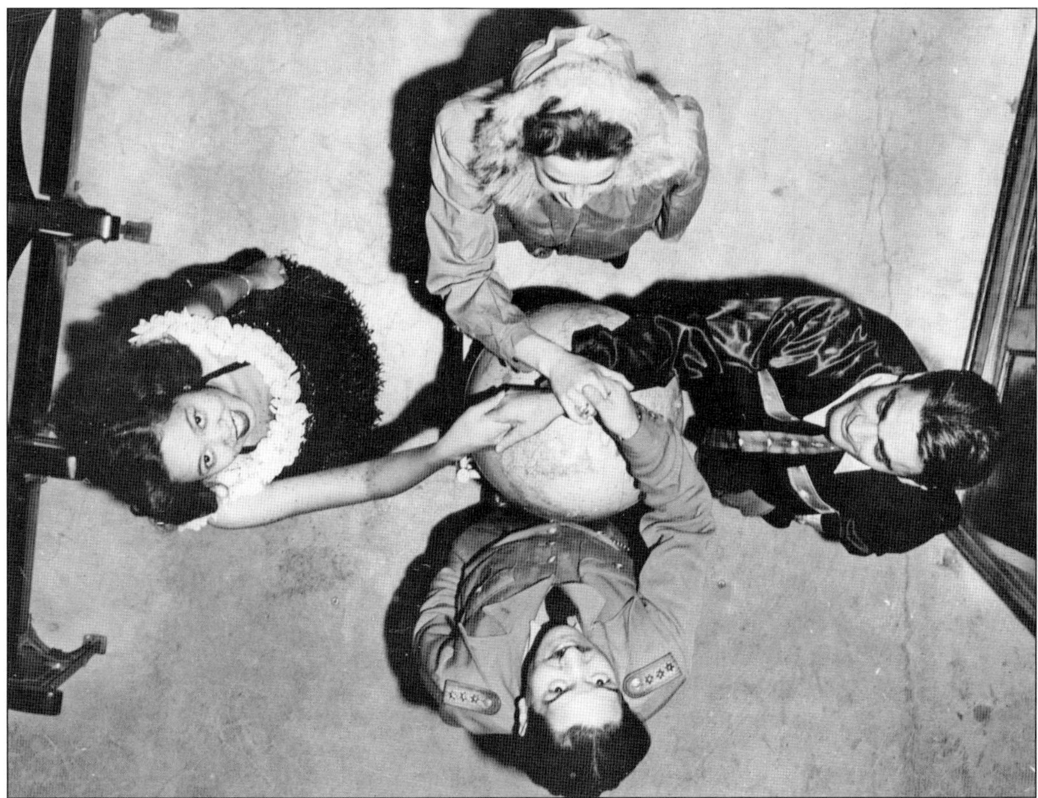

Every year, the university's impact on the world expands. Students become alumni and new students arrive, widening connections. Here, students and a faculty member shake hands across the globe—representing, clockwise from top, the North (Pat Smith, Alaska), East (Haikaz Marcan, Persia), South (Prof. Jose Guzman Baldivieso, Bolivia), and West (Julinda Batungbacal, Hawaii) around 1947. Baldivieso was a Bolivian consul and delegate to United Nations in 1945.

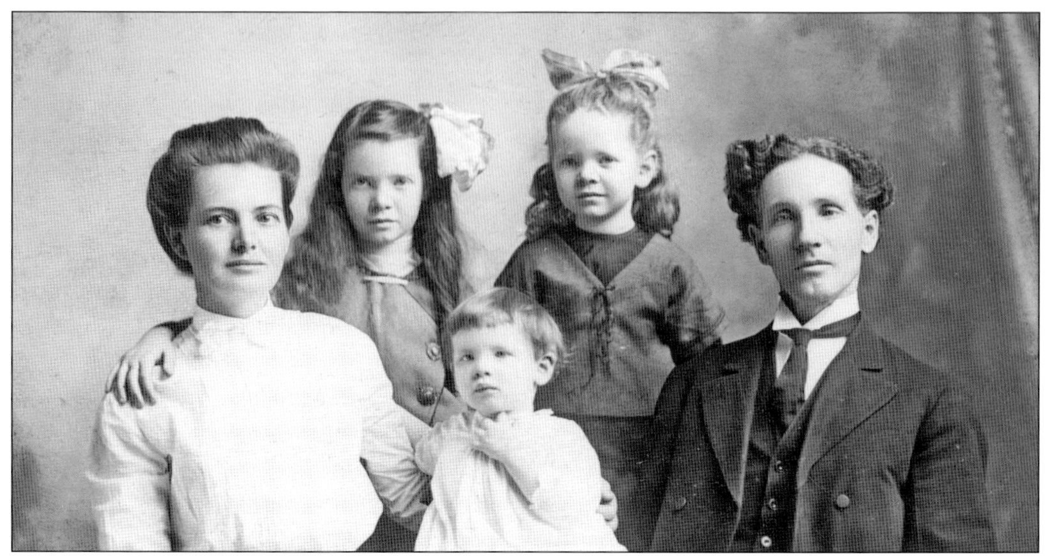

Dr. John Wilfred Snapp was the university's financial secretary and dedicated his career to the Methodist Church. He was the first to start the tradition of the Coyote Cane, given to the eldest living alum. Other cane carriers included Edith Collins Hagerty Bishop, Charles Burch, and Napoleon Dible. Snapp's wife, Anna Viola, is the last known alum to carry the cane, acquired during the 1960 commencement. The cane's head was carved of walnut, and sunflowers wrapped around the staff. Pictured above is the Snapp family: John Wilfred Snapp, Anna Viola Perrill Snapp, and their daughters Katherine, Vivian, and Marion. Pictured below around 1926, students participate in a joint trip of the YMCA and YWCA to Estes Park, Colorado. Katherine Snapp was president of the campus YWCA. (Above, courtesy of the Robert Sturgeon family.)

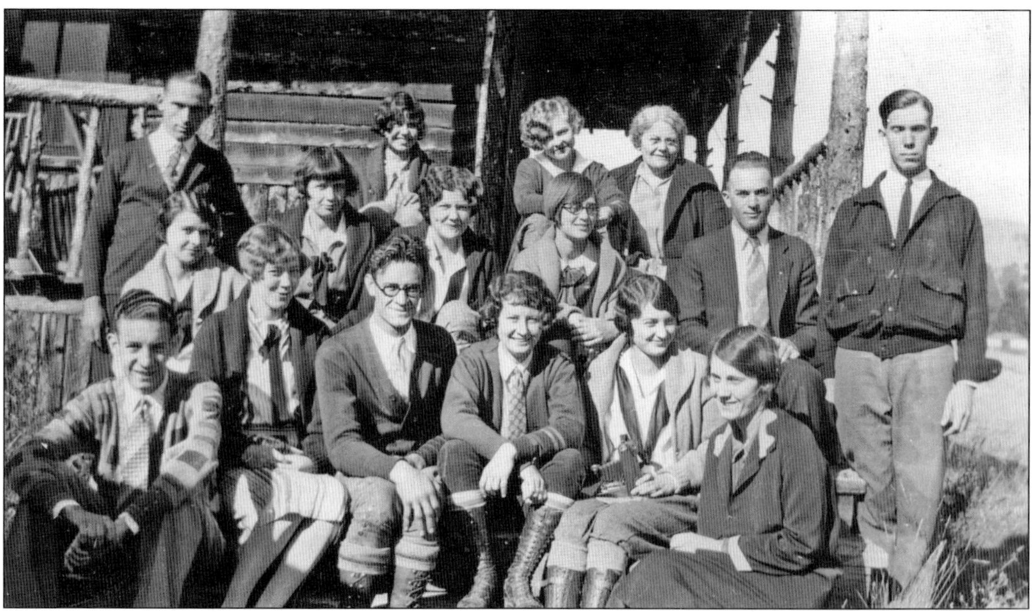

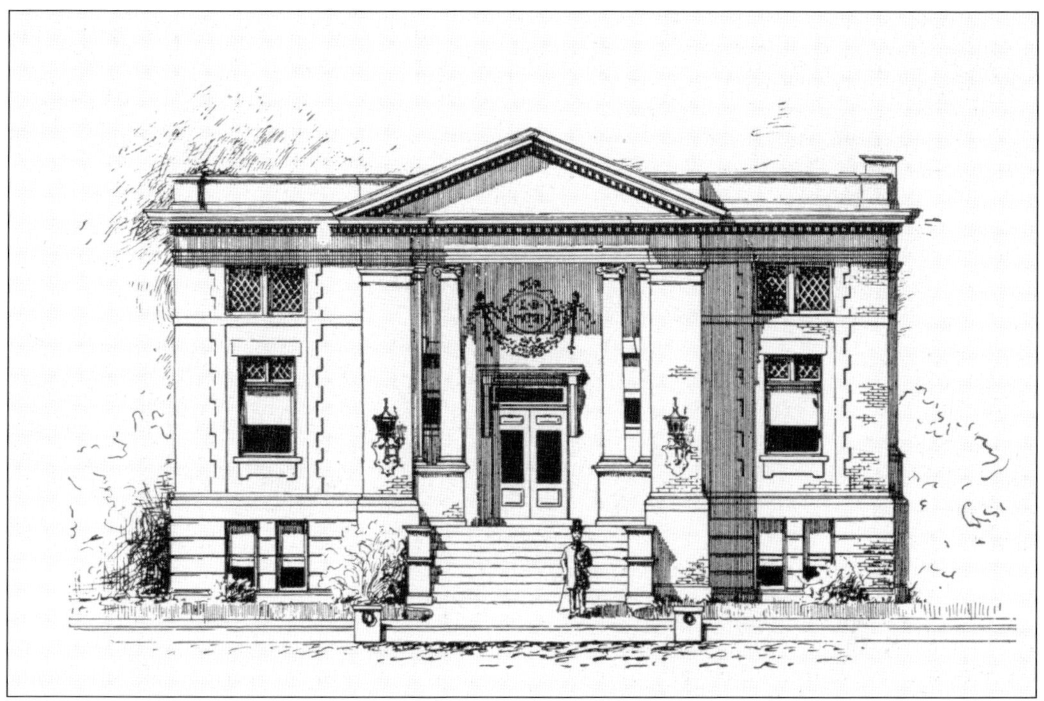

Bessie Page VanWinkle's uncle Pres. Thomas Roach was instrumental as Salina mayor for the development of the town's Carnegie library. Bessie was Salina's first paid librarian, alumna of the business college, and sister to Prof. Clayton Page, namesake of Salina's Clayton Hotel. Prior to the construction of the Carnegie library, Salina's library was housed in multiple locations. Bessie managed the library when it was housed in the business college from 1901 to 1904.

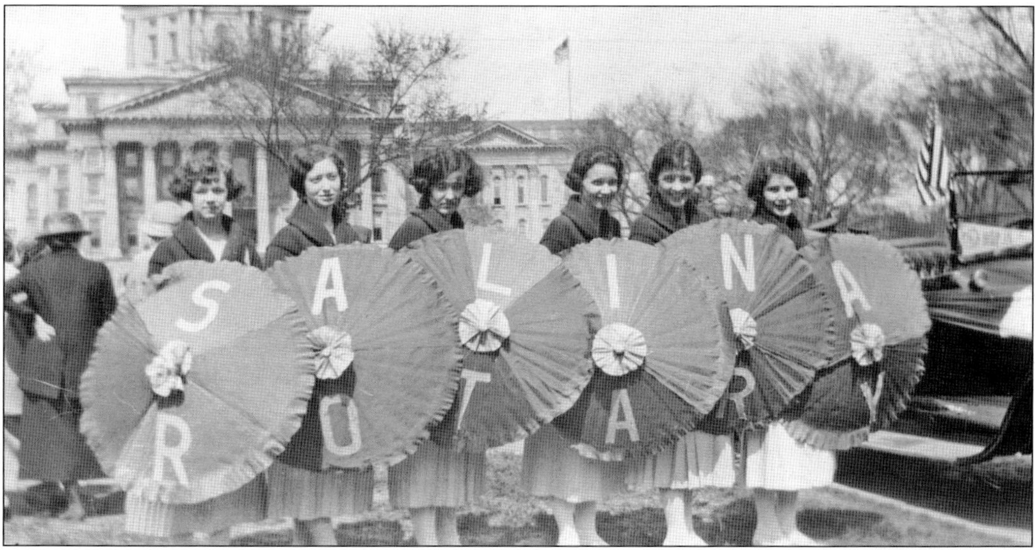

In April 1924, over 2,000 Rotarian and Rotary Anns gathered in Topeka, Kansas, for a state Rotary convention. A parade was held, followed by a speech by Bishop James Wise. The parade coincided with two days of conferences, club meetings, and orchestra concerts. These Kansas Wesleyan University students accompanied Salina Rotarian delegates.

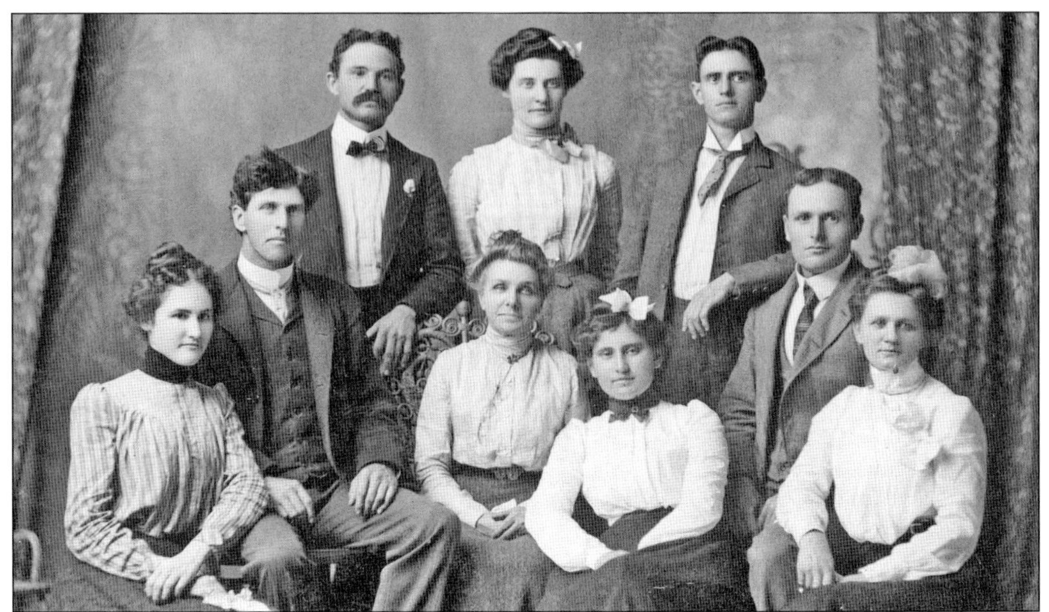

During the school's formative years, the Brown sisters Hester Templin, Charlotte VanSickle, and Margaret Corbett Roberts were strong university supporters. By the early 1920s, these sisters were proud to have one of the largest families to attend the university. Above are Margaret (center) with her immediate family and son John H. Corbett (left), who served as the Salina School District superintendent for many years. Pictured below in 1959, the legacy continues as Pres. D. Arthur Zook dines with alumni in Portland, Oregon. Ethel Templin Norene (standing back) is the daughter of Rev. Joseph Templin and granddaughter of Hester Templin. Other alumni pictured include Rev. Asa Mundell, Jane Rogers Smith, Rena Mickey, Mabel Shoemaker Jones, and Rev. James Smith. (Above, courtesy of the Smoky Hill Museum.)

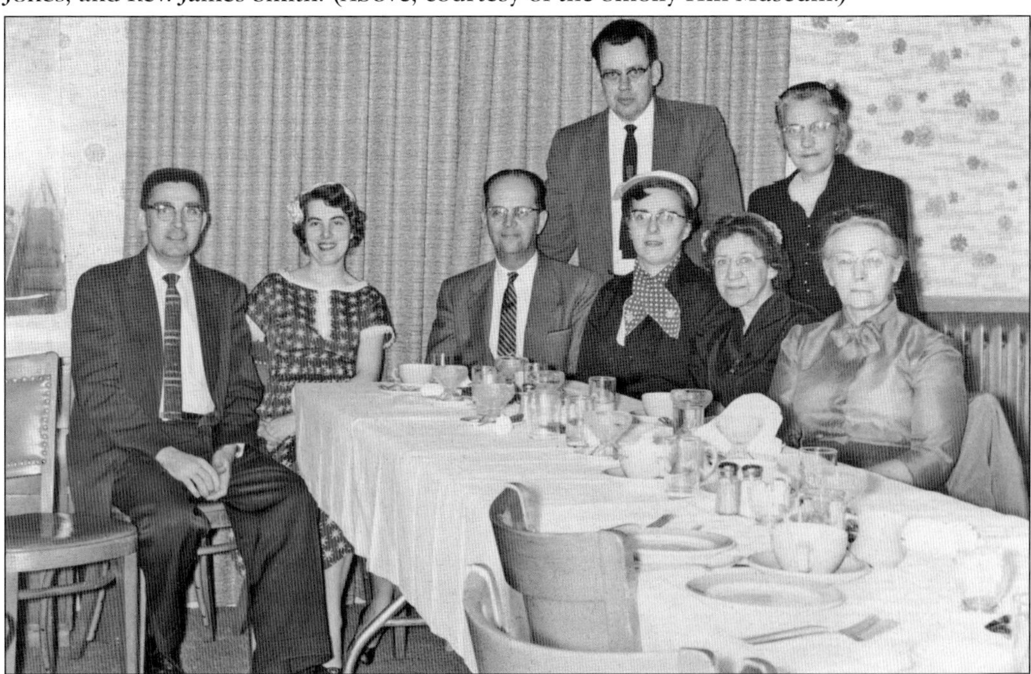

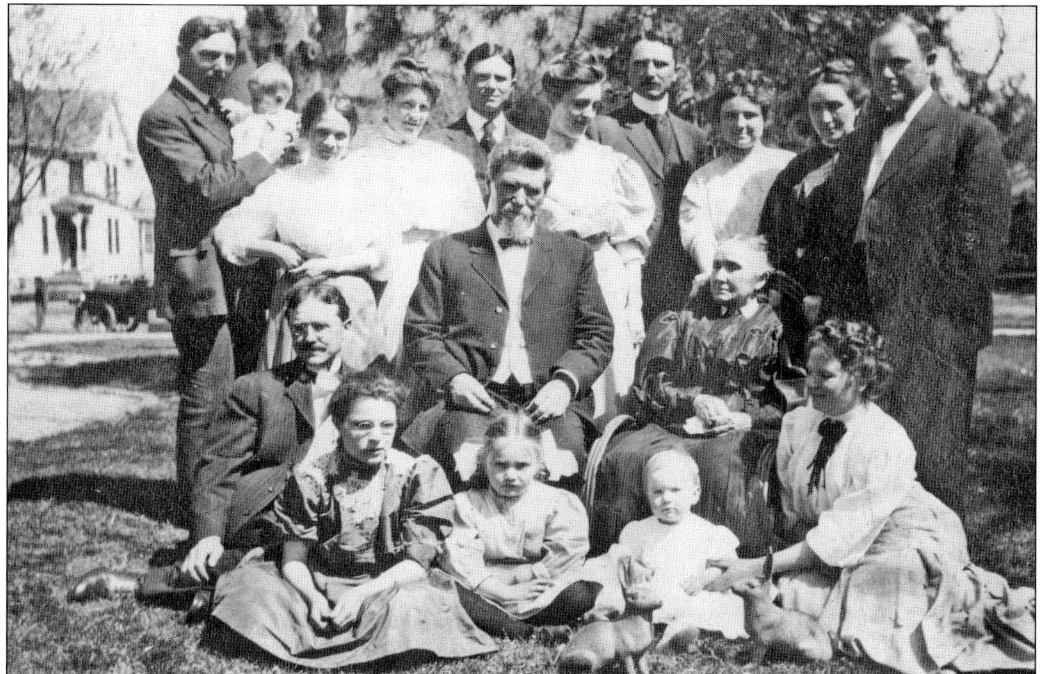

Christopher and Anna Lampert Eberhardt moved to Salina in 1867. They were avid supporters of Kansas Wesleyan endeavors. The Eberhardts advocated for education in the Salina community, and their heirs proudly attended the university. In 1923, at Christopher's bequest, a lot on Santa Fe Avenue was left to Kansas Wesleyan. In 1925, Christopher's heirs donated a home, Eberhardt Hall, at Highland and Kirwin Avenues. (Courtesy of the Smoky Hill Museum.)

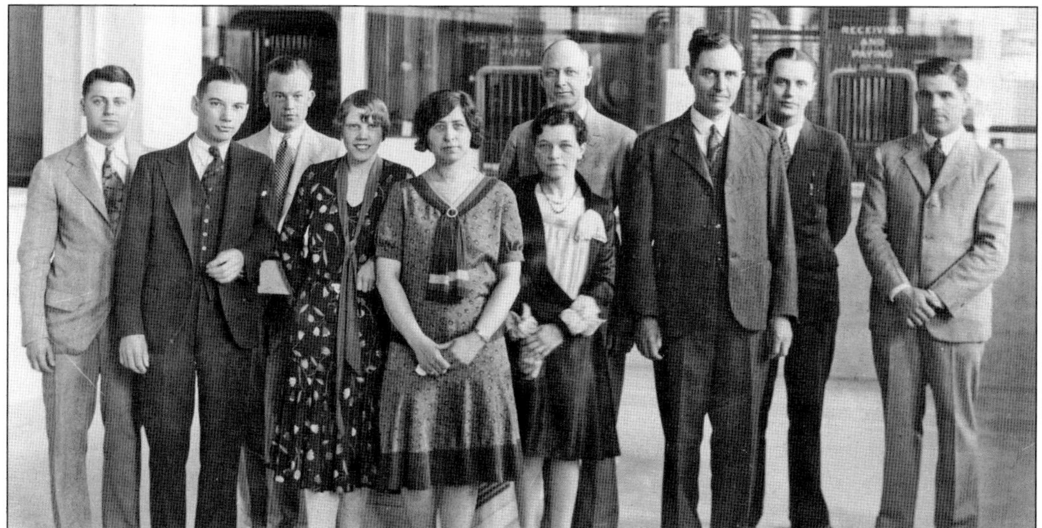

Kansas Wesleyan Business College alumni work at National Bank of America around 1928. From left to right are Eldon Oegerle, Dean Brown, Tom Adams, Dorothy Sharps, Helen Clarke, Esther Grensing, Walter Lindblom, J.C. Reed, Fred Kelly, and Wayne Dailey. Dailey and Oegerle accepted temporary positions that led to 45-plus-year careers in executive positions. In 1959, Clarke was the first woman to receive an award from the Kansas State Bankers Association.

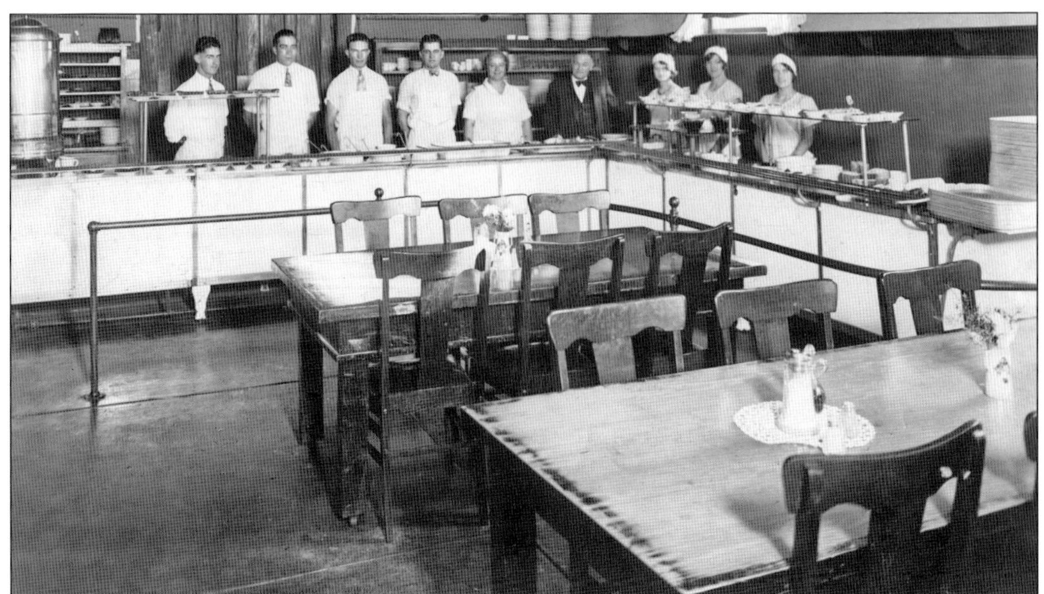

In 1907, Kansas Wesleyan Business College built an annex to the Roach Building for the College Inn, which served as a cafeteria and frequent university meeting place. During World War I, Jenkins Music Company leased the building from Thomas Roach. In 1919, Albert Austin Shelton and his wife, Cora, reopened it as People's Cafeteria. Cora's later pursuits as Kansas congresswoman kept connections to campus. Student cafeteria workers are pictured around 1920.

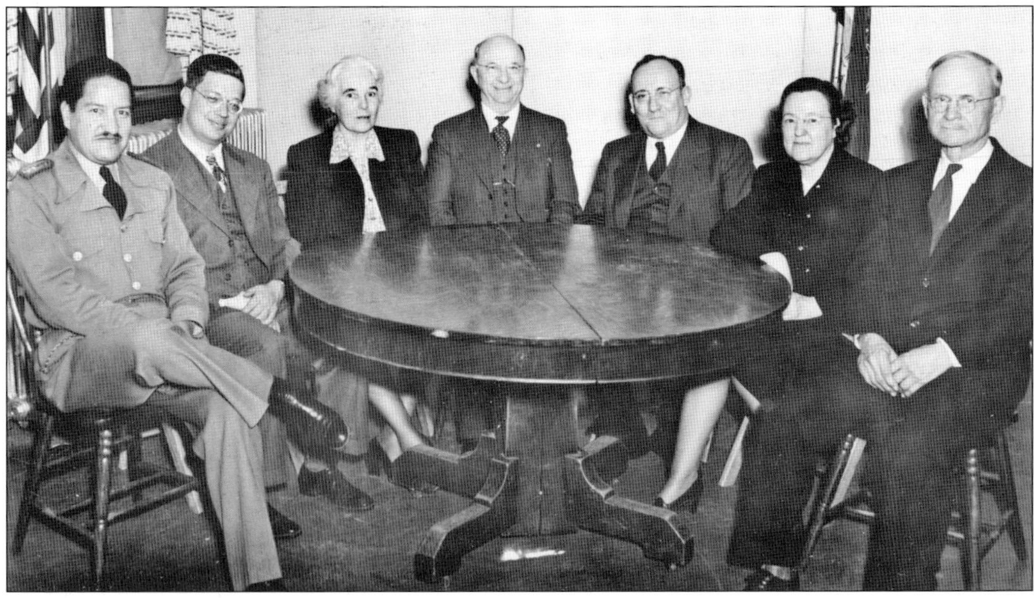

In the beginning, Kansas Wesleyan's founders relied on guidance from Ohio Wesleyan University. The Honorable Andrew Perry Collins graduated from Ohio Wesleyan in 1860. At least four university presidents and athletic director Alexander Brown Mackie attended Ohio Wesleyan. Pictured in 1948, the following faculty (seated from left to right) are Ohio Wesleyan alumni: Capt. Jose Guzman Baldivieso, John Hickson, Julia Russell Reed, Frederick Conrad Peters, Louis Otte, Georgia Haswell, and Walter Long.

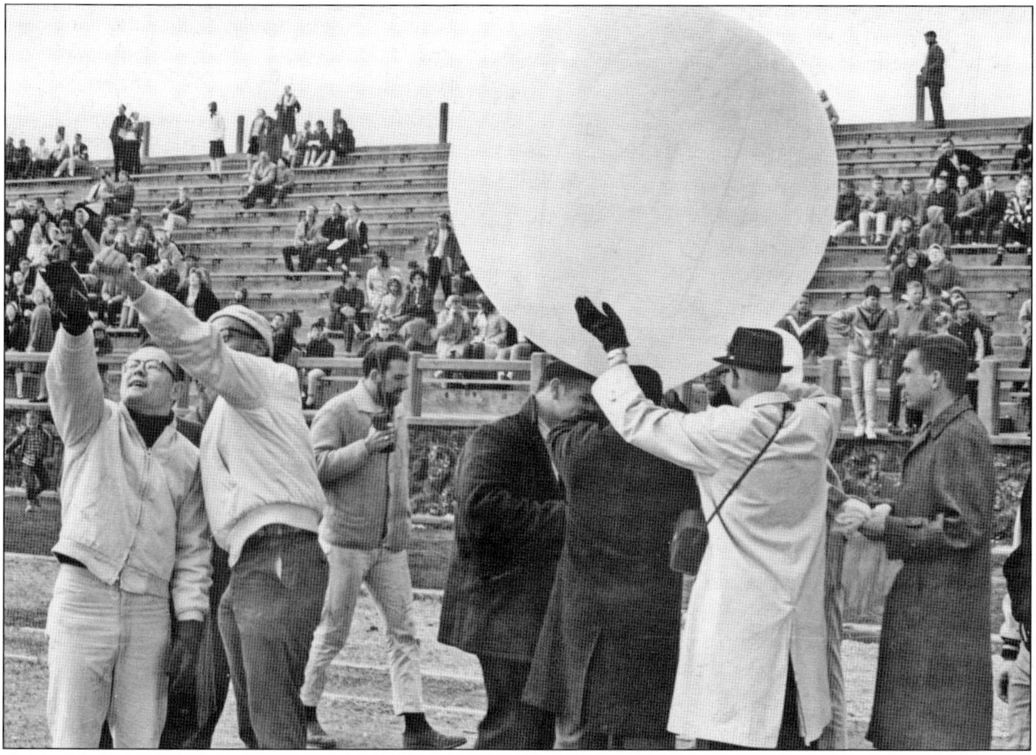

The university hosted science fairs where elementary and high school students had the opportunity to engage and learn more about science. Nick Koengeter passes by with a radio while Bob Hart and Oliver Green (left) watch the weather balloons released during the science fair at Martin Stadium around 1964. Green was student council president and was head laboratory assistant in the chemistry lab.

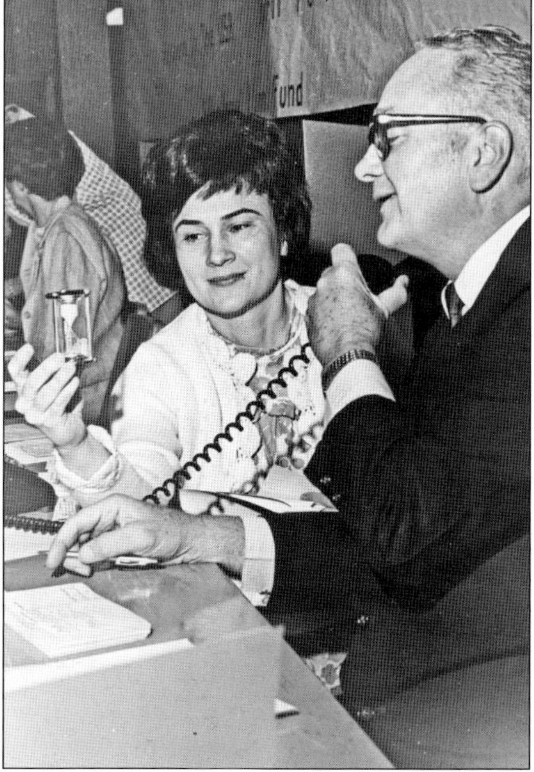

In the spring of 1969, the university held a Dial-a-Classmate fundraising campaign with a goal to raise $40,000 from alumni. Hoping to reconnect with them and raise funds for the university, over 80 volunteers called alumni. Calls were timed for three minutes using an hourglass. J.P. Smith, a member of the Kansas Wesleyan development staff, is pictured on the phone while Virginia Synder Vishneske holds the timer.

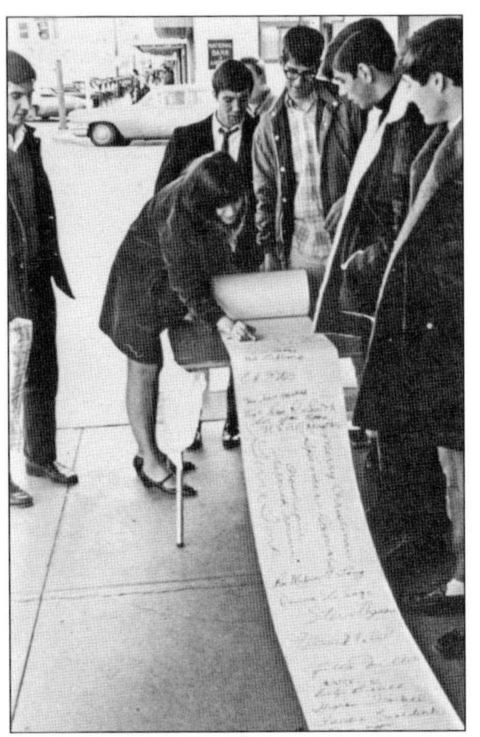

In December 1967, members of the Pi Sigma Upsilon fraternity gather together in downtown Salina along Santa Fe Avenue encouraging people to sign a Christmas card for soldiers in Vietnam. Measuring approximately 570 feet long, this endeavor was named the Longest Christmas Card to Vietnam and included over 1,200 signatures.

In 1988, the Neighbors in Education program began providing students at the university with the opportunity to provide service to the community. The Neighbors in Education program was recognized with Golden Achievement Award by the National School Public Relations Association. Here, Robert Jackson speaks to students at Hageman Elementary School.

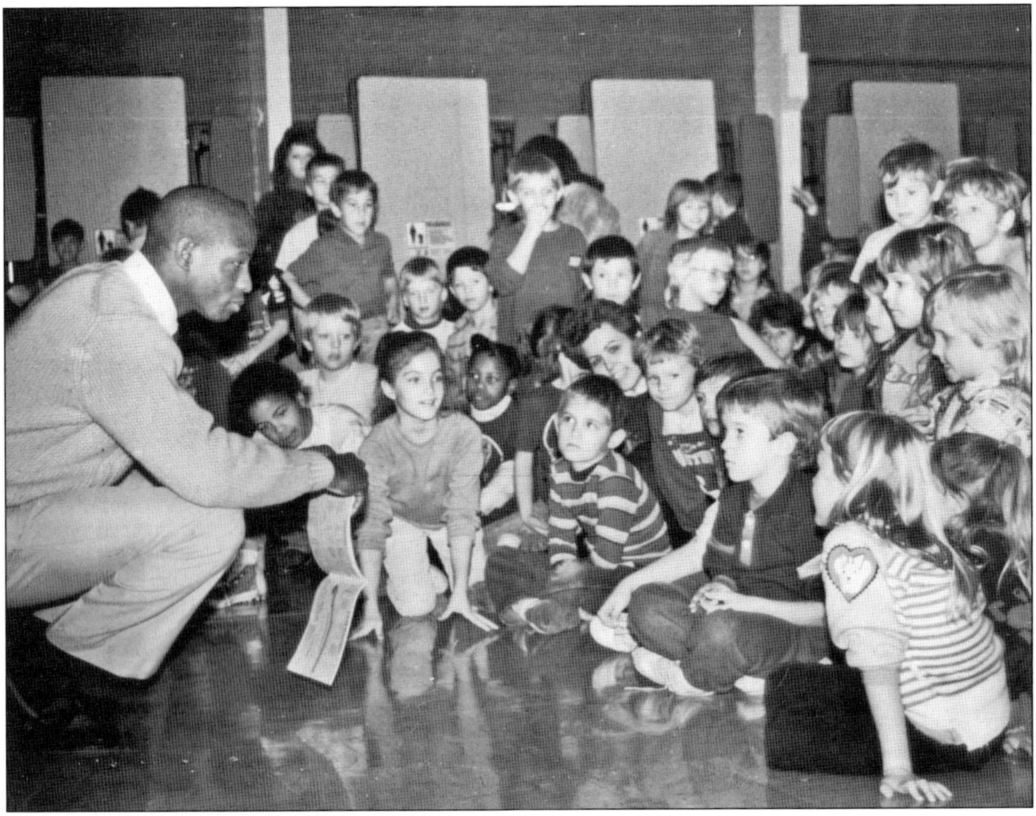

Ten

The Power of And

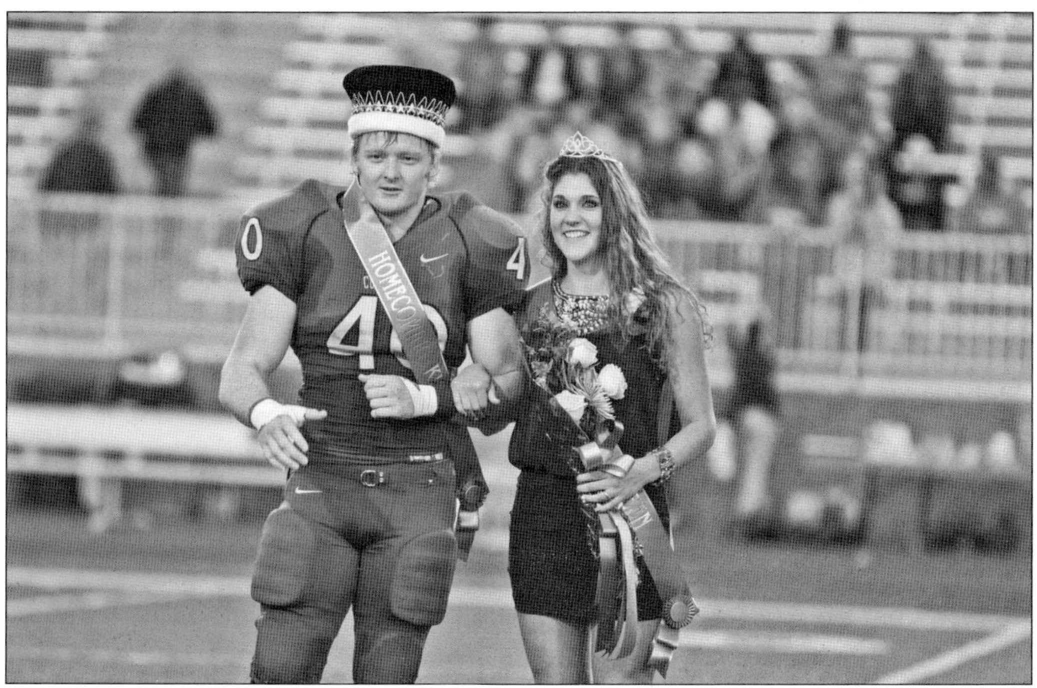

Brady Harwell and Vanessa Kresin were crowned Homecoming king and queen in 2013. The small campus and family atmosphere allow everyone to feel like a part of the bigger picture. Students are encouraged to be as involved as they want. Harwell played football for Kansas Wesleyan and was involved in HPER Club and athletic training. Kresin played basketball and was a campus leader.

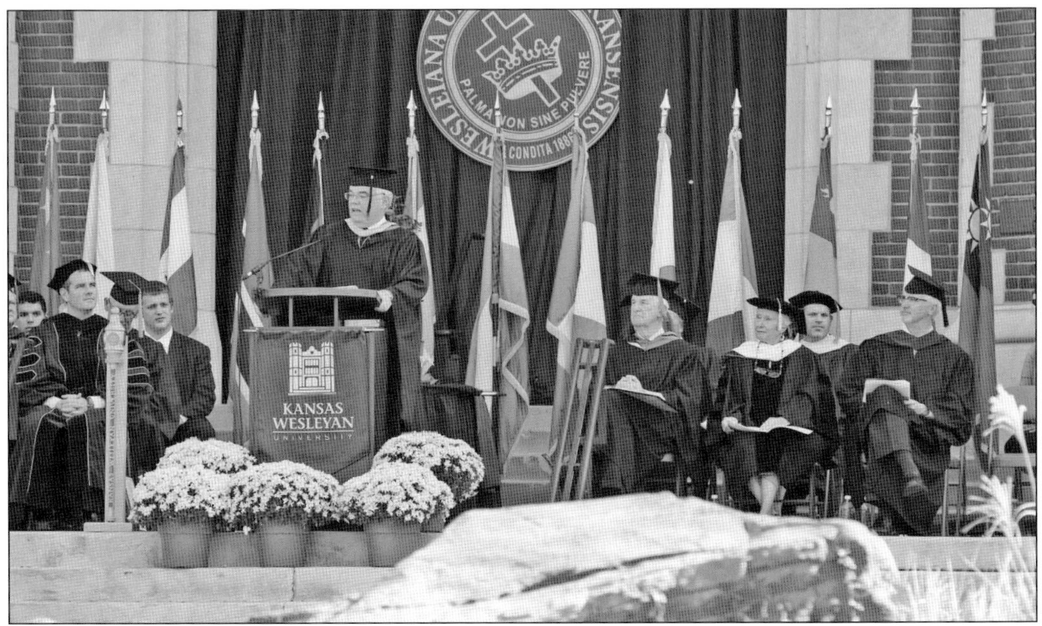

Matthew Thompson was inaugurated as the 19th president of Kansas Wesleyan on September 27, 2013. Alumnus Dr. John Burchill (above), class of 1980 and faculty presiding officer, spoke at the inauguration ceremony. With the assistance of his wife, Jennifer, President Thompson (below, center) received the presidential gown from board of trustees chair Jim Nelson at the ceremony. Thompson's daughter (below, right) Darcel presented the presidential cap to her father. As part of the inaugural festivities, the campus hosted a family carnival along Claflin Avenue featuring a Ferris wheel in the middle of the Santa Fe–Claflin intersection. Thompson champions academic excellence and has launched several initiatives, including the Wesleyan Experience, Wesleyan Journey, and Wesleyan Heritage programs. The university has embraced the "Power of And," which gives everyone the ability to be involved in more than one way on campus.

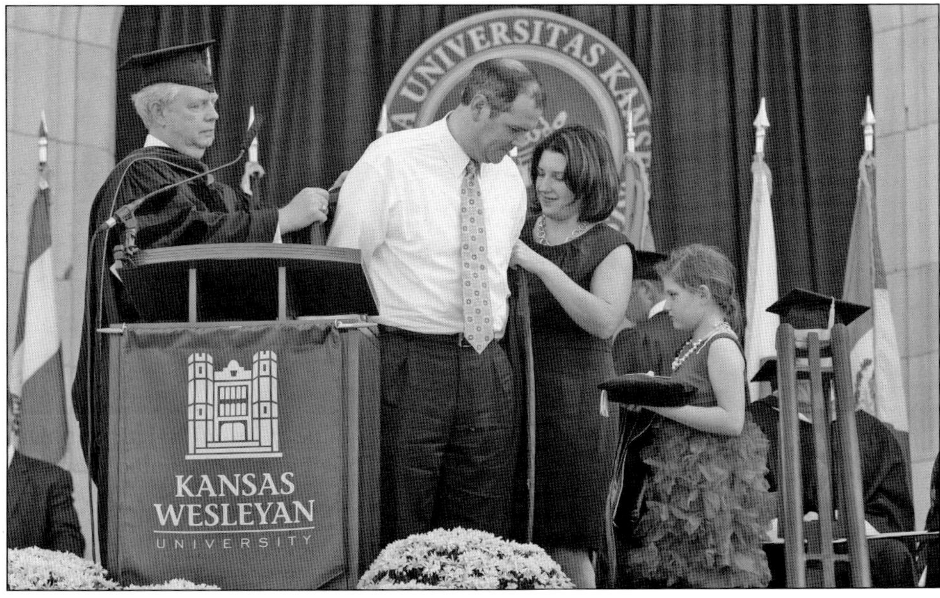

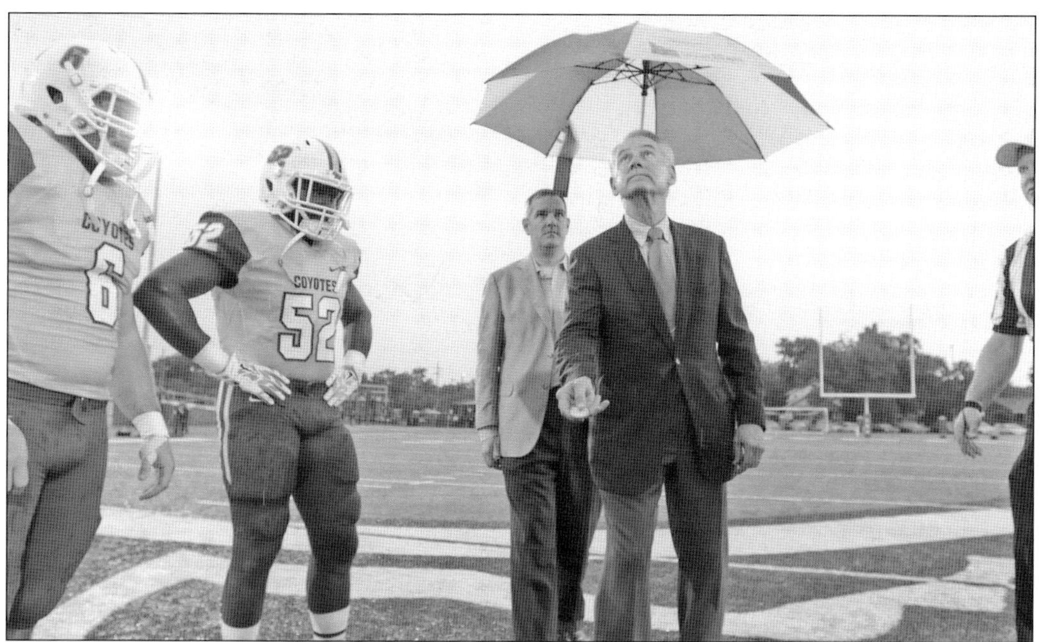

In September 2016, the university celebrated its 130th anniversary during Homecoming and Family Weekend. The university hosted a family carnival along with several other activities. Prior to the football game, the Graves Family Sports Complex was formally dedicated. Bill Graves (above) flipped the coin prior to the game. Graves's great-uncle was Henry Milton Mayo, the first graduate of Kansas Wesleyan. Success is often attributed to alumni who honor their alma mater. Many pay tribute with "O Wesleyan." Around 1909, the university published a book containing over 50 Kansas Wesleyan songs, and its foreword surmises a song is the most "effective expression of college spirit." Songs included are "Wesleyan Memories," "Hi-Ki Wesli" and "Kansas Wesleyan Forever." Below, Ken Hakoda leads the choir.

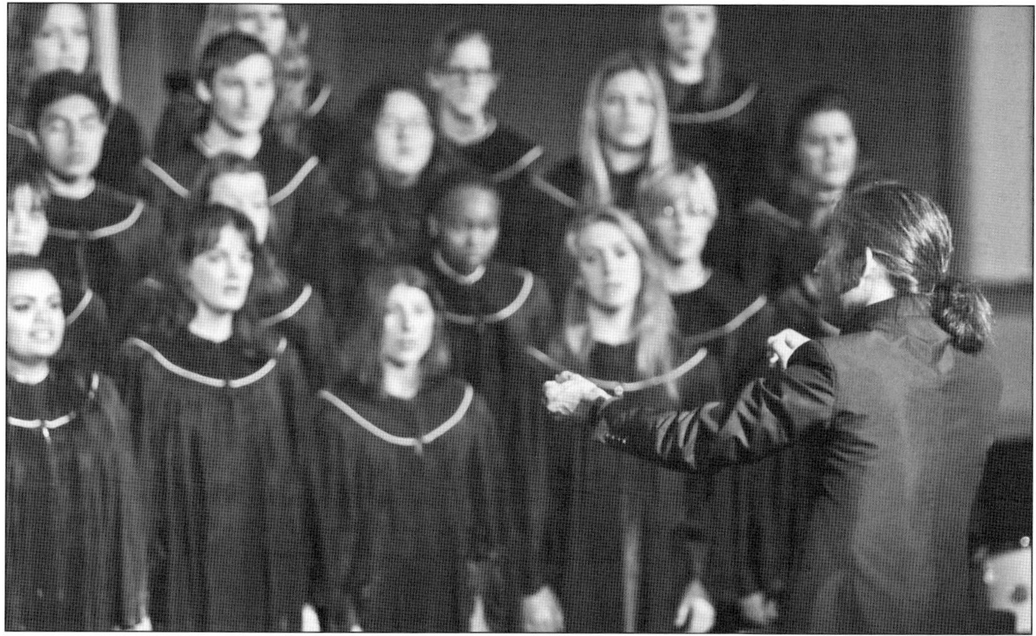